P9-DHB-530

DATE DUE

APR 2 9 2008	
JAN 1 9 2010	
APR 2 6 2011	
APR 2 5 2012	

Politics and
Propaganda

Politics and Propaganda

Weapons of Mass Seduction

NICHOLAS JACKSON O'SHAUGHNESSY

The University of Michigan Press
Ann Arbor

Copyright © Nicholas Jackson O'Shaughnessy 2004

Published in the USA in 2004 by
The University of Michigan Press
839 Greene St.
Ann Arbor, MI 48104

The University of Michigan Press edition
published by special arrangement with
Manchester University Press
Oxford Road, Manchester M13 9NR, UK
www.manchesteruniversitypress.co.uk

CIP Data applied for

ISBN 0-472-11443-3

Printed in Great Britain

Contents

Preface

This book is not an attempt to commission a new concept but to recommission an old one. The term 'propaganda' faced conceptual extinction because it had become an anachronism. How could a cynical, media-literate cadre ever respond to its histrionic excess as earlier, more naive generations had done? The word had disappeared because the reality it signified was apparently no more. Yet ideas do not die, they merely hibernate. From the taunting videos of Osama bin Laden to the euphorias of the embedded journalist, from the lucid rhetoric of the anti-globalisation movement to the empire of spin to the scalding polemics of US campaign advertising, propaganda is back, centre-stage. What other literary formula might we use to evoke the theatre of imagery which we inhabit today? The whirligig of fashion applies to concepts as well as clothes.

This book is thus an analysis of the meaning, content and significance of the word 'propaganda' today. Its focus is primarily on the current world order, though history, and indeed the history of the word, is a constant presence. The content of its subtitle, 'seduction' (in Latin, a leading to oneself), is deliberately chosen because that describes the *art* of the process. Effective propaganda is often seductive propaganda. Propaganda is not usually a lie (because a lie is not instrumental to its ends), but persuasion, and not the seeking of truth, is the objective. In fact there is no 'unvarnished truth' anywhere, and even the success of ideas is inseparable from the fact and process of their propagation. If our current reality is indeed socially constructed, in Searle's sense, then this must imply a formative role for communication, and for propaganda as a sub-set of communication.

There is an ideal book about propaganda that has yet to be written. This is not it, neither does it pretend to be. But it is original in a number of ways. It applies a conceptual approach to propaganda, and then grounds this analysis in a series of contemporary case studies, ending in an assessment of the role of propaganda in the remorseless new conflict which began on 11 September 2001. The book also recognises a need to treat the subject more broadly than hitherto, since its conceptual identity has become localised in totalitarian regimes or wartime hyperbole. As Rampton and Stauber (2003) suggest, 'what mass media, public relations, advertising and terrorism all have in common is a one-sided approach to communications that can be best thought of as a "propaganda model"'.

Moreover the book focuses not just on describing this phenomenon but according it some explanatory depth. The approach is both descriptive and analytic. For example, one key idea is that, like the seducer, the effective propagandist will not assault but insinuate, not challenge values directly but package the thought to fit the perspective. And we argue that propaganda texts are not necessarily meant to be taken literally but rather represent a fantasy we are invited to share (often a fantasy of enmity, where we seek self-definition through constructing our antithesis).

Finally, I would like to thank my many friends, mentors and colleagues, but in particular Morris Holbrook of Columbia University, Jeannie Grant Moore of the University of Wisconsin, Nigel Allington of Gonville and Caius College Cambridge, Bruce Newman of De Paul University and Phil Harris of the University of Otago. They have waited patiently for this book. Here it is.

N.J.O.

Introduction

The idea of propaganda

Before the spring of 2003, propaganda as a concept had been relegated beyond the marginal to the irrelevant. Its conceptual identity was lost amid the new academic lexicon of persuasion, communication theory and the manipulation of consent; the concept of propaganda in popular imagination relegated to the monochrome, stuttering imagery of bolsheviks and storm troopers. Then began an awakening recognition, a cumulative cultural drift; for in a culture where image is sovereign, where symbols matter, where the hair of public figures becomes a nexus of political symbolisation, it could not be long before an old word that could interconnect these phenomena would be rehabilitated. For we seemed bereft of a concept that could give a unitary understanding to the perplexing new realities of our own social back yard – from Wall Street analysts wrapping dot.com and high-tech shares in a cling-film of myth to the evolution of the accounting and finance profession (Arthur Andersen, Enron, Worldcom, Tyco) from purveyors of fact to narrators of fiction, to the ascent of 'spin' (the affixing of determinate labels on to indeterminate events).

 Then there was Iraq. The word propaganda, like a lexical Rip Van Winkle, awoke to a new era. Everywhere, commentators claimed to detect the hand of the propagandist – in the embedded journalist, the elaborate propaganda ministry at Qatar, the 'Coalition of the Willing' and other rhetorical bric-a-brac of the allies, and in the myths – of the Hussein /Bin Laden link, and of the Weapons of Mass Destruction.

 This book differs from other books on propaganda in the elasticity it attributes to the term; orthodox literature has erred in restricting meaning to explicit texts such as the polemical tirade or 'black' propaganda (like the secret wartime radio station, Gustav Siegfried Eis). So the proposition is that 'propaganda' is not synonymous with mere overt polemicism, but informs many cultural products, including such apparently politically neutral areas as entertainment or documentaries – and, while this explanation via cultural phenomena complexifies the subject, it enriches it as well. Goebbels himself would have agreed, since he attempted to conceal propaganda in entertainment vehicles like *The Adventures of Baron Munchausen* or *Lucky Kids* (Rentschler 1996).

One clear problem in the recognition of propaganda is the frequent difficulty encountered in distinguishing it other than retrospectively. Propaganda in the social environment is often 'naturalised' and we are unaware of it. The merit of seeking to redeploy the term in critical discourse once again is that it does duty as a sensitising concept. Foulkes (1983) drew attention to 'invisible propaganda perpetuating itself as common sense', and quotes Orwell: 'all art is to some extent propaganda'. Thus for Foulkes the Nazi:

> has long ceased to be a real historical being. He now inhibits the demonic twilight of the entertainment world; the mass-produced collective subconscious within which Zulu Warriors coexist with invaders from outer space and the Waffen SS ... Propaganda does not often come marching towards us waving swastikas and chanting 'Sieg heil'; its real power lies in its capacity to conceal itself, to appear natural, to coalesce completely and indivisibly with the values and accepted power symbols of the given society.

The explicit propaganda of earlier generations would strike people today as merely comical.

The role of propaganda in human affairs has been underplayed by the limitations of its contemporary definition. The aspiration here is to refresh propaganda as a distinct generic entity, and claim new territory for it as a pervasive attribute of technological mankind. For words direct perception. What we lack a word for we fail to perceive, and for a considerable period of time the word 'propaganda' appeared to have become defunct, to be replaced by terms like 'persuasion' or 'advocacy'. We view reality through the language and conceptual formulations currently in circulation, which integrate the apparently disconnected into coherent patterns, and thus enhance the conceptual richness through which we see things. Otherwise we neglect the interconnectedness of modern communications phenomena, from 'spin' to the Afghan and Iraq wars.

The attempt to insert a new phrase into the political lexicon, as well as elucidate the meaning and conceptual anatomy of that term, is no frivolous activity. With the 'right' terminologies, much else might follow – more nuanced debates and clearer and more rigorous bases for empirical studies. Words are our tools; for example, the phrase 'presidential government', something that Tony Blair has certainly been accused of, condenses many meanings and debates – on Americanisation, the cult of personality, the demise of cabinet government and parliamentary accountability – into a *perspective*. Concepts may be right, wrong or half true, but without them argument would be the more impoverished as we search for verbose formulae to describe the phenomena that we can only dimly apprehend.

Contents

The structure of the book is conceptual rather than narrative-descriptive in approach, and the text is organised round an explanatory schemata. Myth, Symbolism and Rhetoric, the foundation concepts of propaganda, are discussed in detail and seen as animating and structuring the core edifice, or integuments, of the concept, such as hyperbole, ideology, emotion, manipulation, deceit, the search for utopia, otherness and the creation of enemies. Then the focus moves to a series of specific case study analyses of recent political phenomena that embody these elements – the phenomenon of 'Symbolic Government', the rise of single-issue groups, negative political campaigning, and the recent wars in Afghanistan and Iraq. The organising paradigm is thus: foundation concepts – *myth, symbolism, rhetoric*; key elements – *hyperbole, fantasy, emotion, enemies, manipulation, deceit, utopia*.

Summary review of the key themes

Defining propaganda
The attempt is first, and necessarily, to try and define propaganda, an elusive mission, given the vernacular charge carried by the word. The problem is that in the vernacular 'propaganda' is merely a term of opprobrium. Yet definitions are critical – how we define something illuminates the theories that we hold. In one sense, of course, the entire book is a definition of propaganda and its domain. Is it merely, as Schumpeter (1966) says, any opinion with which we disagree? There is unintentional propaganda, press photographs for example, and what is propaganda to one person is not propaganda to another: meaning is negotiable. The issues of definition are also ones of scope: many things, for example a libel case (McDonald's), can be propaganda. Education, especially secondary education, is another theatre of propaganda, where state objectives are sought under the guise of the factual pedagogy of truth. This more elastic definition of propaganda also involves aspects of state activity that would not normally be included in more orthodox reviews, but such official vices as the manipulation of statistics, or the control of information, are surely legitimate candidates for a propaganda category. The state is inevitably one of the principal instigators of propaganda, since in a democracy it cannot resort to coercion alone or

[handwritten margin notes: Scorn / Contempt / Severe / Criticism]

even at all, and all governments, even non-democratic ones, seek at least the passive acquiescence of their people.

The claim is that 'propaganda' is emphatically not merely another word for advocacy, is distinguished from mere marketing by its didacticism and its ideological fervour. Whereas marketing is rooted in consumer response, propaganda asserts, and ideology is seldom submerged, although it may be reinterpreted to fit the particular cultural paradigms.

Explaining propaganda
The book then continues by seeking to explain the phenomena that it has sought to define. The essential argument is that the propagandist drama-tises our prejudices and speaks to something deep and even shameful within us. Propaganda thus becomes a co-production in which we are will-ing participants, it articulates externally the things that are half whispered internally. Propaganda is not so much stimulus–response as a fantasy or conspiracy we share, the conspiracy of our own self-deceit. The force of propaganda is also the forcibility of the utopian vision.

We argue that utopian visions are the underlying presence in much propaganda – the thirst for utopia creates an illusion of a perfect or per-fectible world order. This is manifest in phenomena as diverse as socialist realist painting or the advertising industry. And the successes of propa-ganda are unintelligible without the recognition that the persuasion strate-gies propagandists espouse are in the main emotional. Emotion is seen as the antithesis of reason, and the power of propaganda is largely the power of the emotional appeal. It is difficult though not impossible to speak of a 'rational' propaganda, and propaganda appeals proceed less by argument than by assertion and affirmation. Propagandists exploit, in particular, cer-tain emotions such as fear and anger; and eschew models of man as a rational decision maker.

Foundation concepts: symbolism, rhetoric, myth

This review of what are seen as the foundation concepts of propaganda is extensive, and the conceptual basis for the applied case studies that follow on. It would be impossible to imagine a propaganda devoid of these ele-ments. Effective propaganda is the synthesis and manipulation of all three. These chapters examine the definitions, meanings and debates over these terms, and their salience in propaganda.

Rhetoric
This chapter seeks to explain the enduring success of rhetorical forms of persuasion. We are concerned with how rhetoric works – the constituent

elements of good rhetoric: ideas such as the co-production of meaning, the power of ambivalence and the workings of rhetoric subversively within a value system rather than as an external challenge to it, and the distrust of the power of rhetoric from the time of Plato expressed in the half fearful, half admiring description of Pericles ('a kind of persuasion played on his lips'). Particular attention attaches to the importance of metaphor as the key tool of persuasive rhetoric.

Other ideas of particular interest: the concept of 'resonance' (Tony Schwartz): good rhetoric 'smoulders in the mind'; the notion that rhetoric is not merely a conduit of meaning but actively creates it; and, related to this, the concept of the Rhetorical Vision (e.g. 'Star Wars', 'Axis of Evil'); the Hall Jamieson thesis on the feminisation of rhetoric; the power of partisan language to embed itself in everyday discourse and thus appear natural, neutral and objective; the easily overlooked rhetorical forms such as 'bureaucratic' rhetoric (today the propagandist use of language often has obfuscation as its objective, such as the phrase 'no clear proof' of animal–human infection in Britain's BSE crisis); the propaganda use of language to change perceptions, as with the pressure group which says that it advocates the 'ethical theft' of mahogany products (a perverse juxtaposition that seeks to ethicise the unethical by a linguistic strategy that places it in a fresh perspective).

The political and social impact of rhetoric is critical – such as the language strategies used to persuade in the environmental and genetically modified food debates ('Frankenstein foods') and in the American 'civil war of values'; its historical impact, with examples of great rhetorical events like Reagan and the *Challenger* disaster; and the rhetoric of war, both the language of dynamic metaphor as in Hitler's images of blood pollution or Roosevelt's 'day that will live in infamy' to the evasive technical jargon of modern warfare which deliberately aims to detach people from the human realities, as with 'collateral damage'.

Myths

Nor could propaganda exist without the myths that rhetoric articulates. Myth, defined as the sound of a culture's dialogue with itself, expresses the key values of a society in story form. We see myths as critical to society's integration and sustenance, and to destroy a society's myths is to destroy society.

The impact of myths on history has been critical – for example, the German militarist myth of the 'stab in the back' by democrats at the end of World War I – and the core methodology of propaganda has been the creation and sustenance of myths, such as the myth that the US constitution enshrines the right to bear arms. It does no such thing, yet the popular belief that such a guarantee exists has had incalculable impact on the debate over gun control in the United States. Yet myths are fluid. They can be created, fabricated, resurrected, and the art of propaganda is to do this, since myths always have open texture. Thus there can be myth entrepreneurship, such as the Goebbels manufacture of Horst Wessel, or the (alleged) Soviet authorship of the myth that AIDS was conceived by US scientists as a deliberate way of harming minorities.

And sometimes myths and history are elided. We view history not objectively but through the prism of its own self-presentation. Queen Elizabeth I ordained how we should see her: the imperious white mask swathed in silk and jewels. Our imagery of history is the creation of its propaganda – we imagine Lenin arriving at the Finland station in worker's cap to be greeted by the 'Internationale'. (Actually the train was not 'sealed', he was wearing a homburg and the band was playing the 'Marseillaise': Figes 1997.) The past is thus self-mythologised (sometimes with significant consequences for the present).

Symbols

A symbol is condensed meaning: consumer brands, for example, are symbols and their extraordinary power is the power of symbolism. A symbol is a heuristic or cognitive short cut: why read a treatise denouncing Nazis when that poster of a caricature German officer with a hanging corpse reflected in his monocle (Rhodes 1993) did it so much more vividly and concisely. As a pre-literate form of meaning, symbols can communicate with those for whom the act of reading is a chore. Symbols can and frequently do express, embroider, simplify or resurrect myths. The claim is that their attraction to the propagandist is as an immensely cheap form of gaining recognition, capable of endless duplication – for example, the wartime Victory V sign, and non-fixed in their meanings, eluding precise scrutiny and creating possibilities of multiple interpretation. They also have an inherent plasticity: they can be reinvented, endowed with new meanings.

Judicious choice or manufacture of symbols and symbolic strategies is an important part of the propagandist's work. Political propaganda texts are studded with symbols, such as Eisenstein's symbolic construction of the film *Battleship Potemkin* with its literally faceless Tsarist Guards, but so also is our popular culture – the Marlboro cowboy an obvious example. Symbols can be resurrected, as with the reworking of the raising of the Stars and Stripes from Iwo Jima to Ground Zero (with a detour via denim advertisements: Goldberg 1991). Or they can be given a new and even contrary interpretation.

Key elements of propaganda

The trinity of Myth, Rhetoric and Symbolism undergirds other major elements of propaganda, and we explore other principle themes in some detail, in particular:

Manipulation and deceit

To say that propaganda is manipulative is to define a necessary but not sufficient characteristic of the term. Propaganda in the populist vernacular sense of the term is equated with the idea of manipulation, even duplicity, but never truth seeking. Objective 'facts' are irrelevant, or at best subordinated to persuasive advocacy. Deception is not some essential essence of propaganda's definition, but it is critical to the popular understanding of propaganda. Deceit and forgery are widespread, from the 'Zinoviev letter' (its alleged forgery is now disputed) in the British general election of 1924 to the present day – for example, with the use of technological resources to distort, as in some modern US campaign commercials. One aspect of this manipulation explored by the book is the idea that in propaganda we are being invited to share a fantasy. Propaganda does not necessarily make the error of asking for belief: instead, exaggeration is presented for us to join in as a shared experience.

Another aspect of manipulation is censorship and the exclusion or control of information. In the first Gulf War, for example, licensed groups of journalists were strictly supervised, others were excluded altogether. Thus another important form of propaganda today remains state censorship, the denial of information. And then there is passive (bureaucratic) propaganda, the use of reports, statistics, etc., to manipulate perceptions.

The social construction of enmity

Propaganda is a consequence of our need for enemies: they are not just there but necessarily there: they give coherence and definition to our values and they motivate us to action. They provide someone to blame when things go wrong. Their common humanity is reducible to a mere cipher, such as communism's top-hat image of the capitalist. It is indeed difficult to imagine a propaganda without enemies, for enemies are essential to a compelling narrative structure, but the choice of enemies is inherently political, for Hollywood producers as well as newspaper editors.

Case studies in modern propaganda

The conceptual framework is applied in the second part of the book to a series of review analyses of contemporary theatres of propaganda. The list is hardly exhaustive, but does represent some of the significant phenomena of propaganda that have structured and continue to direct our political culture. Today the old extrovert propaganda, in all its naivety, has been replaced by something more insidious – more akin to the art that conceals art. Spin and sound bite, negative advertising and single-issue groups suggest a pervasiveness of polemical forms of persuasion which amounts to the propagandising of our public culture; even business is drawn into the vortex.

Single-issue groups

We begin with single-issue groups since they represent an extraparliamentary political force of supreme power. They shape our times, and they do so through their mastery of the arts of propaganda. Victory goes not to the most, but to the most vocal. Their poverty makes them entirely reliant on the creativity of a visible public symbolism. The consequences of issue group propaganda, social and political, are very real and tangible. Since public opinion on many things is ambivalent, final victory often goes to those who possess the best propaganda. Many mainstream political issues – Green, feminists – originated not in political parties but in single-issue groups and their masterly proselytisation techniques. The major ideological and value civil wars such as abortion have been fought outside the parties and with the tools of propaganda.

Negative advertising

Never was the word 'propaganda' more apposite as descriptor than in the case of US election campaigns, and this is an area where our discussion of the enmity thesis would apparently have singular relevance. Negative political advertising is a tried and tested device and a sinister exemplar of propaganda today. At one time it seemed to have become the preferred mode of choice in US politics. Everyone knows about the Willie Horton advertisement, but the level of saturation of mainstream US politics with negativity is less well known internationally. Citizen alienation apparently does not find a lenitive in rational discourse but in thirty-second diatribes. A culture of contempt may be the achievement of propaganda even if it is not the objective: but negative advertising also has its cogent defenders.

Symbolic government

But campaigns cost. In most countries, politician and party are a materially impoverished actor limited in their ability to purchase media. The fight is therefore for a favourable media account, testing politicians' propagandist skills to the uttermost. The recognition that no public event is capable of one sovereign interpretation, combined with the observable susceptibility of the media to bandwagon effects, has meant the expertise of governments increasingly becoming not operational management or policy entrepreneurship but communication skill, that is, 'spin'.

Democracy is a political system and a social ethos where we seek persuasion rather than coercion, and it is the recognition that the interpretation of events can be managed or even foreordained that has informed the work of the Blair government in Britain, which has become a supreme practitioner of this craft – replacing, for example, half the heads of civil service information offices with partisan evangelists. However, we identify spin as part of a broader idea, the Symbolic State, embodied in the apparent solution of problems at the rhetorical level alone, preoccupation among politicians with generated imagery, the manufacture of symbolic events and concomitant devaluation of the roles of ideas and ideology in politics.

Marketing war

Afghanistan/Iraq

Both the motivation and the conduct of these wars were inspired and structured by communication, i.e. propaganda, objectives. Again our conceptual formula is used to illuminate the meaning of these events. It seemed at times that 'asymmetric' warfare would be fought on an imagistic as well as a military plane. Uniquely for a terrorist organisation, Bin Laden spoke in a symbolic language instantly intelligible to his allies and enemies – to recruit, of course, but also to terrorise, not just by the act but by the imagery, specifically Bin Laden himself as serial role player and personality cult. There was the 'propaganda of the act' – Nine-eleven – but also classic polemicism – hyperbole, rage, an enemy to hate. Those vivid tapes, and the Taliban's posture as peasant underdog against the global superpower, made some commentators early on suggest that the Taliban/Al-Qaeda were winning the propaganda war. The US had been taken off guard. There was a general recognition that a global culture had sponsored global propaganda and the US had to master this if it was to retain hegemony in a global order. In Iraq the US sought to meld very old propaganda forms – battlefield leaflets, radio stations and the like – with some remarkable new ones: the 'embedded' journalist, the Hollywood stage set at Qatar and direct approaches via e-mails to enemy commanders, abetted of course (at least in the US) by shamelessly partisan media. New insights on propaganda emerge such as the importance of the coherent integrating perspective, or the problem of imagistic control in wartime.

Afterword

The book concludes with a brief review of the measurable impact of propaganda, both as an influence on the direction of current events and as a guiding hand in history. Certainly the failures in propaganda campaigns are not difficult to identify. 'Measurement' remains an insuperable problem, but the great successes must give us pause. There is no final word. Debates such as these can never be concluded, only taken further. But that propaganda has been in history, and remains in our society, an important social phenomenon that deserves to be called by its true name, and studied as part of a general education to equip the citizen for society, is not in doubt.

Part I

Defining what and reasoning why

1

A question of meaning

This chapter teases out the meanings of the term 'propaganda', a task complexified by its common usages and connotative content. We orient and nuance the definition through a number of primary categories: rational persuasion, manipulation, intent, breadth. The chapter seeks further clarity of definition by exploring the complex and ambivalent relation of propaganda to the mass media, appraising some of the limitations of the analytical methods that regularly convict media texts of the ideological determinism associated with propaganda. Subsequently we engage in a summary discussion of the conceptual elasticity of the term as embodied in such diverse cultural theatres as education, the arts, bureaucracy, war, journalism.

Defining propaganda

Propositions on propaganda. This is a dull chapter. No book purporting to explain propaganda can shirk the imperative of actually trying to define the term, a maddeningly elusive task which necessarily involves a recitative of competing definitions. We begin by reviewing the key propositions which summarise the principle debates about the definition of propaganda; a definition that must remain open ended since there can be no closure when a concept comes laden with so much historical baggage.

Problem of definition: no agreement

It is inevitable that there will be no collective agreement about the definition of propaganda in the sense that we might have accord on the meaning of many other words. Our task is to extract what seems most reasonable from the competing interpretations of the term. Since propaganda is a social phenomenon, to define it is to prescribe its social signification and also to accept or reject the utility of the concept. There is also debate on meaning, since we have no rigorous scientific source or juridical authority for the term but only historical usage. To attempt to define propaganda is to tread lightly upon a conceptual minefield. How we define propaganda is in fact the expression of the theories we hold about propaganda. For Franklin (1998) there are no agreed, mutual uncontentious criteria which allow the separation of propaganda from information. Schumpeter (1966) said that the contemporary usage of the term 'propaganda' refers to any statement 'emanating from a source that we do not like', while Jones (Singh 1989) affected to see no difference between propaganda and the institution-bound transmission of information. What in marketing is 'selling', in school is 'teaching', in the church is 'proselytising', in politics is 'propagandising', in the military is 'indoctrinating'. Foulkes (1983) comments that propaganda is an elusive concept to define 'partly because its recognition or supposed recognition is often a function of the relative historical viewpoint of the person serving it'. Thus many investigators limit themselves to extreme situations such as war. Foulkes further argues that the recognition of propaganda can be seen as a function of the ideological distance which separates the observer from the act of communication observed.

According to Pratkanis (Pratkanis and Aronson 1991), the first documented use of the term occurred in 1622 when Pope Gregory XV established the Sacra Congregatio de Propaganda Fidei in the wake of the Counter-Reformation. Militaristic methods were failing and propaganda was established as the means of co-ordinating efforts to bring men and women to the 'voluntary' acceptance of church doctrines:

> the word propaganda thus took on negative meaning in Protestant countries but a positive connotation (similar to education or preaching) in Catholic areas . . . the term propaganda did not see widespread use until the beginning of the twentieth century when it was used to describe persuasion tactics employed during World War One and those later used by totalitarian regimes.

Colloquial uses

Nevertheless the definition of propaganda is complicated by the fact of a colloquial usage wherein propaganda is always associated with the idea of excess, and only a term of abuse, signifying the hyperbolic, extreme, declamatory. The pre-war anti-marijuana film *Reefer Madness* represents in its hysteria the kind of excess popularly ascribed to propaganda texts, or the rumours, the outrageous fibs that yet fester in the gutter of human consciousness – that the Holocaust did not happen, that Nine-eleven was a CIA or an Israeli plot, that the lunar and Mars landings were enacted in a

Hollywood studio. Another illustration would be so-called 'black' propaganda, such as the Japanese campaign against Sunkist lemons in which Japanese agricultural groups 'spread the rumour via the media that American lemons were laced with Agent Orange' (*Chicago Tribune*, 12 June 1995). A major reason for this elusiveness of meaning is that no working definition of a concept can ever be separated out from its colloquial uses. Hyperbolic aspects are really particular uses of propaganda rather than descriptions of some essence of propaganda itself. Nevertheless such colloquial usages cannot simply be set aside.

Hence attempts to discuss the term objectively are distorted by the accumulated meanings of the concept through history, its associations with the Third Reich, for example making dispassionate analysis difficult. Drescher (1987) argues that 'propaganda' conjures up images of governmentally inspired lies, often either in the context of a 'hot' or a 'cold' war. Usually, Americans in particular think of propaganda as an activity that is engaged in by authoritarian or totalitarian governments. In fact, as Drescher points out, propaganda may involve the truth, even though it falls into the category of 'boo' rather than 'hurrah' words. That the idea of propaganda remains one in which elements of guile, cunning and duplicity are not foreign is apparent even from the objective definitions.

Can there then be no meritorious propaganda? The genre itself is viewed by many as inherently immoral and even its wartime uses consigned to the historical limbo of necessary evil, like the bombing of cities. Examples of a virtuous propaganda are more numerous than we would imagine, and propaganda is not merely a psychotic expression of our social dysfunctionality . There *can* be a virtuous propaganda, when for example propaganda represents an alternative strategy to legal coercion, as demonstrated by the comparison between the very different attempts to deal with the scourge of illegal drugs and that of cigarettes.

The scope and complexity of the idea of propaganda have often been neglected in such parochial definitions that invest it with its familiar and narrow vernacular meanings. The word is not value-neutral and its strong connotative associations need to be interrogated if it is to be used critically rather than rhetorically. If I choose to speak of something as 'propaganda' I do not mean necessarily that it is worthless; it may be worthy because the aspiration to establish the cause as a legitimate one is worthy. Words are tools. To use tools effectively demands not the search for the perfect tools we do not possess but rather that we recognise the limitations of those we do. The term 'propaganda' may be conceptually flawed, but it is not thereby redundant.

Clarity

Propaganda generally involves the unambiguous transmission of message: 'clarity' may not be an essential adjunct to the definition of propaganda but it is certainly a normative one. Propaganda carries this inherent contradiction, that it is a complex purveyor of simple solutions. Schick (1985) relates propaganda to 'media whose symbol systems are visible'. Foulkes (1983) could thus argue that a propaganda doctrine, socialist realism, could portray only those problems and conflicts for which the system ostensibly has a solution, and he also relates this phenomenon to western mass culture.

In *Rhetoric, Language and Reason* Michael Meyer (1994) argues that manipulation and propaganda proceed as if the question they were dealing with were solved. However, good propaganda may disguise the fact that it thinks the issue solved. Meyer is perhaps referring to the uncritical nature of propaganda: other forms of advocacy can betray elements of self-doubt, but propaganda cannot. For other critics, language becomes propaganda not so much by its inherent structures and devices as by the ideology it champions. Propaganda is shameless advocacy.

Distinguish from communication and rational persuasion

Propaganda is often defined, however, by its antithesis, by what it is not, and its essence is viewed as primarily emotional and not rational persuasion. Indeed, it is difficult to imagine what rational propaganda would actually look like: propaganda may sometimes appear rational via mimicry of the forms of reason, but that is not the same thing. It represents the supremacy of the visceral emotional appeal in persuasion. Propaganda seeks out our emotional sensitivities at their deepest with associations both compelling and even irrational: 'a land without people for a people without a land' was a vision, a bewitching slogan, for the early Zionist pioneers, to summon a reality that did not exist before its rhetorical promulgation. But where mythical truth is turned by the alchemy of rhetoric into embedded fact, and when the dream ignores the context, the consequences can be destructive – here an entire people arbitrarily wished away.

And since a great writer can articulate our deepest emotions with an eloquence far beyond the talents of any stump politician, it follows that *littérateurs* are better propagandists than either journalists or politicians. Describing the political impact of Yeats's play *Cathleen ni Houlihan* on the Dublin working class in 1902, Marreco (1967) comments:

> thus Yeats persuaded Maud Gonne to play the part of the mysterious old woman who appears to the hero, Michael Gillane, on the eve of his wedding in the troubled days of 1798 and causes him to abandon all human happiness

for the sake of Ireland. No one who saw Maude Gonne in the part ever forgot the climax of the play when Michael follows the old crone out, and, when his father asks him if he has seen an old woman going down the path, replies, 'I did not. But I saw a young girl and she had the walk of a queen.'

Many authorities claim to perceive a strong distinction between 'propaganda' and the more usual 'communication', 'information' or 'persuasion'. Ellul (1973) certainly distinguishes between propaganda and communication; Moran (Schick 1985) sees them as existing in opposition to one another. The Institute for Propaganda Analysis, an influential force in the United States in the late 1930s, deliberately chose the word 'propaganda' rather than the more emotionally neutral 'communication'. While the term 'propaganda' is sometimes used erroneously as a substitute for other categories of persuasion, it is not synonymous with persuasion as such and is in fact a highly distinctive form of advocacy. There are many examples of non-propagandist persuasion. Authorities – Jowett (Jowett and O'Donnell 1992), for example – do distinguish propaganda from persuasion: 'propaganda tends to be linked with a general societal process whereas persuasion is regarded as an individual psychological process'. Propaganda is 'mass suggestion', and its targets are the multitude, and this, as Jowett says, is what distinguishes it from persuasion.

Propaganda is also seen as the obverse of 'reason', or rational persuasion, often expressed by the word 'information'. Thus some have claimed to perceive an elemental bipolarity in the language of politics, that political language has two essential strategies, the one emotive, that uses rhetorical-emotional appeals (propaganda), the other passive (rational and informational). Propaganda is certainly not rational persuasion. The appeal to reason, where it occurs, is just another propaganda strategy.

When we define propaganda in the attempt to distinguish it from advocacy, we also say that it carries a 'sense meaning' rather than a bounded or lexical definition – the recognition that 'I know it when I see it'. To some extent one is really seeking to try and define propaganda by what it is not. As a sealed discourse, the concept excludes notions of intellectual exchange. Smith *et al.* (1946) distinguish between propaganda and education by arguing that the former is concerned with attitudes on controversial issues whereas the latter is concerned with attitudes on non-controversial issues. According to Salmon (1989), 'the problem with this distinction is that it assumes the *status quo* as non-controversial, which it is for the haves of society'. Teachers and others, Salmon believes, are also manipulative and benefit from socially sanctioned labels which conceal persuasive intent.

Yet other critics see 'propaganda' as having no conceptual content distinct from 'mere communication', but propaganda is more specific than 'communication', a word which refers to any transmission of information without judgement as to whether this transmission is biased, hyperbolic or deceitful. The relation is therefore of set to subset. Schick (1985) cites the communication theorist George Gordon, who argued that propaganda was merely a value-free subset of communication, 'good if its ends are good, and bad if its ends are bad'. To make no distinction between propaganda and communication is to demand a language that is itself judgement-free. Yet language must be a tool to elucidate meaning, otherwise we accept a bland formulation whose utility as tool of expression is dulled. For Taylor (1990) 'Propaganda is simply a process by which an idea or an opinion is communicated to someone else for a specific purpose. Speeches, sermons, songs, art, radio waves, television pictures, one person or millions of people — none of these things matter here for purposes of definition.' In fact he appears to see self-interest as the core definition of the term: 'Propaganda uses communication to convey a message, an idea, or an ideology that is designed to serve the self-interest of the person or persons doing the communicating. . . . Propaganda is designed in the first place to serve the interests of its source.' Definitions such as this are merely particular types of propaganda rather than descriptive of some conceptual essence of propaganda itself.

Manipulation

Propaganda represents the antithesis of the objective search for truth. Truth itself is not a motive but another rhetorical formula. But propaganda seldom succeeds by a direct assault on cherished beliefs, and works best by subversion. All propaganda is manipulative, and it would be meaningless to speak of a non-manipulative propaganda, since that would render the term conceptually redundant. For example, Elizabeth I recognised her people would mourn the banished cult of the Virgin Mary which her Protestant Reformation had confiscated from them. What better policy, therefore, than to substitute an earthly virgin for the celestial one, and she promoted the soubriquet 'the Virgin Queen'.

Most scholars almost invariably draw an association between the word 'propaganda' and the idea of manipulation. They see manipulation as the core of propaganda. Drescher (1987) notes that 'the withholding of relevant information is planned to result in the persuasion of outsiders, hence it is propagandistic'. Pratkanis claims that the ancient roots of propaganda lie in Catholic counter-reaction, its modern forms in duplicity, especially the British duplicity of World War I. Its origins lie in deceit: now he sees it as influence via the manipulation of symbols and the psychology of the individual.

Jowett and O'Donnell (1992) define propaganda as a 'careful and predetermined plan of prefabricated symbol manipulation to communicate to an audience in order to fulfil an objective'. Propaganda is 'the deliberate and systematic attempt to share perceptions, manipulate cognitions, and direct behaviour to achieve a response that serves the desired intent of the propagandist'. The word has attracted negative connotations 'and now refers to the form of communication in which a communicator manipulates others, often without their being aware of the manipulative effort, for the source's own benefit rather than the benefit of the receiver'.

Philip Boardman (1978) also attempts a number of definitions of propaganda that focus on deceit:

> from this earlier neutral (Roman Catholic) meaning, propaganda has now gone the way of the word rhetoric to mean language and verbal strategies which are deceptive and misleading, or which misrepresent the true motives . . . propaganda is that language – most easily a slogan, but perhaps a White Paper, a Manifesto, an editorial, a book – which influences the false doctrine or serves a false ideology.

The author defines propaganda further: 'while propaganda might once have referred to the political exhortation or patriotic speech (propaganda of the faith), it now generally implies some element of deception, either in the statement itself or in the motives of the speaker. Thus there is a very fine line between political oratory and propaganda.'

Although by their very selection of examples these and other authorities refine their definitions, sleaze would appear to be the common denominator. This would also be true of its vernacular meaning. Yet, while propaganda is certainly something more than advocacy alone, manipulation is a vague term indeed, a universe that incorporates everything from selectivity of facts to the extremities of fraud. All advocacy manipulates. Inherent in these discussions is the notion that propaganda does so in a more extreme form, which may be necessary to effective persuasion, but does a disservice to the cause of truth.

Intent

Is 'intent' essential to the definition of propaganda, and can one indeed produce unintentional propaganda? The point is not a frivolous one, since the range of phenomena embraced by the term propaganda would be vastly expanded were we to extinguish the requirement of intent. The attribution of intent as a motive would ascribe an introspection, a level of self-analysis which many proselytisers and evangelists do not possess; the possessors of a private monopoly of truth do not see themselves as propagandists but as truth tellers. Yet accepting this point also complicates the problem of definition, inflating the term's conceptual expanse to embrace the work of hordes of journalists, television producers and the like, and, indeed, accusing them of something they were not aware of committing. The journalist Paul Johnson, for example, in his lurid propagation of the views of the author of *The Bell Curve* (*Spectator*, 18 February 1995) would never have seen himself as a propagandist.

Jacques Ellul (1973), the French theoretician of propaganda, regards all biased messages as propagandist even when the biases are unconscious. He would not impose the criterion of deliberate intent. Ellul thus makes an almost exact equation between propaganda and bias. This is rather extreme. All propaganda is necessarily biased, but not all bias is necessarily propagandist. This view is somewhat controversial. How can something be propaganda if the communicator is not even aware that the messages are functioning as such? The best propaganda is sometimes the most unconscious. The consumer, or the historian, of propaganda might judge a text to function thus even when the producer did not: all those school books and stories which once extolled the glories of the British empire were not necessarily seen by their authors as propaganda. They thought they were telling the truth or obeying the proudest voices of conscience and profession: the effects of their work may have been manipulative, but the intent may not have been. The question of the relationship of intent to propaganda, then, admits no easy resolution – particularly in relation to education, whose pedagogues see themselves as communicators, yes, persuaders sometimes, never propagandists.

Most authorities disagree. For such critics, propaganda is defined by intention, its authors seek a particular political effect on a particular audience. For Lee (1986), propaganda is communication, but it implies that the communication is purposeful. And Taylor (1990) argues that 'by propaganda I mean the *deliberate* attempt to persuade people to think and behave in a desired way. I recognise that much propaganda is accidental or unconscious. Here I am discussing the conscious, rational decision to employ techniques of persuasion designed to achieve specific warlike goals.' These sources, then, would see one distinguishing property of propaganda as being this deliberate intent to influence, but the same could be said of much human communication – rarely indeed is the communicator entirely indifferent to the consequences of the message. Indeed, if propaganda were only purposeful communication, much would be included, in fact most kinds of advocacy.

Unintentional propaganda is produced all the time, much of the best, in fact. A propaganda event may boomerang and be conscripted by antagonists against the cause that sponsored it. This is exactly what happened in the case of Sir Robert Vansittart's polemic *Black Record* (1941), which contrived to fulminate not merely against the German government but against the German race. Dr Goebbels promptly printed and distributed it. The remark of a US officer in the Vietnam War, that it was 'necessary to destroy the village in order to save it', circumnavigated the globe, a self-inflicted wound.

Another illustration of how propaganda can transmute into counter-propaganda is afforded by George Bush's landing on the aircraft-carrier *Abraham Lincoln* to declare the Iraq war over. (In fact more Americans were to die in the guerrilla epilogue than in the war itself.) This was combustible advertising material for Senator Kerry (*New York Times*, 11 November 2003): the spot opens with a quick shot of the 'mission accomplished' banner featured on the carrier. It then shows Bush on the flight deck in an olive-green flight suit and with a helmet tucked beneath his left arm. Inspirational music kicks in as the spot continues. An announcer runs through Kerry's record while the advertisement goes on to flash images of him at various points in his life: making his presidential announcement before the carrier *Yorktown* in South Carolina, receiving a combat medal as a young navy officer, speaking with voters, speaking at hearings and writing at his desk. The *New York Times* comments, 'the commercial does not bang viewers over the head with the image. In fact, the script does not refer to it once. Campaign strategists said that is because the moment speaks for itself and provides a good curtain-raiser for a spot that highlights Mr Kerry's vast experience as a soldier and politician.'

Propaganda can be indirect, and a text can be usurped as propaganda even when the intent was neutral – the creation, for example, of an image in photo-journalism. Key images from the Vietnam War were scorched on to the consciousness of world opinion: the napalm-burnt girl, naked, running in terror; the South Vietnamese General Loan (Eddie Adams) firing a gun into the head of a helpless Vietcong suspect; the John Filo image of the college girl kneeling over a lifeless body at Kent State (Goldberg 1991). Whatever the intent of their original photographers and publishers, these images circulated internationally through many media as classic atrocity propaganda; their perceptual construction helped determine how we interpreted the war then and how we remember the war now.

One communication vehicle that particularly raises the question of intent in propaganda is the documentary. This announces in advance an intent of objectivity, addressing burning issues of the day. While nobody would suppose that a documentary film maker would properly lack a sense of mission, the ostensible purpose is truth telling and it is therefore a particularly appropriate vehicle for the confection of lies.

Television documentaries can mutate into propaganda by the very measure of their selectivity, and without, necessarily, any conscious intent on the part of the producers. Lesley Garner, the reviewer of a BBC-2 television documentary on euthanasia, *Death on Request*, pointed out that the merciful, self-chosen extinction exhibited in this film is still one end of a long moral spectrum which could end in the deliberate deaths of the disabled, old, unwanted (*Daily Telegraph*, 16 March 1995). In this case, the film makers recorded the relief *in extremis* of a Dutch motor neurone disease sufferer, Cees van Wendel de Joode, in an ostensibly powerful documentary about the organised ending of a human life. We are profoundly moved by his suffering, and convinced by the humanity of his official executioners, but the film is about a single case, and it does not seek nuance or debate about the complexities of euthanasia. At what stage does this, a partisan argument, mature from advocacy into propaganda? An interesting point of comparison is an overtly pro-euthanasia propaganda film called *I Accuse*, directed by Wolfgang Liebener, which premiered on 29 August 1941. The Nazi functionaries implementing Hitler's 1939 (secret) euthanasia decree explained it to Liebener and requested a film (Herzstein 1978), since Goebbels had sensed disquiet among many over the regime's policy, especially among Catholics.

I Accuse is about the deterioration under multiple sclerosis of a young woman whose husband grants the release she craves by killing her, something doctors have refused. Her husband is put on trial. The concluding scene illuminates the arguments for euthanasia that the regime had sought to mobilise. The doctor changes his mind. Comments Herzstein:

> the dialogue in this scene is extremely effective, intellectual as well as emotional in its appeal, and apparently calculated to let the audience make up its own mind about the problem. No one is portrayed as a hero or as a villain, audiences left the theatre feeling sympathetic for the accused and his action. Eliciting this reaction was precisely the aim of the regime.

In *I Accuse* it is the law that is made to seem barbarous, not the administrators of euthanasia. The German film is intelligently made propaganda, designed to precipitate a change of the general climate of opinion by raising doubts.

Both films use the core idea of a helpless, suffering person who wishes to die at a time and under circumstances of their own choosing. Is the 1995 documentary thereby propaganda as well (even though unlike the Nazi one it is not perverted in the cause of licensed murder)? The intent is not sinister, whereas the Nazi film was made to legitimate a euthanasia programme where the victims had no choice: in fact its pretence that choice was everything is a masterly deceit. However, the rhetorical mechanisms are similar, since both films simplify the euthanasia debate and ignore the ambiguities which lie at its heart.

Whether or not something is to be regarded as propaganda should also be judged by context as well as technique and intent. Richard Attenborough's 1982 film *Gandhi* (Carnes 1996), for example, employs many devices which associate with propaganda – the idealisation, the caricature of the British enemy, the dwelling on that enemy's atrocities while simplifying the causation – but it is not propaganda. The imperialism it denounces is long defunct, nor is there any cause in the contemporary world for which it could be seen as symbolic advocacy. In this it is different from another Attenborough film, *Cry Freedom*. Had *Gandhi* been made in the days of the Raj it would, indeed, have been propaganda.

Breadth

However, Pratkanis and Aronson (1991) note that as scholars began to study the topic in more detail many came to realise propaganda was not the exclusive property of totalitarian regimes, nor were its contents limited to clever deceptions. The word had evolved: it is communication of a point of view with the ultimate goal of the recipient coming to voluntarily accept this position as if it were his or her own. Many critics define propaganda very indulgently. Lee (1986), for example, includes the press, since it:

> emphasises the existing and superficial and neglects socially important economic and political developments. . . . International affairs are stereotyped or caricatured, reduced to positive and negative generalities . . . political campaigns for office or for reforms are dramatised in simplistic and personality terms with basic issues avoided, glossed over or presented in a biased manner.

Then there are such things as the 'development of obviously kept researchers, often under contract to prove specific policy contentions or to plot special interest social strategies'.

Ellul (1973), similarly, sees propaganda as an omnivorous force; arguing that his definition is too broad, Drescher (1987) criticises this tendency to see virtually any form of communication as propaganda: 'In Ellul's views everything is propaganda. Under these circumstances, it is equally useful if nothing is propaganda.' Ellul, Drescher argues, would consider the multinational corporation to be propaganda, but surely it is only indirectly political in its expression.

Any label is rhetoric. Inscribed within it is both a perspective and a domain, but labels also have inherent plasticity and they remain open to conceptual repackaging. The word 'propaganda' needs redefinition as well as definition. No longer can we dismiss it as merely something to do with *Der Stürmer*, Leni Riefenstahl, *Pravda*, *Izvestia* or even the occasional party political broadcast. Today it assumes myriad disguises and reinvents itself, now as an objective video news release on animal rights, now as the latest management fad or popular treatise on pseudo-science. The purpose of reclassification is to alert us to the new possibilities it has colonised.

Propaganda, interpretation and the mass media

Perception

No attempt to discuss/define propaganda can ignore the special relevance of the entertainment industry. Entertainment is historically the most successful propaganda genre, because narrative momentum compels interest and (sometimes) disguises intent. But only a minority of entertainment products are made to service a distinct political agenda. These may be either subtle or explicit, but they are still political – films such as Gillo Pontecorvo's *The Battle of Algiers* (1966) or the Chinese anti-colonialist epic *The Opium War* (1997).

But we reject the vogue notion that is everything is political. Most entertainment either eschews politics or exploits them either for narrative purposes or to establish the ethical content of the text. It can seldom be overtly political because politics is a signal which activates a defence mechanism. The broad social liberalism of many entertainment products – racial integration, harmony, social esteem for different segments of the community – represent an ethos. This ethos may be celebrated overtly: it is more likely to be simply a benevolent narrative assumption. But it is not propaganda. 'All entertainment is propaganda' would be a nonsense, the notion that since entertainment is manufactured by commercial interests it will invariably celebrate the *status quo*. The Frankfurt School in particular viewed all entertainment as propaganda for a dominant social order – as gratifying to the masses and therefore contributing to their further enslavement. This is a gross simplification. As a cultural product entertainment must seek out novelty and therefore subversion, since continuous celebration of the *status quo* would bore.

Drescher *et al.* (1987) argue that what we classify as propaganda is also a function of receiver perceptions: 'the same message may function as objective information or as a persuasive statement in a different context', and 'whether the message is interpreted as fact, propaganda, or noise depends on the perspective of the receiver. . . . A sender may also transmit a message with the intent that it serve more than one function. . . . Messages may also be transmitted with the knowledge that Nation A will regard them as statements of fact while Nation B will find them to be persuasive in nature.' Thus Drescher argues that 'the speech that to some sounds like simple patriotic praise may be perceived by others to have self-serving and propagandist motives' (Boardman 1978). Many apparent cases of propaganda 'will be interpreted differently by different readers'. There are ambivalent cases which provide both information and fog – for example, the newspaper which announced that 'inflation in March rose 3.2 per cent, continuing the trend of declining rates of interest'! Films may be propaganda only in the sense that some of the audience would choose to react as if to propaganda, since that is the meaning they have chosen to appropriate from a repertoire of possible meanings. A literary or musical piece, such as Mozart's *Marriage of Figaro* which satirised the aristocracy on the eve of the French Revolution, can be used as propaganda (Perris 1985), and as political propaganda it was the more beguiling, and the more dangerous, because clothed in a language that was not verbal but musical and therefore both meaningful and imprecise.

Derrida (1981) claimed that no single interpretation can claim to be the final one. He demonstrated this not by revealing how the text's meaning is reconstructed but instead by deconstructing a text in the sense of showing its failure to be interpreted unambiguously. Of course this is not true of much historical propaganda, one of whose characteristics is that meaning is indeed non-negotiable. Even in the war propaganda realm we do indeed meet examples where an openness to interpretation exists: the subtlety of a film like Powell and Pressburger's *Life and Death of Colonel Blimp* (1943) introduces us to layers of meaning. And Cook (1992) has described how – partly through the agency of para-language – the message and story line of much commercial advertising is ambivalent. For example, Calvin Klein advertisements would seem deeply vulgar if put into explicit words (see J. O'Shaughnessy 1995) . This coheres with the Hovland thesis that people are not passive receptors but active participants in the creation of meaning (Hovland and Janis 1959). The most extreme version of this view sees all meaning as a ultimately a co-production between text and viewer-receiver (see Kellner 1995).

An apparent propaganda event can turn out to be anything but. Responses – how people choose to interpret material – may diverge from what the producers intended or what logic would anticipate. This was, for example, true of the television film *The Day After* (Adams *et al.* 1986), about the aftermath of nuclear war. It had the distinction of the third highest viewing audience in US television history, and therefore (potentially) some social significance. The prediction was that it would foment opposition to the policy of nuclear deterrence. The reverse happened. The share of people seeing Reagan as the more dangerous President declined appreciably, from 36 per cent to 27 per cent. This can be explained on several levels. First, the film was not the explicit propagandist evocation of nuclear armageddon predicted by the political right. In fact it was rather anodyne. Second, nuclear holocaust was shown as survivable, which may have surprised people, since Americans already accepted the destructiveness of nuclear war. Third, the film had received considerable publicity, sensitising viewers to possible manipulation, and making the film anticlimactic. Researchers were unable to detect even a trivial shift on the key questions.

Moreover, ideology itself is perhaps a more complex matter than heretofore. To say that a cultural text today is ideological-propagandist is to assume that ideology itself has remained clear-cut, but ideologies can and do meet and merge in a complex theatre of ideological pluralism; political opinion becomes less definite when people hold a portfolio of right-wing and left-wing positions rather than coherent ideological packages. This is a consequence of components of the 1960s counter-culture being absorbed into the political mainstream. For example, elements of the figure of Rambo himself – long hair, bandana, androgynous breasts – are derived from it (Tasker 1993), while for Webster (1988) 'the countryside is a symbol that unites the contemporary ecologist with the old blood-and-soil Right (hinted at in terms like hick-chic)'.

Propaganda and interpretation

Each producer of a message relies on its recipients for it to function as intended. This assumes they know how to interpret the message. Meaning is always negotiated in the semiotic process, never simply imposed implacably from above by an omnipresent author through some global code (Hodge and Kress 1988). This is where the didacticism of much classic propaganda fails in persuasive terms, for example Soviet propaganda, which assumed a hypodermic model of opinion modification; Goebbels in contrast sought to disguise propaganda as entertainment. Traditional semiotics errs in viewing the relevant meanings as 'frozen and fixed in the text itself', to be extracted and decoded by the analyst by reference to a coding system that is impersonal and neutral and universal for users of the code (Hodge and Kress 1988).

The media text does not have one meaning but has to be interpreted, Rambo for example, within the social and political context that gave birth to it, so that the complete meaning of a propaganda event therefore emerges only when we study the society that produced it. Like many cultural theorists, Kellner (1995) argues that the audience is not 'a passive receiver of pre-digested meanings'. The domain of communication and culture cannot be clinically separated, and in Kellner's view they are an interactive system.

There are dominant, negotiated and oppositional readings. For the propagandist this presents the problem of the unintended reading, and the audience may not find a propaganda text stimulating in the ways expected. For example, propaganda texts are a great source of counter-propaganda. The Nazi epic *Triumph of the Will* was an imagistic warehouse for anti-Nazi propaganda, storing easily retrieved vistas of menacing aggression. Audiences can resist a dominant interpretation and appropriate images to create their own meanings; thus, for example, men in a New York homeless centre were antagonistic to a movie sympathetic towards the police (this accords with Gramsci's model of hegemony and counter-hegemony: Kellner 1995). And when Michael Moore's *Roger and Me* (Bateman *et al.* 1992), an undeniably propagandist film, was shown to a group of Japanese students, they actually reacted slightly favourably towards business in their own country.

Negotiation of meaning

Much in film eludes precise study: it can be described but its nuanced nature makes analysis difficult. How do we dissect 'atmosphere' or tone? What ideological function do we ascribe to stylistic devices that qualify or even subvert a dominant ideological reading, such as a certain playfulness? Tasker (1993) complains of 'standards of truth against which popular films have been judged, standards which rarely admit the complexity of terms like fantasy'. The new critics' focus on surface forms provides, it is argued, 'a valuable qualification to a political understanding of popular texts as an uncontested space for the play of dominant ideology', since specific formal devices do not carry an innate or essential meaning.

Attempts to stigmatise the mass media as propaganda are usually doomed to failure because of the ideological elusiveness of much of their content. Yet, if political fixity is a characteristic of propaganda, it is rarely to be found in the popular cinema (Tasker 1993). As a consumer product, media must please target markets which are usually ideologically heterodox: seldom therefore do they issue an ideological clarion call, more an enigmatic invitation to interpretation. Entertainment is both an important source of propaganda and encapsulates the conundrum of its definition. Much entertainment that is characterised as propaganda by right and left-wing critics is seldom consumed as such by its audience, since such critics are really searching for a rhetorical bullet in an ideological war. Critics are much too willing to discern in texts the hand of the propagandist and this involves them simplifying the entertainment product in the cause of an ideological argument, such as those who dismissed the film *Michael Collins* because it had pre-invented the car bomb and other pedantic details. The entertainment industry knows that it is entertaining a politically plural audience, redneck as well as New York bohemian. Interpretation is left open. Classification as propaganda may represent the coercive imposition of a rigid interpretation that the facts do not support if 'facts' are taken to include the complete ensemble – narrative structure, surface decoration of texts, stylistic devices, dialogue, meaning brought to the role by actors from their previous roles. The result is a complexity which does not so conveniently sustain classification as propaganda.

Nor does the mere possession of a dominant ideology – such as Clint Eastwood's *Dirty Harry* (1971) persona, for example – necessarily amount to propaganda. The fact that people appropriate it as propaganda does not amount to the same thing at all. For example, *Blackhawk Down* is primarily a generic action movie, celebrating bravery, military comradeship, self-sacrifice. It could be 'read' as patriotic celebration or conversely as an indictment of failed political policy for which the soldier is made to pay. The plasticity of the Reagan-era *Top Gun* (1986) is more easily categorised as propaganda.

Alison Griffin (1995) discusses this in relation to the Welsh-language soap opera *Pobol y Cwm*, which raises the question of intent and negotiated meaning in propaganda, since it is a programme that subtly portrays an array of different attitudes and offers a dominant ideology, yet presents materials that can be used by nationalists as a source of support: 'competing pressures and subtexts indicate the ideological complexity of the soap's engagement with topical issues'. Issues, including socio-political ones, which, like cottage burning, gained in importance in the serial from 1988 remain 'negatively unresolved' and 'as a site of discursive struggle' meaning in *Pobol y Cwm* is not transmitted in any fixed or static way. Viewers 'produce' determinacy from non-determinate materials. A good example is the in-migration to the village of the boorish Birmingham publican Ron Unsworth, who wishes to bring strip-tease to the pub: yet the locals are seen to tolerate him. According to Griffin 'students interpret elements in the series as anti-English invader propaganda', adding that respondents told anecdotes antagonistic to English in-migration: 'there was little ambiguity in the respondents' reading of the "invasion" story-line and its invited ideological argument'. It is also possible to dwell excessively on the openness of texts to interpretation. While all texts are interpretable, it is important to recognise the concept of a dominant reading.

David Thorburn (1988) issues a number of important cautions against tendencies to discern in the media text the hand of the propagandist – or, at least, 'the fashion for seeking out what are said to be the ideological structures controlling cinematic discourse'. He believes that this risks severing itself from the way in which such texts were conceived and experienced by those who created them and by the audience who consumed them, and he adds, 'a scholarship insensitive to aesthetic features of the medium would be radically enfeebled'. In particular, he criticises Barnouw's work on the connection between 1960s spy series and US imperialism, since Barnouw regarded series such as *Get Smart* as US propaganda. Thorburn claims that in fact four of these six serials have a subversive and parodic energy and that Barnouw falls into errors of interpretation because of his indifference to their aesthetic character, to tone and atmosphere, failing to perceive alternative textual interpretations such as their satire of the conspiratorial world view embedded in 'straight' or serious spy fiction

Thorburn accuses Barnouw of seeing only that the series envisaged Americans as living among unscrupulous conspirators who required a response in kind; camp villains were part of no core interpretative essence but simple surface features in ideological fables. He claims such readings are in fact typical of social science analyses of television (for example, at the Annenberg school): a more sophisticated school, Raymond Williams and his imitators, also would surface television's ideological substructures as apologia for advanced capitalism. Thorburn suggests that ideological pressures are not dictates; television in the Third Reich, by contrast, was being planned as a propaganda instrument, to be kept out of private hands and confined to public spaces. Television and film are 'consensus narratives', so created by myriad interactions between the text, its ancestors, competitors, authors, audience and socio-economic order. This communality explains their unoriginality and also their power to articulate the wisdom of the community: 'that inherited understanding is no simple ideological construct, but a matrix for values and assumptions that undergo a continuous testing, rehearsal and revision in the culturally licensed experience of consensus narrative'. (But if the meaning of such cultural texts were clearer they might indeed function as propaganda.)

Categories and scope of propaganda

As we have seen, critics differ in the elasticity of definition that they would ascribe to the word 'propaganda'. While we cannot permit a definition so broad that it ceases to possess an independent or operational meaning, our perspective is that current understandings have erred in restricting its meaning. To illustrate this breadth, we discuss the propaganda endowment of such diverse subjects such as war, architecture, music, bureaucracy. For even the date of an intended event can have propaganda merit and be nominated for that reason: 911, the emergency telephone number in the United States, was picked by Al-Qaeda with truly diabolical cunning; another example is Admiral Wemyss, with all the savvy of a Madison Avenue executive, choosing 11–11–11 as the moment – month, day and hour – for the conclusion of World War I. Even a coin can function as propaganda, such as the minting of the Vichy French coins which substituted for the anachronistic 'Liberté, egalité, fraternité' a new formula, 'Eglise, famille, patrie', to condense and express the values of the regime. Since propaganda is the denial as well as the evangelisation of message, censorship also functions as propaganda. For example, no legal case in history can have quite so bizarre a title as 'The Government of the United States versus the Spirit of the American Revolution', but in 1917 the crime of depicting the British as America's enemies even in the context of the War of Independence was sufficient to merit a substantial (three-year) jail term (Kammen 1978).

Propaganda and the arts

The problem of dissecting the concept of propaganda lies also in its breadth, since so many theatres of human activity exhibit propaganda content. Architecture, for example, cannot be excluded from any discussion of propaganda – to involve it is not to extend the boundaries of the term, but to attempt to give it a completeness of definition. The fact that the master propagandist himself, Adolf Hitler, was such an enthusiast for architecture should suggest the *prima facie* existence of a connection between his twin passions. The Great Dictators were sponsors both of a massive conventional propaganda industry and architectural monumentalism in the pseudo-Romanism of Albert Speer, Stalinist baroque, or the triumphalism of Italian Fascist construction. Architecture is not merely associated with the propaganda of totalitarian dictatorships. Lutyens's New Delhi, though actually built largely after the publication of the Montague–Chelmsford report which started the clock ticking for the Raj, is an extraordinary and studied essay in imperial superciliousness: it is propaganda in stone.

The arts can also function as propaganda and, again, to apply the term is by no means to imply condescension. Manifestly, the greatest art has sometimes had propaganda intent: El Greco and Titian were propagandist celebrants of the Counter-Reformation, glorifying the wealth, power and renewal of the Roman church. David, similarly, was propagandist for Napoleon, evoking the radiance of his imperium. Shakespeare was an apologist and occasional propagandist for the Tudors in general, and in particular for Elizabeth I and for that brilliant conception of monarchy and legitimacy which was so beguiling to her court. Thus to say that art is 'propagandist' does not consign it to being mere crude iconic representation. Propaganda does not inevitably preclude the kind of nuanced subtleties critics find endearing. (Art ceases to be propaganda when it becomes art?) For example, the fierce dejection and fatalism evoked by Byron's *The Prisoner of Chillon* is art, a melancholic analysis of one man's fate, but also an impassioned curse on the authoritarian regimes which do this to people, i.e. propaganda, its meaning is both individual and universal (political). And the arts can be deliberately suborned for political purposes: the Information Research Department of Britain's Foreign Office, for example, had Orwell's

Animal Farm, an anti-communist allegory, translated so widely that it could even be read in Telugu and Norwegian (Adams 1993).

Categories: academic and education

Propaganda has normally been juxtaposed with education. The difference between propaganda and education 'lies in the idea that propaganda teaches people what to think whereas education teaches people how to think' (Smith *et al.* 1946). In fact education is seen as the real antidote to propaganda, but, as Taylor (1990) suggests subversively, 'they might sometimes however be one and the same thing'. For example, Nazi mathematics textbooks expressed problems in terms of calculating the angle of attack of a dive bomber (Grunberger 1991). All education programmes have their biases – in Spain, for example, the Armada of 1588 is portrayed as a trivial sideshow – yet many of the debates on education are ultimately about ideology and therefore, potentially, the use of education as propaganda. Some critics claim to see the content of modern education as at best an ideology of secular humanism, at worst liberal propaganda. For example, for some social conservatives (Chris McGovern, *Daily Telegraph*, 18 January 1997) 'much of the so-called British history boils down to little more than a mass of amorphous social history common to the whole of Europe. It is permissible, for example, to mention Nelson, but do not assume this means the battle of Trafalgar. It is as likely to be conditions below deck.' What then is propaganda? One could indeed argue that secondary education is overdetermined by partisan value systems, neither offensive nor subversive in themselves but certainly in tension with values that stress competitive national achievement both in war and in other theatres. This (more nationalist) perspective was sanitised from the syllabus. The preference for social as opposed to political history is the articulation of a value preference, one moreover which is the subject of great debate among professional historians. If such a debate, it is argued, has not been 'won' among the community of historians, why does the mass juvenile curriculum assume that it has?

Are we not in fact back in a world very familiar to historians of education themselves, that is, the use of education to perpetuate a dominant orthodoxy, in this case liberal but in the nineteenth and early twentieth centuries nationalist and imperialist? 'The purpose of textbooks was to inculcate patriotism, plain and simple' (Kammen 1978). The Victorian schoolboy knew all about the pantheon of national military heroes and their victories; he had also absorbed the ideology underpinning it, that England's cause was always just, and the empire existed for the betterment of the human race. Similarly, his literature – which he often had to learn by heart as poems – reinforced this ideology: he would learn Newbolt's 'Drake's Drum' and 'Vita Lampada' or 'The Burial of Sir John Moore at Corunna' or 'The Last Fight of the *Revenge*'. There might indeed be a tentative literature of environment ('Woodman, Spare that Tree') but social histories, if taught at all, would be limited to Arthur Bryant (1942) vistas of stout English yeomen, their apple-cheeked children and blazing cottage hearths. A different age, perhaps, and one where the propagandist thread in education is readily identified, but is our own school history any more objective? Can only one ideological hege-mony flourish in the education system at any one time, is there no value or possibility of ideological pluralism? Nowhere does this question of differenti-ation between propaganda and education arise with more acuity than in academia itself: for when does an academic discipline become special plead-ing or group interest advocacy, and when does *that* become propaganda? Academics may be involved in the disinterested search for truth, but they also partake in a ferocious battle over the distribution of resources: their aims, mission, findings and subject discipline are sold and sometimes over-sold – for instance, by the claim that something (sociobiology, for example) is in fact a 'science'.

Journalism

Dr Goebbels, no slouch when it came to the analysis of propaganda, very properly observed, 'even the *Times*, the most democratic paper in the world, makes propaganda in that it deliberately gives prominence to certain facts, emphasises the importance of others by writing leaders or comments about them, and only handles others marginally or not at all' (Herzstein 1978). Goebbels understood, for he was contemptuous of explicit propaganda, dis-missing the *Mythos* of Alfred Rosenberg as 'ideological belch'. The distinc-tion between conventional journalism and journalism-as-propaganda is well illustrated by David McKie's (1995) contrast of the style of the *Mirror* and *Sun* newspapers in the 1992 general election. The *Sun*:

> campaigned with a style and a brutal wit which the *Mirror* rarely matched. The difference between the panache of the *Sun* and the *Mirror*'s predictability was the difference between the *Mirror*'s election-morning 'Time for a change' and the *Sun*'s 'If Kinnock wins today will the last person out of Britain please turn off the lights,' illustrated by a picture of Neil Kinnock's head in a light bulb.

Categories: direct action

Propaganda, one would imagine, is popularly identified with the macro-organisations of the powerful corporation, the nation state, the press mag-nate, the totalitarian empire. Given the particular course set by twentieth-century history, it is hardly surprising that propaganda is seen as an activity of the omnipotent monoliths, and that perhaps we should be grateful to them for not using its persuasion alternative, coercion. The identity of propaganda in the late twentieth century shifted fundamentally in so many ways. It is especially true that propaganda is now no longer the exclusive prerogative of the holders of power: communications technology, particularly the internet, makes self-authorship possible. Everybody now can be a propagandist. Not even money is entirely necessary. All that is needed is determination.

Seen in this light, the idea of propaganda becomes more demonic to some and more acceptable to others. Propaganda is not only a means by which states and organisations can sustain their power and continuity, but also offers their miniature enemies a means of opposing them, such as the propaganda of direct action, and also, for anyone who can afford a computer, cyber-propaganda. Modern propaganda as a genre is a resource both of the powerful and of the puny. Propagandist direct action which is provocative enough, such as lesbian activists abseiling into the House of Lords, will stimulate public attention. Many intelligent citizens, who would never see themselves as victims of propaganda, are nevertheless members of single-issue groups: not everything those groups do is propaganda, and nor are those of their activities which can be described as propaganda always contemptible. Often such acolytes simply do not accept that what their group is in fact doing is engaging in propaganda. (It is necessary to enlighten them?) At its furthest extreme, direct action becomes terrorism and is represented by groups such as the Real IRA or, on a more diminutive scale, the Animal Liberation Front. Such groups eschew constitutional process: they do engage in conventional propaganda but spike it with acts of violence. For Schmid and de Graaf (Crelinston 1989) 'Terrorism cannot be understood only in terms of violence. It has to be understood primarily in terms of propaganda. Violence and propaganda, however, have much in common. Violence aims at behaviour modification by coercion. Propaganda aims at the same by persuasion. Terrorism is a combination of the two.'

Bureaucratic propaganda

War propaganda and revolutionary propaganda should be seen not as the (almost) exclusive contexts for propaganda, but rather as particular variants of it. Other kinds of propaganda might include, for instance, bureaucratic propaganda – the official accounts promulgated by government departments but, also, the way they manipulate information. Thus during the 1980s the definition of 'unemployment' was changed about fifty times by the British government. Altheide and Johnson (1980) assert that bureaucratic organisations through official accounts of themselves (propaganda) create a self-justificatory world. They describe how bureaucrats draw on and reaffirm a socially constructed reality by exploiting the logic of 'official' information – statistics, annual reports and so forth (Rakow 1989). There is no such thing as neutral information?

The political forms of propaganda – political in the sense of being directed by the state itself – have been less overt and crude with the demise of the great dictatorships, but present and insidious nonetheless in this form of bureaucratic propaganda. 'Research' is manipulated and information massaged: measures of air pollution, for example, may be taken in streets where there is no traffic. 'Information' can also be ideological in character, such as the so called 'Parents' Charter' mailed to every single British home under the auspices of the former Conservative Education Secretary, John Patten. Then again, information can be censored or withheld, even ancient information. The British government long concealed items from World War I such as details about the trial of Sir Roger Casement, or even the sinking of the *Lusitania*, or information about Ireland in those years. What, for example, was the identity of that master spy who from 1884 to 1922 gave Dublin Castle full details of the activities of Irish nationalist conspirators? We still do not know (Richard Bennett 1995).

Some of what bureaucracy does is actually a propaganda activity, with the aim of increasing its power and diminishing its inconvenience. Bureaux seek the exercise of power for its own sake and to vindicate the magnitude of that power; and bureaucratic success is measured by the size of budgets and numbers of officials employed. Bureaux are organisations that seek permanence by self-perpetuation, they are thus their own self-justification and they seek their ends via, essentially, the control of information (in such methods as the denial of journalistic access). Incompetence is hidden, energy is invested in preventing secrets, such as the bombing of Cambodia, from being released (for example, the official persecution of 'Spycatcher' Peter Wright).

Bureaucratic propaganda is a fact of life in all societies. The official lies, evasions and bureaucratic fog often thrive beyond the radar screen of propaganda textbooks precisely because they seem to be the antithesis of what is publicly imagined to be propaganda, not high-decibel polemic but silent, mannered and arcane. Conventional propaganda is equated with lurid language but here is manifest the reverse – bureaucratic language actively seeks to sedate and it is therefore ignored. Bureaucratic propaganda delights in the language of obfuscation and obscurity, evasion and denial. It does, especially, seek to present itself as 'rational'. Administrative jargon masks ideological rigidities, proposals are made to seem logical and self-evident – indeed, the entire Nazi enterprise was often veiled in such bureaucratic formularies. 'Neutral' vehicles, e.g. reports, statistics, carry ideological messages. The 'normality' of bureaucratic propaganda is enhanced by its espousal of bogus rationalism, such as the claim in Britain's BSE crisis (Harris and O'Shaughnessy 1997) that there was 'no clear evidence' that BSE could move from animals to humans (as if the requirements of scientific and civic veracity were the same). Moreover bureaucratic language is depersonalised, the author not an individual but a system.

War as propaganda

War is communication. The aim is seldom the complete physical extermination of the enemy but to persuade them to surrender: the object of war is therefore the enemy's morale. The activity of warfare is structured by propaganda objectives, and, partly because of this, wars are conducted inefficiently.

Strategy itself is often dictated by symbolic aims – the symbolic meaning of the place, rather than whether it is the easiest route or the most easily defended. The strategies of World War II are in particular a theatre of symbolism. For example, General Mark Clark's determination to capture Rome in 1944 rather than advance up Italy allowed Kesselring to regroup. Clark could, potentially, have cut off their retreat, but was more interested in the propaganda value of capturing Rome. In the Spanish Civil War Franco's strategy was distorted by the propaganda imperative of capturing the Alcazar of Toledo. This point could be made by innumerable other examples from the most famous campaigns in history: that propaganda value is a significant military objective and often overrides a rational military calculus. Notably of course there is Hitler's inflexible refusal to make a strategic withdrawal at Stalingrad when the Wehrmacht was trapped; Stalin, conversely, would hold the right bank of the Volga at any conceivable cost. Stalingrad was the symbolic pivot of World War II – and upon its outcome hung the future of the war. In World War I the equivalent was, perhaps, Verdun.

Thus propaganda and war are inseparable. In the twentieth century war had meant the mobilisation of vast civilian populations. They had to be convinced. For example, by the end of 1944 Dr Goebbels even withdrew 100,000 men from the front lines of the dying Reich – the size in effect of the current British army – to make a colour epic about Prussia surrounded during the Napoleonic wars, *Kolberg* (Herzstein 1978). Propaganda also muffles the reverses of war, as with Churchill's conversion of Dunkirk from physical defeat into a great (moral/rhetorical) victory.

Symbolic sites can be murderously contested when they engage with national myth. Nuremberg, the great stage of Nazi rallies, was militarily valueless but still the target of a notorious air raid. Battle may be sought purely for the imagery it generates. The 1968 Tet offensive by the North Vietnamese was, military, a failure, and the United States was the unambiguous victor. Yet the US public – with Vietcong appearing even near the US embassy itself – were persuaded otherwise (Gustainis 1989). This victory became a US defeat because it was perceived as such. Thus propaganda is not just a branch of military activity. Military activity itself is inherently propagandist, in part, or entirely.

There can be no final closure in the debate on the meaning and definition of propaganda and there will always be those who regard the idea as bogus. But if the word has no meaning, under what other terms can we discuss the phenomena it purports to describe? More neutral forms and formulations give neither coherence nor intellectual direction: a word is a classification system, and definitions are meaningless if they would include everything from Goebbels to the 'Lost and found' column of the local newspaper in the same conceptual breath. Words focus perceptions, we cannot be said to 'know' what we lack a language to describe, and without this particular word we become desensitised to the ubiquity of its operation. For example, when Governor Pataki asked that New York schools should teach the great Irish famine as a Holocaust, that is, of deliberate causation, he is both undermining the historical primacy of the Jewish Holocaust and teaching children an erroneous lesson. The real comparator, with the 20 million dead of Mao's Great Leap Forward (1958–1961), and the derivative lesson on the rigid imposition of fundamentalist economic ideologies, is completely lost. Where propaganda is the text students come out of education not the less but the more ignorant. Why not, then, use the term?

2

Explaining propaganda

'Why propaganda?' This chapter seeks, if not to answer, then at least to understand that question better – or, more particularly, the persistence of propaganda into our own time. The salience of propaganda texts and events in history is not in doubt, although the measure of its impact is impossible to gauge and therefore permanently subject to dispute; the visible continuity of propaganda as a mode of social mobilisation beyond the wars and dictatorships of an earlier generation and into our own age does, however, require us to seek some explanation. Where the entire communications context is controlled, as in the old totalitarian dictatorships, as in the 'hermit kingdom' of North Korea today, the reasons for propaganda as a ubiquitous form of social control need little elaboration. What is more mysterious is why propagandas should still flourish in modern democracy, among a better-educated generation, one incubated moreover amidst the cacophony of mass media. Our cultural conditioning in Western countries includes the acquisition of learned defences against the blandishments of advocates and advertisers of every kind; indeed, did we not learn to filter out many of their messages, our reason and even our sanity would be in doubt. Yet propagandists continue in business via emotional appeals that exploit our uncertainty, stimulate our fantasy and take advantage of our credulity: we ask for belief, and the request is answered.

Propaganda, as has been discussed, is no recent, or ephemeral, historical phenomenon. The crusades, for example, were propelled on a cascade of ecclesiastical propaganda after Pope Urban's sermon at Claremont in 1095 (Taylor 1990), since the church wished to externalise the destructive energies of the delinquent knights who were ravaging early medieval Europe. While propaganda in some recognisable sense of the term has actually been a characteristic of all societies since people first formed organised communities, and developed the ability to create the symbol systems that could lend them cohesion, the twentieth century may be called in particular the propaganda century – with as much legitimacy certainly as it might be termed, say, the 'scientific century' or 'the American century'. The explanation for the significance of propaganda as a driving influence on earlier twentieth-century history is not difficult to find. The coalescence of literacy with urbanisation and manufacturing and new tools of communication meant that authority was now more often negotiated than merely imposed. Hierarchical social orders found themselves challenged, or displaced. The need to persuade was now a necessary concomitant of the ability to command. The great dictators found persuasion not the less but the more necessary, their police states monitored not only or even primarily by policemen but by citizen informants, galvanised by propaganda. Moreover the nation state now sought more from its citizens – total mobilisation for total war, conscription, social ownership and even collectivisation. The need for mass persuasion arose out of the recognition that the threat of violence alone could not attain the ends the dictators sought

This does not really explain the success of propaganda today, in less naive and more open political cultures. A primary explanation for the persistence of propaganda in stable, supposedly rationally based and technocentric societies is the power of the impassioned emotive appeal alone with no reference to empirical evidence at all, and the tenacity of irrational beliefs once they have been acquired. The Chicago School idea of the rational public is derived from the eighteenth-century Enlightenment. But there are other views of the public as irrational, and these raise possibilities of manipulation via communications technologies (Robins *et al.* 1987). For this authority 'the modern state is, necessarily and inescapably, the propagandist state'. People are in general not skilled critics of logic and argument, and we do not train them to be so. They may detect the lie and still behave as if they believe its truth; propaganda research has consistently demonstrated that people can respond favourably to a message even when it is obvious that it is biased.

Propaganda is also utopian. While it is impossible to ascribe a set of characteristics which would be comprehensively descriptive of the genre, in the sense that every propaganda text would embody them – since no such set of universal characteristics exist – the utopian idiom approximates closest to such a universal. Propaganda is, usually, an articulation of idealism and idealism is unthinkable without some vision of that end, the world picture, which is the object of idealist striving.

Thus in this chapter we first advance a theory-based argument that (1) the continuity of propaganda today lies particularly in the emotion-driven nature of our response to stimuli; that is, the emotional not the rational appeal that affects us at almost every level of our activities; (2) in spite of the cynicism that may be derived from the spectacle of failed utopias, the utopian vision, the perfectibility of things, still arouses the activists and sometimes the targets of their activism; (3) then there are aspects of our cognitive processes – the way we deal with information – which may account for the continued vulnerability of our societies to propaganda, such as 'default beliefs', self-deception and fantasy, and the permanent possibilities of interpretation and shifting perspectives. In the second section of this chapter we explore how the continuity of propaganda as a genre is explained by the contemporary context – the delegitimation of coercive control, weakening of parochial loyalties, explosion of information sources, the ascent of single-issue groups as a dominant mode of political expression. In such a context, all loyalties are tentative and therefore the possibility of defection is ever-present, for where allegiance is rented it has to be continually renegotiated and thus the activity of persuasion cannot cease, making propaganda activity not the less but the more likely.

Why propaganda? (1) Theoretical approaches

Emotion: the supremacy of emotion over reason

Most propaganda is primarily emotional rather than rational in content. For Hitler, persuasion was only about the generation of collective emotion. 'They are like a woman, whose psychic state has been determined less by abstract reason than by an emotional longing for a strong force which will complement her nature. Likewise, the masses love a commander, and despise a petitioner' (Blain 1988). Emotion is the core of propaganda.

The notion of human decision making, whether political or consumer choice, as rational and not emotional has been the governing paradigm not only of economists but also of political science and marketing. Yet economists long clung to models of man as a utility-maximising rational decision maker: 'but as Searle (1995) argued, it is implausible to claim, in deciding what to eat in a restaurant, that we have some set of antecedent well ordered preferences and perform a set of calculations to get on to a higher indifference curve' (O'Shaughnessy and O'Shaughnessy 2003). In fact – as Laurence Moore demonstrated in *Selling God* (1994) and Marc Galanter in *Cults* (1989) – people can be entirely won over by a message even though it is totally bereft of any rational content at all, and the appeal is simply to social and emotional satisfaction. Velleman (2000) contradicts such theories as those which present political, social and consumer decision making as a calculus of pluses and minuses for the various options. Instead he sees deliberation in decision making as in the main descriptive – we think in terms of self-described or other-described images of the choices available, whether a product or whatever. If decision making does indeed rest on multiple alternative descriptions, propaganda's opportunity to persuade lies in composing them. Faith can be based exclusively on trust without any real understanding. This is particularly true of the less well educated, who tend to use the 'likability heuristic', choosing primarily on the basis of feeling – the implicit favourite model – and then finding other evidence to justify choice. The search for evidence becomes subsequent, and not antecedent to, conviction.

The rational model of decision making ignores the power of emotional prejudice to outweigh illuminated factual truth, our ability subjectively to decry a fact as false even when we know it objectively to be true. In a study by Rozin *et al.* (1986) people willingly ate fudge shaped as a disc, but much less so when it was configured as animal droppings, and similarly with sugar which they saw poured from a bowl and into a box which was then arbitrarily named 'sodium cyanide'. Known facts cannot bleach out negative associations and the powerful emotions they inspire. The power of the emotional appeal in persuasion also arises partly out of our difficulty in resolving uncertainty, where there is no logical path but only multiple risk. Take the case of genetically modified foods. The concerned citizen remains mystified. One set of partisans point to the potential of GM crops to liberate the Third World from hunger, they argue also that fewer pesticides are required, less land needs to be cultivated, allowing more of the natural environment to flourish. Their opponents also claim closure in the debate by simple reference to the rhetoric of 'Frankenstein foods'. Previously we have argued (O'Shaughnessy and O'Shaughnessy 2003) that people do not react in proportion to the probability of some particular outcome: epistemic emotions exist independently of assessments of logical probability – in fact simply to imagine an event causes emotion, even if the probability of it occurring is in fact zero. Even when there is a recognition that some outcome is highly unlikely there is always wishful thinking, while insecurity and uncertainty create a vigorous market for dogmatic reassurance.

Today there is no real reason to believe that rationality in public discourse has greater sway than in the past. Some would argue that today there is a cultural drift towards more extrovert emotion-driven forms of behaviour and therefore of persuasion, with our inquisitorial media, confessional talk shows, etc. Many public manifestations of a mood of anti-science make no attempt at reason; the rejection of genetically modified crops, while in itself not irrational, was hyperbolic in expression. If human beings were indeed rational decision makers there would be little need for propaganda. Since all decisions imply goals, they therefore invoke values, and the emotions that express, power and undergird those values. Decisions involve choices and trade-offs and these are seldom value-free or devoid of emotion. It would be a very peculiar, unique perhaps, propaganda that relied on reason alone – a superficial, or social, assent might be secured by mere logical exposition, but often not conviction and the commitment that flows from conviction: indeed, rhetoric and feelings have by a tradition going back to Aristotle been viewed as the opposites of reason and logic, even gendered opposites, feminine and masculine. Persuasion and propaganda may involve tactical appeals to reason, but in general a process of logical exposition is peripheral to it. Rarely can a process of logical demonstration entirely convince, since it cannot remove all doubts – and where there are doubts, reassurance and therefore further persuasion are needed. We have claimed (O'Shaughnessy and O'Shaughnessy 2003) that in symbolic logic, by contrast, there is only one solution – answers are demonstrated, errors exposed, in a deductive process. In life, decisions both trivial and life-changing must often review different perspectives, different interpretations, so that persuasion becomes possible.

Thus the appeal of propaganda is in general to emotion and not to reason. It proceeds by dogmatic assertion, as if there could be no debate on the propositions advanced: in Le Bon's words 'an orator wishing to move a crowd must make an abusive use of violent affirmation' (Herzstein 1978). Dogmatic assertion does convince, it elevates mere value judgement to the status of truth or law and, contrary to Petty and Cacioppo (1981), people are persuaded by such when they are content to delegate their thinking to others, be it pundit, priest or politician. Constant assertion can stun consciousness, naturalising the perverse as normal and interrupting internal dialogue to prevent counter-arguing. For propaganda is not a nuanced production; in it assertion has little qualification and the arguments of opponents are parodied rather than rebutted. There is frequent recourse to *ad hominem:* opponents presented as either bigoted or self-interested; repetition, simplification and black–white polarisation. Reagan, for example, would use anecdote and metaphor rather than argument, introducing citizens who had performed some selfless act, promulgating a never-never land of trickle-down effects and Laffer curves. Evidence is not to be assessed or explained, but manipulated or invented. Propaganda texts contain scant recognition or capacity for intellectual abstraction, they are actively antagonistic to abstract thought, eschewing the tentative, the complex line of argument, the weighing and debating of evidence. The concern of the propagandist is not with how we think but how we feel.

There are numerous instances of propaganda and advertising exploiting this fear of emotional manipulation by claiming an appeal grounded purely in reason. This is, of course, an emotional appeal in itself. Governments are

particularly prone to making it in the face of some catastrophic error, con-
trasting their reason with their critics' emotion, and this is the rhetorical
core of the propagandist argument whenever the state or big business has
committed some wrong and will not own up to it: whether the victims of
nuclear tests, victims of Gulf War syndrome, BSE, particular drugs or much
else. Propaganda aimed at sophisticated targets has, however, long found it
necessary to page homage to reason. As Taylor (1990) suggests, 'Allied
propaganda in World War II did not give up the blond beast and yellow peril
strategies, but took into greater account the need to explain what people
were fighting for and what institutions they were defending.' Even Goebbels
felt impelled to create an 'intellectual' weekly, *Das Reich*, to counterbalance
the intellectually moribund Nazi media.

Utopia

Much propaganda would seem to register the existence of a utopia – it can
be a hoped-for utopia, or a utopia irretrievably buried in the past. Many
political extremists are disappointed utopians, and the vision of a perfect
world or world order, its possibility, perfectibility or existence in the past, is
the undisclosed presence behind propaganda. This would account for the
harshness of some propagandas and their rejection of any offer to compromise, as the achievement of whatever utopia their creators have in mind
continually eludes their grasp, as, in an imperfect world, it is bound to do. It
is the impatience with the messiness, fluidity and compromise of the real
world that marks the propaganda order. Thus activists rejected the claim of
the first deaf Miss America, Heather Watson, to be ambassador for the deaf
(*Sunday Telegraph*, 26 March 1995). Hard-line advocates of cultural deafness resented the fact that she had learned to lip-read such that it was difficult to guess a disability. The current orthodoxy dictated that sign language
is the only acceptable form for communication for the deaf. Deaf advocates
protested, saying that she had no right to represent people whose culture
she was unfamiliar with. In the words of one deaf ideologue, she might be
clinically deaf, but she didn't have the social identity of a deaf person
   A vision of the perfectible does sustain belief. It assuaged the insecurities
of the newly urbanised twentieth-century publics, and helped satisfy
mankind's need for meaning and a coherent value system. This would perhaps help explain fundamentalisms with their contempt for the ambivalence of the secular world. From socialist realist art to the imbecile ecstasies
of consumer advertising, the 'dull footage' is edited out, in Schudson's
(1982) terms, a Panglossian best in the best of all possible worlds. Adams *et
al.* (1986) have analysed Reagan's 1984 election campaign as a 'manipulation of romantic pastoralism'. One photograph that appeared in *Time*

depicted Reagan beneath a huge mural of 'Reagan country' – hills, farms, rivers – symbolic of the virtues for which Reagan ostensibly stood – thrift, hard work, patriotism, etc. Such imagery occurred in his television advertising and campaign biopic: 'America had wandered, he told us, and the symbolism of traditional rural life becomes a way of telling us what we had left behind.' But this need for utopia is what unites, conceptually and stylistically, all propaganda. A yearning for the primordial, for the pure – for a perfect world, in fact – is prelapsarian fantasy.

For Mircea Eliade (1991), we long for something altogether different from the present instant, something either inaccessible or permanently lost, in fact he argues that it is really a yearning for paradise itself. On this argument, behind the hectoring, the meanness perhaps of much propaganda, lies the search for paradise, rage at its loss and some half-articulated idea that it once existed. Hence, for example, Rubin (Kevles 1994) summarises Rachel Carson's vastly influential *The Silent Spring* (1962) thus: 'such popularisations have an excessively evangelical tone, akin to that of the temperance movement, which urges environmentalism upon us not only to preserve the earth but also to achieve a kind of personal salvation'. Nostalgia is one form of this paradise – in Eliade's view, the most abject nostalgia discloses the nostalgia for paradise. This, I think, is true of many political cultures – for example, the yearning in later Rome for the pristine, ascetic-heroic virtues of the Republican era. This is no mere romantic speculation – Wiener (1981), for example, in his *English Culture and the Decline of the Industrial Spirit* demonstrates the way a yearning for a lost rurality, an arcadia of Merrie England, permeated the culture, with negative consequences in his view. In World War II this rural England was, time and again, the symbol in posters and films such as *Mrs Miniver*. But nostalgia is not perhaps exactly the right word to describe what is going on in propaganda. As Webster (1988) says of populist rhetoric, it is important to see it as a 'strategic mobilisation of the past rather than nostalgia'. Indeed, the pasts of the propagandist bear little relation to the historical past – the Nazi creation, for example, of aboriginal 'Germania', was largely an exercise in fiction, and Webster argues that the American 'new right' was a mass of contradictions. It managed to conscript a mythologised past social community in the service of free-market rhetoric. Reagan 'has been said to speak for old values in current accents' and 'like the nation, of which he is such a representative figure, he is a contradiction in terms – a hero of the consumer culture preaching the Protestant ethic'.

The anthropologist Mary Douglas (1996) argues that the most basic choice that a rational person has to make is the choice about the kind of society to live in or, if you like, his or her preferred life style. People are viewed as continuously trying to bring about their ideal form of community life. In other words, the superordinate value for any person is his or her ideal form of community and it is the emotional attachment to this idea which dominates as a concern. Douglas would view human beings as innately utopians, so much so that she even infers the co-ordinating principle in all consumer purchases as being protest against other competing ways of life. If this is so, and it is certainly a minority view, the utopianism inscribed in much propaganda becomes not merely explicable but perhaps essential to its persuasive force.

Always open to persuade:
why the activity of persuasion can never cease

We are always, at least potentially, open to persuasion, and therefore to that variant of persuasion known as propaganda. We may on occasion disobey the most dearly held principle or ideal, since principles are never specific commands but general rules, thus raising the possibility of deviance in any particular instance. We may be environmentally conscious shoppers but lapse on occasion: as Levitin and Miller (1979) show, the relationship between general ideology and specific choice is not strong. Our choices are not linear projections from our principles – if they were, our beliefs would be extraordinarily tenacious and saturate every action we undertook. Many decisions are complex and ultimately incoherent, drawing upon myriad beliefs and values, some contradictory, some changing in intensity according to context. If our principles do represent imprecise general rules rather than specific commands, the possibility of persuasion must exist in perpetuity, since there is always a potential openness in the application of the general rule to the specific case, a flexibility propaganda can always exploit.

The art of propaganda lies in changing perspectives, and to change perspectives we have to alter interpretation, to interpret the emotion-arousing situation in a different way so people reassess its significance. This is a debate not about the truth of facts in themselves but about their meaning, and there is no challenge offered to values *per se* but to value judgements, which are reinterpreted. This process is in its fundamentals emotional, not, as de Sousa (1990) says, some sequence of logical inference but of emotional argument with the aim of persuading the audience to share a perspective or conjure up a certain experience. Only then, when both parties are conscious of sharing the same perspective, can rational argument and logical inference proceed. The cunning propagandist will not proceed by assault. The targets and values will appear to have been left intact and the new argument will stress how the new interpretation coheres with the old values. For example the Irish Georgian Society sought to combat nationalist prejudice against the preservation of Irish country houses as relics of colonial rule by proclaiming them the handiwork of Irish craftsman and artisans, and thus worthy of celebration. In this sense, good propaganda is subversive, since only by subversion can effective persuasion proceed. Commercial ads, for example, may seek to assuage guilt through reinterpretation, particularly violations of the rules acquired from past authority figures like parents, hence Kentucky Fried Chicken identified its core marketing problem as guilt, which it sought to assuage with the slogan 'It's nice to feel so good about a meal' (Aaker and Myers 1989). We see examples of this attempt to shift interpretation all the time. Opponents of the death penalty in the United States, for example, now castigate it as another case of government incompetence. Why should we trust government to be any more efficient at organising death fairly and effectively than it is at any of the other activities it undertakes? They are speaking the language of the political right in the service of a liberal cause.

Propaganda does not try to change values, it attempts to conscript them. Every advocate knows that values are almost impossible to alter overnight, they move slowly over time as a result of exposure to rival arguments and mature reflection. This is because values are difficult to change, since they are not open to factual correction. We do not refer to Mill's 'proof' of liberty but to his magnificent defence of liberty. Values can be neither proved nor disapproved. They are also part of a structure – to alter one is to alter the relationship of all the variables in the system, a potentially life-changing event. Propaganda seeks only to interpret those values to yield different value judgements.

Default beliefs

Propaganda can also be irrational but effective because it mobilises an individual's system of default beliefs; discarded thoughts and the fragments of defunct ideology may still survive, shadows that flit about in the recesses of our minds. They may come back, if for example conditions change, challenging more recent structures of belief and even demolishing them. This is why today, although antisemitism seems almost invisible, we shouldn't still fear it as a past fact and as a future possibility. The same is true of academia; rejected concepts and theories may linger on even after their intellectual rejection, to become what Thompson (1979) calls 'excluded monsters' – for example, Weber's thesis on Protestantism and the rise of capitalism.

Thus explanations for the effectiveness of propaganda may lie in the fact that many beliefs and attitudes exist unknown to us. Propaganda is often effective where it 'resonates', surfacing (Schwartz 1973) half-submerged, barely articulated fears and aspirations that lie beneath the level of everyday consciousness. Thompson's *Rubbish Theory* (1979) has relevance here.

In this theory, people who do not transport some relevant belief to the next stage of some plan of action are regarded as 'throwing away' the belief. The belief may stay 'hidden' in the mind, existing as a kind of default belief, and it is to this that propaganda can appeal, arousing ancient enmities that had been buried. The example of the Balkans is pertinent here, where a war which had occurred within the context of World War II was refought, with a recrudescence of the old labels and the old warpaint. It is also true of stereotypes, which do not die so much as hibernate; propaganda refreshes and reinvigorates them. Clinton, for example, had not been 'high tax, high spend' but that image of the Democrats can always be easily resurrected by their Republican antagonists.

The impact of propaganda can be very long-term indeed, encouraging adherence to a cause long after defeat has become inevitable or even already occurred. Hopeless causes still have life left in them, testament to the enduring power of propaganda. There are many reasons for this:

> we do indeed have aspirations to bring about something but, on occasions, recognise our goals will never be realised (e.g. to reintroduce laws prohibiting pornography) but pursue hopeless causes because it makes us feel we are doing something to bring about our vision; the cause may be lost, but it is not silent. Lost causes litter the landscape of history and pass on from one generation to another. Expectancy theory is impoverished when it ignores the expressive meaning of action, with expressive meaning involving the emotions. Expressive action contrasts with instrumental action. While instrumental action is a means, designed to get things done, expressive action permits us to ventilate our feelings or emotion. (O'Shaughnessy and O'Shaughnessy 2003)

Second, whereas beliefs may be changed by new information, emotions do not necessarily cohere with them, at least not straight away. They may continue to carry the charge created by past propaganda; beliefs have an after-life as well as a shelf life.

Self-deception

A further explanation for the persistence of propaganda is its role in self-persuasion; the propagandist, whether party activist or Mormon missionary, internalises adherence by the activity of propagandising. In other words, the function of the propaganda can degenerate into servicing the psychological needs of those who produced it in the first place. Thus Herzstein (1978) has argued that 'by 1944 Goebbels was making propaganda as much for himself and the leadership as for the masses'. He argues that the later products of Nazi cinema and the slogan 'Victory in death' represented 'visions of salvation'. For the Nazi elite films such as the colour film

Rite of Sacrifice, where at the end eternity beckons with a heavenly chorus, were allegories of the end. The aim was to transcend the doom-laden present via belief in an immortality conferred by the approving judgements of history and future generations of Germans.

Self-deception is thus another consequence of propaganda: it may also be an intentional objective. We can become co-conspirators in our own self deceit. 'Self-deception' is not necessarily always motivated by an aversion to some truth but, on occasions, simply motivated by affection for some particular falsehood. (This is particularly true when through self-deception we neutralise an ethical dilemma.) Some, for example, continue to believe that the practice of the Roman Catholic religion was once illegal in Ireland, although it never was. Self-deception involves refusal to face facts, or to lend them an utterly perverse but self-serving interpretation. Often the deft propagandist wants us to do this, the aim of the propaganda being to serve up plausible reasons for that frivolous interpretation, or for those 'facts' being untrue. And the potential is endless. The historian David Irving, for example, can describe Auschwitz as a labour camp with an unusually high mortality rate (*Daily Telegraph*, 13 April 1994). Presumably he seriously believes this. And any evidence can be twisted round; he can assert that Hitler gave no recorded, direct instruction for the Holocaust (true, but in the context meaningless). When challenged with the lack of evidence for a world Jewish conspiracy, for example, the paranoid antisemitic will claim that this merely illustrates the cunning of the Jews. While we see this as mere self-deception or irrationality, there are also other explanations. The truth can be impossibly painful – and self-deception may thus be a necessary strategy for survival: we are seduced by the propagandists because they offer us a way of coping. People thus persist in adherence to beliefs despite all the evidence to the contrary. So Germans continue to believe in the essential decency of the German army, the Wehrmacht, in World War II while fully accepting the evil of the overtly Nazi institutions: many found great difficulty in accepting the extent to which the army itself was complicit in Nazi atrocities, as the outraged reaction to an exhibition on this theme in Germany revealed (*Crimes of the Wehrmacht: Dimensions of the War of Annihilation, 1941–1944*, Berlin Institute of Contemporary Art, November 2001). Moreover self-deception may mean simply adherence to dominant values, avoiding the social awkwardness of questioning them, at least publicly, and the embarrassment of standing out: self-deception can be a group phenomenon and not just apply to the individual. If propaganda succeeds with part of a community, it can in fact impact all of a community since even majorities can be tempted simply to 'go along' with the strongest opinion rather than the most representative.

Fantasy

Hyperbole does not make the mistake of asking for belief – it is a fantasy which we are invited to share, explicit and even paranoid, but the fantasy does nevertheless affect perceptions of the reality. One form of hyperbole is classic atrocity propaganda, for example the British claim in World War I that the Germans melted bodies for fat. Such exaggerations work not because people necessarily believe them but because they are willing co-partners in a process of self-deceit of which they may be fully conscious. They want to see their own darkest fears and angry broodings made visible and luminous. Propaganda does that for them. In other words, there is a political truth that exists independent of the objective factors in a given situation. Propaganda is hyperbole – not all propaganda, certainly, for hyperbole is a manifestation rather than a condition of propaganda. The aim of hyperbole-fantasy is to trigger self-persuasion by getting people to imagine some event, encounter or person; they talk themselves into believing or desiring something via this process of self-imagining. Much consumer advertising is also an invitation to share a fantasy, with the hope that imagining using the product will create an inner dialogue. Hyperbole became the rhetorical reflex of Serb media in the fragmentation of ex-Yugoslavia. For some time before the Serb invasion of Kosovo, the Serb media carried anti-Izvet propaganda claiming that he would establish a Muslim state. Pointing out that non-partisan sources of information such as the BBC were available to Serbs, Zimmerman (1995) claims that people did not want to know the truth: they seem to know the difference between news and propaganda, yet when a choice is available most choose propaganda.

The argument is that propaganda is often a co-production and that people lend to it a suspension of their disbelief, and they have a need to see what they recognise as their own fantasies reflected in equally fabulistic media, their own lies to themselves reflected and sustained by the larger lies of the public space. When critics claim that propaganda is 'manipulative', they perhaps envisage a passive recipient. While some propaganda exchanges may resemble this hypodermic form, what is often going on in the propaganda process may be more subtle. The idea of people willingly misled strikes at the root of the concept of man as a rational decision maker, yet surely this is what occurred in Serbia, Rwanda and elsewhere.

While much propaganda can be said to involve exaggeration – that, almost, is part of its definition – and indeed active misrepresentation, undeniably it sometimes involves the manufacture of falsehood to the extent that its texts are even forgeries. Here we are in the realms of active fabrication and deceit. Yet propagandists can do this almost openly with the audience even conscious of the falsehood being perpetrated, becoming willing co-conspirators of an act wherein they themselves are in a sense the victims. Once again the explanation is that they are really being invited to share in a mutual fantasy of anger, a point missed by critics who too easily reach for words like 'gullible' and 'naive', assuming the audiences have no recognition of the techniques being used. An example of this is 'morphing' (Johnson 1997). When Professor Harold See stood in the 1996 Alabama Supreme Court election, one advertisement showed a skunk fading or 'morphing' into the image of Harold See with the words 'Some things you can smell a mile away ... Harold See doesn't think average Alabamans are smart enough to serve on juries.' Stamped on his face were the words 'slick Chicago lawyer'. A self-styled 'Committee for Family Values' produced an advertisement claiming that See had a secret past and had abandoned his family, allegations he strongly disputed. In fact, he won. Another case, in California, related to the murder of twelve-year-old Polly Klaas. In 1996 one of the Democratic candidates for Congress, Professor Walter Capps, was attacked thus by commercials: 'when the murderer of Polly Klaas got the death penalty he deserved, two people were disappointed . . . Richard Allen Davies, the murderer. And Walter Capps.' Commercials showed images of Davies and Capps with the labels Davies 'the murderer' and Capps 'the liberal'. Davies and Capps were 'run' as a kind of double ticket. Congressman Vic Fazio found that the face of Davies was morphed through computer graphics into his own even though he had not voted against the death penalty for several decades (Johnson 1997).

Why propaganda? (2) Modern conditions

Social control

Propaganda, whatever else it may be, functions as a form of social control in the modern world, a substitute for social coercion and for more passive forms of social persuasion. Some social control is always necessary, but its potentials remain both liberal and illiberal, given the question of its form, extent and source (who wields it). Propaganda is 'soft' social control, prison is 'hard' and generally the most extreme alternative. Ellul (1973) sees propaganda as made necessary by technological society and that its end 'is the integration of man into the technological system'. He believes that we should teach people to live in and against Technology. Many have echoed him. Thus 'propaganda is subsumed into the form and structure of social control' (Robins *et al.* 1987). Propaganda is seen as a key element in the ability of advanced industrial and post-industrial societies to organise and integrate themselves and exert some sort of authority over their individualistic publics: otherwise 'how can we have a public body but not a public mind?'

and this is because 'coercion has been delegitimised' (Robins *et al.* 1987), yet modern society is very heterogeneous, so that 'the engineering of consent is one of the great arts to be cultivated'. Propaganda is the cheaper way of doing this (Lasswell 1971).

Social change

Change entails uncertainty, and it is to the insecurities created by major social upheavals that propaganda has often, in the past, appealed. Such uncertainty can be extreme enough to constitute a national mood – the classic study by Cantril (1963), which examined perverse social/national movements such as Nazism, illuminated the evolution of pan-national moods. In such moods of nervous pessimism we yearn for the security we have lost and the emotional anchors that have been taken from us; there is a huge market in nostalgia, exploited by politicians, and by advertising: 'social change in particular is emotional because there can be no non-users' (O'Shaughnessy and O'Shaughnessy, 2003). The propagandist will thus contrast the turbulent or inadequate present with some imagined Golden Age – this was true not least in the case of the Romans themselves, whose literature and political rhetoric often sought to contrast the degeneracy of the empire with the imaginary austere and stoical virtues of the ancestral republic embodied in figures like Cincinnatus; their habit, the strategic mobilisation of the past to critique the present, found many subsequent imitators. The mood is one of fear as social values erode, the familiar disintegrates, the old loyalties are betrayed, the old truths falsified and people grasp for simple certainties and reassurance, with persuasion by authoritarian figures and didactic assertion rather than logical argument.

The question 'Why propaganda?' may thus be partially answered by reference to the prevailing level of social insecurity; Nazi propaganda, for example, produced a negligible level of response until there were 7 million unemployed Germans. While a society may in general feel secure, particular subgroups may not. In the early 1990s, for example, the previous high level of job security enjoyed by middle managers disappeared along with the mutual loyalty they received from, and gave to, corporations. Suddenly they were being delayered and downsized, and a new kind of populist managerial literature, often anecdotal and anti-empiricist, appeared to minister to their insecurities.

Information overload

Another reason for the rise of propagandistic forms of persuasion in our society lies in the very complexity of life today – the pressure of multiple information sources and the judgements they demand, and the consequent need to digest information quickly. The cognitive environment is certainly information-saturated, with the internet and e-mail, direct mail and so forth. The trend of the entire twentieth century was towards the multiplication of information sources; the Infobahn and 200 channel satellite television and their merging have taken all this to unimaginable new heights. The offer of propaganda is the cognitive short cut. We become, of necessity, cognitive misers. We need, across a whole range of issues, from our consumer decisions to our opinions on the politics of other countries, to depend on the advice of others. Otherwise life would be impossible. As Mayhew (1997) says, a 'realistic account of how influence works cannot ignore the fact that people regularly accept on faith, without independent verification the pronouncements of others'; if every opinion on every issue, if every minor decision, had to be interrogated and researched, we could not function for a single day: 'it is this very reliance on the views of others that offers the possibility of manipulating agreement'.

Ambivalent opinion

The opportunity for the propagandist lies essentially in the confusion, the tentativeness of public opinion. We are seldom without opinions, but, mostly, they are weakly held. That is why the minority church of strong believers in anything from the right to bear arms (NRA) in the United States to the pro- and anti-foxhunting lobbies in the United Kingdom fight the polemical war so vigorously. Perhaps we seek to avoid the intellectual labour of reason and the moral labour of keeping an open mind. Moreover communication has to penetrate noise and contextual density and this in itself is a reason for recourse to the methods of propaganda, since they guarantee us a more likely hearing. For we have become Toquevillean man to excess – only the lurid bestirs us from introversion and petty cares. We also exhibit a latent want for variety, away from that familiar which reassures but also bores us.

Today political action, political participation of every kind, becomes a part of the leisure market, and competes for money and consumers with other kinds of leisure activities. The demise of parties and in particular the class structures which gave them an automatic corpus of support has led, in electoral terms, to a new consumerism in which the loyalty of voters is rented. The coalescence of spending power and New Media creates choices, mass partisanship, of every kind, becomes enfeebled and the inherited wisdom and mythological structures of communities expire with their decline. Persuasion territory is up for grabs. The negotiation of multiple pressures makes people vulnerable, and while local wisdom represented one possible defence against propaganda, departure from traditional ways of knowing makes its ascendancy more likely: mobile, urbanised society becomes a cultural and ethical vacuum and polemic fills the space vacated by tradition. So a trigger for propaganda is the poverty of social integrating mechanisms in techno-centric market-place democracy. The old identities of community are edited out and a decline of social hierarchy leads to the demise also of ritualised, inherited loyalties; persuasion, not the command of traditional authority sources – teacher, parson, parents, or the coercion of community and social pressures – becomes more important. All authority is tentative, and when authority is negotiated, persuasion becomes central.

Single-issue groups

Another manifestation arising out of the fragmentation of the old mono-lithic certainties and the social organisations that were their expression are single-issue groups, and their ubiquity is a driving force behind propaganda (see Chapter 5). They were the political phenomenon of the late twentieth century. It is through propaganda that they are created and sustained and impact the legislative agenda. Single-issue groups arise as an organised response to an emotional call to action: a consequence of propaganda therefore further becomes a manufactory of it, for it would be difficult to describe the literature and generated imagery of single-issue groups in any other terms. Some of them are now actually bigger than the political par-ties, as animal rights, abortion and so forth intrude on to mainstream agen-das and usurp them (Richardson 1995). The emotional satisfactions of adherence to a single-issue group are stronger than party activism for many because there are fewer ideological compromises. They exert an immediate emotional appeal. For an issue can be personalised in the way a political party cannot be, the issue becomes 'our' issue, and participation becomes a hedonistic consumer activity, and also an act of social display. There is thus a symbolic aspect to single issue membership, it becomes part of our identity, one of the ways in which we articulate our social self.

News manufacture

A further reason for the pervasive extent of modern propaganda lies in the press's need for a condensed story with a hero and villain and a moral so that the press is enlisted, though perhaps unintentionally, as participant in a propaganda battle. This demand for a story is inherent in the organisation and culture of the press itself, and derives from both the imperative neces-sity of news 'production' and humanity's deep-seated need for myths that give structure and meaning to the fluid, amorphous events of life. The love of a good story, with plot, character, dramatic suspense, powerful conclusion and eloquent moral is so universal among cultures, of such antiquity as a human activity, that after Pulitzer (see below) first recognised the value of story as a framing device in the nineteenth century it became the dominant pattern of press discourse. This does not make the press story axiomatically propaganda, but it does explain why the press often appears to become self-conscripted as a propagandist agency. Its need for heroes, villains, scandal, lessons, its self-conceived role as moral agent and bringer of retributive justice, scourge of the hubris of power, make its product sometimes indistinguishable from propaganda.

Under this melodramatic quest narrative, the antecedent complexities of situations are ignored because they cannot be expressed in simple story or metaphor. News is quite literally produced – material must be fabricated round pre-existing narrative structures – and all nuance is avoided. Events – such as the savings and loan debacle in the United States, whose genesis was long maturing – appear nevertheless to happen suddenly. In line with this, there is often a need to identify some evil individual or community and likewise a hero combating them, with the finality of closure, and if villains cannot be identified they can be conjured up via the rhetoric of implication with phrases like 'no proof yet'. As Crelinston (1989) has remarked, 'it is increasingly recognised by people both within the industry and by people who study the news that the distinction between news and entertainment is not a sharp one'.

One term for this can be the 'news manufacture' approach, and while 'news manufacture' is not conceptually identical to propaganda the two have obvious affinities, and sometimes they become one and the same. The blame for this – if indeed blame there should be – lies with the introduction by Joseph Pulitzer of emotion into staid narrative: he brought drama to the news, with plots, story and colour. Newspapers hitherto had contained dry accounts of government activity, but Pulitzer authored blaring headlines, big pictures and eye-catching graphics: emotional immediacy is striven for rather than rational exposition (Vanderwicken 1995). As Crelinston argues, 'contextualising incidents bores people'. News is a commercial product sold in a competitive market place, and to succeed it must be vibrant, original, emotional and easily understood – classic attributes, in fact, of propaganda.

At times even a free press can conspire to present a powerful 'dominant view' against which all other opinion is perceived as deviant. When opinion becomes universal among major press protagonists like this, not only the techniques but also the effects resemble those of propaganda. Such an occasion was the British general election of 1992, when the Labour Party under Neil Kinnock was leading at the polls. The press decided to crucify him, with for example the *Sun* newspaper's eight-page extravaganza 'Nightmare on Kinnock Street' (see Chapter 6)

Postmodernism

The explanation for the continuity, even renaissance, of propaganda can also be understood in terms relevant to the postmodernist – the universe of postmodernism is also the universe of propaganda. The extremer (i.e. French) postmodernists tend to reject notions of objective standards, for them there are no absolutes and there is no sovereignty of truth, everything becomes a matter of interpretation. Since reason is more suspect, emotional judgements at once acquire greater legitimacy, the Enlightenment reverence for reason, the rational vision of Max Weber, for example, are superseded by greater faith in the validity of our feelings. In asserting this, such postmodernists would claim to be describing the world they find, as well as justifying it at the intellectual level. In abandoning notions of objective truth, the more radical of the postmodernists credentialise propaganda. If there are no absolute standards, a balanced, rigorous analysis is of no greater account than emotive speculation. A propaganda text is accorded greater respectability, it is interrogated for meaning and significance, but it is not despised because it is propaganda. Moreover, since no truth is absolute, the search for truth becomes less pressing as an objective, or even ceases to be an objective at all. The relationship between propaganda and postmodernism lies in the confusion of the real and imaginary. For the postmodernist, the border between the real and the simulated is confused: we inhabit an era of simulacra, of hyper-reality, a time in which the image transcends the word and television is more significant than print, where traditions and communities have withered and where identity definers are found in exaggerated symbol systems. The postmodernist order both inspires propaganda and explains it, since propaganda is a creative process that focuses on the confectionery of image and symbol.

Explaining propaganda: insights from the social sciences

No work on propaganda could sensibly ignore the insights generated by the social sciences. While this remains a condensed and random summation, and is speculative, it does suggest further possibilities for the analysis of the study of propaganda. We outline some of the principal ways in which psychology and sociology can offer explanatory depth, since propaganda is

(1) a social phenomenon experienced in social contexts, (2) an irrational phenomenon, lending credibility to the incredible.

Explanation in psychology

Behaviourism (see O'Shaughnessy 1992)
Classical conditioning. All forms of behaviourism are based on a presumption that behaviour is caused by external environmental factors that condition behaviour to respond accordingly. Classical conditioning rests on the supposition of the occurrence of involuntary reflexes which are said to make the associations compelling, and the traditional view is that all conditioning assumes unconscious learning. The ceaseless drum beat of incessant repetition may contribute to propaganda's conditioning effects. Napoleon and Hitler used pseudo-classical symbols, but there are also commercial symbols such as the Marlboro cowboy, and such symbols may be said to evoke, on occasion, a conditioned response. For the notion of conditioning is surely plausible in certain circumstances where the weight of previous association is strong, symbols of ethnic and national stereotypes such as, for example, the symbol of John Bull and the range of associations attributed to him. Classical conditioning also has a place in rhetoric, where the loaded rhetorical term creates compelling associations, as when we refer to Dickensian conditions, Rachmanite landlords and so on.

Operant conditioning. Operant conditioning represents a more liberal idea of conditioning. The core notion is that all living organisms are spontaneously enacting behaviour and whenever this action is reinforced it increases the possibility of recurrence; unless the response is reinforced it faces extinction. Operant conditioning implicitly assumes that people behave not so much out of any conscious deliberation or anticipated outcomes but because of the consequences that have followed similar behaviour in the past. Operant conditioning is more useful than classical conditioning as an explanation of the working of propaganda. Advertising often seeks reinforcement by showing social approval of use of the product such as a particular make of car, and the social disapproval of non-use such as a brand of deodorant, and similarly with propaganda. Propaganda films chronicle how desired behaviours (loyalty, heroism, etc.) are rewarded and undesired ones punished, they feature idealised behaviour patterns engaged in by ideal individuals and denigrate others. The function of propaganda is often to remind – of past pleasures, and also of old resentments – and thereby to reinvigorate. The rites of Protestant and Catholic in Northern Ireland, their songs, myths and the marches, are a ritual of reinforcement as they seek to implant sectarian sentiment in each successor generation. Adolf Hitler seems to have subscribed to an entirely behaviouristic theory of propaganda.

Social psychology (see Webber 1992)
Social cognitions of the self; self-awareness. When self-awareness is reduced, we are less likely to act in accord with our values. The state of reduced self-awareness is known as deindividuation, which can be created by stimulus conditions, including immersion in a group, physical or social anonymity or by arousing and distracting conditions. These are the conditions where we are less likely to be influenced by personal integrity. This immersion in a group can be achieved when the propagandist has organisations at his disposal such as the Young Pioneers in Soviet Russia (or even the immensely successful Young Conservatives in 1950s Britain). All these conditions of group emotion, physical and social anonymity and distracting conditions were present at the Nuremberg rallies. Jacques Ellul stressed how critical for propaganda was enrolment in this type of proselytising organisation; propaganda needs a membership list. The success of some types of propaganda such as televangelism stems from precisely this sense of the presence of the crowd. People commit acts after joining organisations such as the Irish Republican Army which they would never contemplate as individuals. The German Nazis in particular focused on the group, and there were membership organisations for everybody (including university professors, on whom punishing demands for physical fitness were inflicted! Grunberger 1991).

Self-motivation. Self-motivation covers the desire for self-consistency. A particularly strong appeal in propaganda is to self-justification (to retain our social prerogatives and deny them to others, for example), and there is often much to justify. Advertising, for example, often seeks to give permission to our extravagance and hedonism, so that post-purchase justification is its critical object. Ronald Reagan provided rhetorical justification for inequality and free-market fundamentalists told the United States that high unemployment was good for it. Another major self-motivation is the protection of self-esteem, which is also serviced by propaganda, and this applies not only to individuals but also to nations. Propaganda is a distorting mirror. Reaganite propaganda flattered, and drew attention away from its civic profligacy. Even Churchillian rhetoric could on occasion ingratiate and assuage national complacency.

Social information. We seem particularly hungry for information about others and rely heavily on several forms of social information. Thus perceptions of traits, or generalisations about behaviour, are universal even though the attachment of a trait as a descriptive label involves the error of ignoring exceptions. Propagandists deploy the Great Leader traits as a medium through which all Leader actions are to be interpreted: such as asceticism (Adolf Hitler), virility (Mao), grandfather of the nation (de Valera), matriarchy (Golda Meir), and other enunciated traits include things like the family man (Blair), the tough Leader (Thatcher), the patriot (Bush junior), the war hero (Bush senior), the holy man (Gandhi), the intellectual (Elena Ceausescu), the virile (Mussolini half naked in the fields). Ordinary individuals are also chosen to represent the traits desired by the regime. Traits are also seized on by antagonistic propagandas such as the sybaritic Churchill of Nazi propaganda or the physical disability of Goebbels.

Stereotypes are generalisations, particularly the attribution to an individual of characteristics ascribed as universal to a group from which that individual is drawn. Stereotypes are much deprecated, but they are also inevitable, since they are heuristics or cognitive short cuts that simplify complexity and ambiguity and absolve us from the intellectual labour of forming balanced judgements. Thus it was an invariable principle for Alexander Korda that his films showed the English not with subtlety but in accordance with the preconceptions foreigners had of them, so that they frequently appear in his films as self-parodic. The manufacture of stereotypes is the definitive act of the propagandist (socialist worker hero, Thatcherite entrepreneur, etc.). It is particularly important that political and national enemies are caricatured. Nazi propaganda relished the stereotype in its images of the English – the cruelty of British imperialism, the effeminacy of the ruling class (*Soldiers of To-Morrow*): they enjoyed crude satires of what they called the English plutocracy, which they inevitably presented as in league with the Jews. In the film *The Rothschilds* a Star of David is superimposed on a map of England. The English loved to depict the Germans as automata: one British propaganda film forwarded/reversed footage of goose-stepping storm troopers to the tune of 'The Lambeth Walk'.

Psychoanalytical psychology (see O'Shaughnessy 1992)
The focus here is on explaining the covert and non-conscious aspects of psychology, and particularly neurosis. The claim is that unconscious motivations are causal mechanisms. The id, ego and super-ego become unbalanced and repression takes place, and neurosis is an attempt to reconcile them. Stability is attained via better understanding. The attraction of psychoanalytical theory over behaviourism lies in the insights into the complexity of motivation that it claims to offer.

Psychoanalysts would have a field day when it came to propaganda. They would be especially fascinated by the propaganda creation of a synthetic family, and the father figure has in particular been the *Leitmotif* of totalitarianism – the ostensible avuncularity projected by Stalin with his pipe, and so forth. Such an all-powerful patriarch is projected as a reassuring figure to the people in times of trouble and anxiety. The patriarch enunciates a fatherhood role celebrated by his propaganda, and a necessary part of this role is that the people feel and act as children. The dictator cares for the minute details of their life in a stern but loving way, as a patriarch would: thus, for example, Adolf Hitler gave workers killed in an accident during the building of the Berlin metro a state funeral (Grunberger 1991), stressing thereby both the enhanced status of the worker under Nazism but also his own role as a caring father figure. It is not merely the dictator who provides the paternity, for father surrogates can also be retrieved from history and perform the paternalistic role from beyond their graves. Nazi films did this very frequently with Führer surrogates such as Bismarck and Frederick the Great. Another way, of course, in which totalitarian propaganda expressed the patriarchal order was in the many instances where dictators were filmed or photographed with children.

The propaganda creation of the political 'family' extends beyond the building up of father figures. Sometimes there are also son figures, and this is particularly popular with revolutionaries – Castro and Guevara, for example, or perhaps the role given to Baldur von Schirach as leader of the Hitler Youth, or indeed in some senses the relation between Lenin and Stalin as propaganda projected it (although Stalin implicitly conceptualised the relationship as Messiah–Apostle). The focus of propaganda remains to enunciate elements of paternity: the idea is of an all-knowing authority under whose benevolent gaze people regress to childhood and the pain of decision making is taken from them. Of course, there are mother figures as well. Propaganda has often conceived of the nation state itself as mother, as fertile provider. Indeed, in war propaganda women often seem to assume the roles of mother to their menfolk rather than the role of lover and wife. Then again, war films made with propaganda intent often seem to create groups of individuals, typically an army unit, who are socially involved with each other but replicate again family roles in a kind of alternative military domesticity. Thus there is the mother role, the baby role, etc. The army is the larger family. Such films even mirror the family life cycle as the 'babies' grow up and rebel and eventually take over the leadership of the family. In US films in particular, such groups of soldiers have often represented different ethnicities and national subgroups, implicitly giving the idea of the nation as family.

Another variant of the family idea which suffuses propaganda is to depict subject or 'inferior' peoples as children, the colonial race then assumes the paternal role. As children, subject peoples are innocent and enthusiastic and babble in a strange way, but have a need for discipline and tutelage. These traits are all visible, for example, in a film like *Sanders of the River* (1935) with Paul Robeson, though Alexander Korda, as former film commissar in the short-lived communist government of Bela Kun in Hungary (Kulik 1990), would probably have denied he was making propaganda for British imperialism. Others would be less sure.

A psychoanalyst would be particularly intrigued by the salience of sexuality in propaganda, both as an inducement but more particularly as a threat. Subject peoples and races are seen as a sexual menace, since they could contaminate the purity of the dominant group and thereby its sense of integrity. The Nazis were particularly worried by the threat posed by the sexually attractive women and men of subject peoples. It is a necessary part, for example, of the construction of a subject people that they are also perceived as promiscuous. Nazi propaganda strove to warn people about the terrible dangers of racial contamination; France, for example, with its African soldiers, was depicted as 'the racial poisoner of Europe' (Herzstein 1978).

It is not merely the sexual attractiveness of enemies we must be warned against. It has often been integral to the social construction of the enemy that he is seen as a sexual violator too, and the theme of sexual violation, especially in atrocity propaganda, is particularly strong. The enemy is implicitly and sometimes explicitly a rapist (for example, the 1918 Hollywood movie *The Kaiser Beast of Berlin*). War and sex seem closely allied, and in propaganda of World War I, German atrocities were often depicted as aggression against women, while the reaction of British soldiers to the execution of Nurse Edith Cavell surfaced the same kind of anger (see Chapter 4). The enemy as sexual violator does indeed seem the common currency of all for propaganda, for example the Italian fascist poster of a black, simian US soldier carrying a classical statue of a beautiful woman (Rhodes 1993): the subtext is obvious. Of course the threat of sexual violence can be used as propaganda by both sides, by the defender to create rage and by the aggressor to instil fear.

The enemy is constructed not merely as sexual violator, but a sexual violator of pure women. It is almost an axiom of war propaganda that the women you are defending are 'pure'; sex itself is present but merely implied. These women are loyal and deeply virtuous, and this trait seems, almost, universal, so that their possible violation enrages all the more. But it is also the case that such women put their men under intense sexual pressure – to fight, that is. The World War I song 'We've watched you playing cricket. . . . We don't want to lose you, but we think you ought to go' is an image echoed many times in propaganda posters and productions with slogans such as 'Women of Britain say Go' or 'Is your best boy in khaki?' Thus soldiering becomes the definition of maleness, not to be a soldier is to cease to be a male, to be emasculated. ('What did you do in the war, Daddy?') Remember too that for the British such modes of persuasion were of critical national importance because conscription was not introduced until the middle of the Great War. Appeals in recruitment propaganda were to traditional concepts of maleness. The genders are allocated unambiguous roles – the men to fight bravely, the women to look after the home: there is suggestion of their virginity, but also the virginity of the motherland itself –

the two are equated. Women are also incarnate as abstract concepts such as liberty ('Madeleine').

There is also an overt erotic stratum in the usage of propaganda. Revolutions, for example, connect with ideas of sexual 'liberation' – the early years of the Bolshevik Revolution or the events of Paris in 1968. Revolutions are often accompanied by proclamations of free love and a sense that the lid has been taken off all 'repressions'. Not only a ruling class but an internal moral order is overthrown and in the period before new authority is established or bourgeois revenge takes place there is a flowering of the avant garde and the bohemian. Sexual appeals are of course the thing in consumer advertising, but they are clearly present in every form of propaganda. The Nazis, for instance, used Germany's Marilyn Monroe, Christina Soderbaum, extensively in their films. Propaganda films often succeed by foregrounding the story of attractive women and their romantic relations with men – the propaganda message is secreted in the background and in the story line. Indeed, it is a tribute to the potential of propaganda and, at its best, its resonance as an art form, that *Casablanca*, probably the most famous film ever made, is also a supreme example of the propaganda genre (though it is seldom analysed as such).

Dictators themselves may be framed in an overtly sexual style, from the circulation of rumours as to their alleged potency to Mussolini parading bare-chested to his people, something which shocked the more bourgeois Adolf Hitler as vulgar. Eroticism can be a strong element in propaganda. The Breughel-like peasants and earth-mother women who clumsily adorn Nazi art are hardly likely to tickle the sensuous fancy, but Nazi iconography also abounds with images of naked women and athletic nudes. Indeed, the male body as a power symbol (physical and temporal) features prominently in Nazi art and propaganda, as in the denim and cosmetics advertising of later generations: Häagen-Dazs and Calvin Klein today would understand those associations. There is an obvious equation between the dominance of the master race and sexual virility. But there is also an overtly pornographic element in propaganda, from the ravings of Julius Streicher's *Der Stürmer* to the lurid tales of Rasputin and the Czarina's court printed and circulated after the April 1917 revolution (Orlando Figes 1997).

Another characteristic of propaganda which could be of interest to psychoanalysts is its obsession with regaining the purity of some ideal, unsullied by the world. Totalitarianism itself could be represented as the wish for regression to some womb-like state of succour. Propaganda constantly assures us that a perfect world is just around the corner, from the myriad utopias of the totalitarian to the sanitised world of material satiety projected by the advertising industry.

Explanation in sociology (see O'Shaughnessy 1992)

Social anthropology

Astute propagandists are best advised to make a message fit another's conceptual universe rather than seek to undermine their well established, comforting set of private truths. Today the term 'phenomenology' is commonly used to cover any method that explains behaviour by interpreting the meaning of that behaviour for the person engaging in it. There is a need to explore the concepts people use to describe and structure their environment, and this would be key for a propagandist, otherwise our encodings are not decoded and there is passive misinterpretation of our meaning or active antagonism towards it.

Exchange theory

Exchange theories borrow from behaviourism the notion of reward and substitute cost for the notion of punishment. The real issue lies not in whether political consumers occasionally behave like utility-maximising economic man – they clearly do – but in how much political behaviour can be adequately explained by such a narrow view of human motivation. In neglecting such important things as feelings, values and sentiments and our sense of obligation, exchange behaviourism shrinks social conduct to the 'behaviouristic hedonism of a reward-maximising, cost-avoiding image of Man' (O'Shaughnessy 1992). Nevertheless there are situations where exchange theory would clearly apply. Consumer advertising often concentrates on economic appeals, the price-wise aspects of the offer, and similarly propaganda makes the focus personal gain or self-preservation in many situations. Revolutionary propaganda particularly stresses the material reward possible once the *ancien régime* is overthrown, and thus Lenin's slogan in the Russian revolution was 'Land, peace and bread'. The idea of expropriating some caste – bourgeois, nobility, Jews – clearly had inherent (material) attractions that propaganda could exploit. Rather more generally, party political propaganda and marketing have always placed a big emphasis on economic self-interest, hence Reagan's appeal 'Are you better off now than you were four years ago?' This is the main thrust of many party programmes rather than appealing to values or idealism, but they err in merely seeking to rent allegiance rather than create converts: they are in the same dilemma as the company which seeks to compete only on price.

War is a particular context where the calculus of self-interest is a major dimension of propaganda. The aim of war propaganda is to get the enemy to surrender, and such items as cards guaranteeing safe conduct are critical, but so also is the ubiquitous fear appeal when people are intensely concerned about their personal survival. German propaganda emphasised the immense destructive possibilities of the German war machine, the marching columns, fleets of bombers, partly as a way of terrorising other potential belligerents. If such fear appeals intimidate, they also represent an invitation to join by connecting to our quisling wish to identify with the most powerful.

It should be stressed that private goals are not the only focus of war propaganda. Altruistic motives and notions of social duty are also critical. Exchange structuralism is the exchange theory of P.M. Blau (1964). This version inflates the concept of 'reward' to embrace intangibles like social approval, esteem – respect and power over others. Thus exchange structuralism is probably a superior descriptor of much war propaganda, with its emphasis on the need for esteem and its broadening of the concept of reward to include such things as social regard, as with the Italian recruiting poster featuring the classic bombazine-clad mother urging her son on (Rhodes 1993). But even here the focus is still egocentric, and it ignores the utility of altruism in political persuasion. Goebbels was at his most eloquent when appealing to community spirit in the middle of World War II, for help for the injured and bombed out, 'Winter Relief' and so forth. It is a paradox of history that Nazi propaganda was at its most convincing and successful when addressing the virtuous instincts of mankind, despite Hitler's earlier claim that virtuous propaganda would always fail.

Conclusion

Propaganda is a way of mediating our response to social phenomena and our relationship with society. It is not viewed in isolation from society; it is interpreted by individuals but their response is influenced by others. The grievances it exploits are social, those of the larger community, as much as personal. Thus it is useful to review some of the insights from sociology and social psychology. But there is no universal 'key' to propaganda via either sociology or psychology. Those who look for a universal theory, a code to unlock, search in vain. The many manifestations of propaganda, styles, appeals, tricks, must be accessed in a similarly heterodox way.

Part II
A conceptual arrangement

3

An essential trinity: rhetoric, myth, symbolism

Rhetoric, symbolism and myth are the interwoven trinity that has under-pinned most propaganda through history. But it is difficult to imagine a propaganda programme which is deficient in any of these even though the individual propaganda text may be.

Great rhetoric never retires. To work effectively rhetoric must 'resonate' with attitudes and feelings within the target (Tony Schwartz 1973); great rhetoric is substantially a co-production between sender and receiver. Rhetoric is a cheap way of reaching the target, since it is relayed by the press. In this chapter we argue that the power of rhetoric resides principally in the power of metaphor. But we will also discuss the arrival of new rhetorical forms such as spin, and we discuss in particular the rhetorical US presidency of Ronald Reagan.

Symbols are another component in this trinity. Ultimately we argue that a symbol can be defined as condensed meaning and as such is an economi-cal form of propaganda, for symbols are universally understood in ways that language can never be; a symbol eludes precise scrutiny and can be 'read' in many ways, endowed with multiple meanings. Old symbols can also be re-used, for symbols have inherent plasticity .

The power of myth is the power of narrative. Propaganda rejects intel-lectual challenge, and it seeks refuge in the structures of myths. Old myths can be re-created, but new myths can also be invented – that is to say, myth entrepreneurship. Myths are a culture's self explanation, and they are a key part of propaganda (stereotype, for example, is a kind of myth).

Rhetoric and propaganda

Seldom does mere logic alone frame our perceptions; it is emotion that is the pathway to conviction. Rhetoric is emotional persuasion and its core is therefore emotion. Rhetoric is a subset of propaganda, but it is often confused with it, and the two words carry many of the same conceptual problems, for rhetoric is also sometimes a term of abuse, and is made to refer to any argument we disagree with. Along with symbolism and myths, rhetoric performs a key role in propaganda and the three are intertwined, rhetoric may be strewn with symbolic appeals that make reference to myths. The trinity of rhetoric–symbolism–myths is the conceptual anatomy of all propaganda.

Thus the relationship of rhetoric to propaganda is tricky to nuance, since an intelligent case could also be made for the notion that all rhetoric is also propaganda. Much depends on how precisely we define rhetoric and the conceptual domain that they both share, especially if we expand the idea of rhetoric to embrace the visual and physical as well as the verbal.

Rhetoric was once the basis of European education. At Eton College, for example, one of the great events of the school year is still 'Speeches', where students dress up to declaim the great perorations of the past (King George III being apparently moved to tears by a recitative of the Earl of Strafford's speech on the scaffold, 'Fickle is the love of princes'). Rhetoric today is as important as ever, and its prime function, to pinpoint, illuminate and showcase the nub of the issue, is unchanged. But the forms are different. For example, the key focus of rhetoric today is the soundbite, its form has become condensed and the art of rhetoric now is one of compression.

Rhetoric, verbal and indeed visual, has been a critical part of the propagandist's armoury since the beginning of recorded history. In Athens the participation of all adult male citizens in the assembly and judicial process made eloquence highly desirable, and rhetorical teachers – sophists – could teach you, write speeches, and so forth. The art of verbal persuasion was the core of sophists' training, it was central to the legal system and in the drama of Greek tragic theatre. Persuasion and its superiority to force were the symbol of high culture (as in the *Oresteia*) and Pericles' funeral oration 'celebrated Athenian willingness to submit political decisions to discussion' (Emlyn-Jones 1991). The wicked charm of rhetoric has long been feared. The theme of rhetoric itself possesses an ancient and distinguished literature, its study and practice dominated Greece and Rome. The Greeks were fascinated by and feared the power of eloquence – a speech which 'delights and persuades a large crowd because it is written with skill but not spoken with truth' (Emlyn Jones 1991), and in his *Encomium* Gorgias depicts Helen as helpless under verbal persuasion as under a powerful drug: this was 'the earliest attempt at theoretical discussion of the psychology of verbal persuasion'.

Early critics

Rhetoric had its critics from the earliest times; for the ancients there was an independent truth, and rhetoric was seen as powerful and dangerous. Many of these selfsame arguments are repeated today, with their proponents perhaps seldom aware of their ancient pedigree, that the rhetorical privileging of belief and feeling over fact finds earlier echoes. The art of persuasion became controversial, it was recognised that eloquence was not invariably an illuminant of the truth: Aristophanes in *The Clouds* depicts the sophists as concerned 'to teach pupils the manipulation of situations by means of illegitimate verbal persuasion' (Emlyn-Jones 1991). Thucydides employed pairs of speeches to enable audiences to choose either interpretation, and his Cleon accuses the assembly of being the victim of eloquence. Thus, according to Emlyn Jones, Athenian speech represented a persuasive force independent of the truth, and a quasi-medical force which acts irresistibly on the psyche. *Mythos*, which means word, also means argument; *peithmei* means 'I am persuaded' but also 'I obey', *denies* means marvellous and persuasive speaker. Thus Pericles: 'a kind of persuasion lived on his lips. He cast a spell on us. He was the only orator who left his sting behind in his audience.'

Rhetoric was pseudo-reason, it invented reasons for the sentimental fancy to achieve self-justification. Rhetoric was seen as the employment of the symbols of rationality to bypass the scrutiny of reason. Plato attacked orators for possessing beliefs rather than knowledge, a criticism that rings true of Members of Parliament today: he thought that truth had a persuasive power irrespective of exposition. As regards late fifth-century Athens, 'never again were the psychological and epistemological premises upon which persuasion techniques are based so thoroughly questioned' (Emlyn-Jones 1991). Another reason for the attack on rhetoric was that it had become partially detached from the search for objectivity and had degenerated into 'mere' advocacy. Hence Plato differentiated strongly between philosophical thought and its specious counterpart, rhetoric. Plato disdained the inflated claims made by Gorgias and the sophists for rhetoric, seeing it as the art form of the fawning manipulator. Certainly it could not be a branch of knowledge, making no distinction between truth and falsehood, analysing no received wisdom nor testing some assertion. Persuasion was simply a means and an end with no higher goal.

When seen as based on the use of questioning, rhetoric ceases to be a form of reasoning. All reasoning implies questions to be addressed, not solved; at least they are answered. Logic works only with answers and their links while rhetoric focuses on the relation between questions and answers. For Aristotle, persuasion is in large measure rhetorical, and he saw rhetoric as synthesising emotion and reason, since both were relevant. For him, rhetoric was about opinion (*doxa*), not the knowledge of which we can be sure (*episteme*). For Aristotle, persuasion comprised the multiple qualities of the persuader:

1 *Ethos:* credibility (reputation, technical expertise, trustworthiness), including the signs of credibility such as intelligence of argument, choice of language, force, eye contact, etc.
2 *Logos* means the rational content of the message and its appeal.
3 *Pathos* is the emotions and appeals based on them.

The claims of the postmodernists would appear to be the lineal descendant of such approaches, as in Foucault's (1975) claim that any distinction between rhetoric and logic is false, since all communication is rhetorical.

Those educated up to and even beyond the nineteenth century were often rigorously schooled in classical precepts of rhetoric. The content of their ideas could never be entirely separated from their rhetorical methods. For example, the impact of the theories of Marx and Freud is partly a consequence of their education in persuasion. Freud was an able orator, though occasions of Freudian oratory were rare. Freud's background and education provided a thorough grounding in classical literature – including schooling in Quintilian and Cicero: 'unlike Marx, Freud left no youthful translation of Aristotle's *Rhetoric* as a testament to his interest in rhetoric. Nevertheless there is good reason to believe that Freud was familiar with the classical notion of rhetoric that Aristotle defined as the study of the means of persuasion in any subject' (Patterson 1996). Freud was educated in rhetoric in his German and Latin classes; the emphasis was on rhetorical declamation. The best students – including Freud – were selected to perform before parents and the school, Freud reciting the speech of Brutus (Patterson 1996)

Why rhetoric?

It has been claimed that today rhetoric is undergoing a revival. As the range of choices and opportunities, in products, politics, leisure and entertainment, expands for the individual, communication becomes much more critical in society with the emergence of a 'persuasion' culture. Another factor is the decline in the authority of Authority, of churches and governing institutions, and the movement from inherited cultural practices – partially tied to rigid class systems – to individualistic choice from a supermarket of stylistic and behavioural alternatives. For Meyer (1994) the revival of rhetoric can be seen as one of the numerous demonstrations of our nihilistic present. The loss of indisputable principles has rendered nearly everything questionable (and I might add thereby vulnerable to propaganda). When values are controversial, and experienced as such, it cannot be otherwise: it is in this historic context that rhetoric has re-emerged. It is thus the uncertainties of our time, the lack of an inherited definiteness, that make us vulnerable to rhetoric. Perhaps it really is the case that, outside the realm of Euclid's geometry, we are permanently in the realm of persuasion. Thus the new uses of rhetoric have evolved because the older assurances have been diminished; when all is open to question, direct methods of persuasion are less relevant and the need becomes to persuade via metaphor rather than logic.

One scholar who has engaged in substantial empirical research on our vulnerability to false beliefs and fallacious reasoning, the source of many rhetorical appeals, is Deanna Kuhn (1991). One of her major findings is the extent of pseudo-evidence; the people who depend upon it believe it to be as powerful as genuine evidence in their quest for truth. Propaganda is of course concerned with such manufacture of pseudo-evidence. Pseudo-evidence scripts serve to establish or enhance the intuitive plausibility of a causal theory by portraying how the causal sequence occurs: they elaborate or spell out the causal sequence instead of providing evidence for the theories' correctness, that is, subjects are often unable to think of what evidence might be relevant and so dwell on elaborating the reasonableness of their position. Much propaganda does indeed do this. Subjects who could advocate good counter-arguments were around half her sample. The author argues that subjects who cannot generate counter-arguments cannot properly evaluate the truth of the theories they do actually hold. In our terms, many people cannot think critically, and they accept and internalise packaged opinions; moreover, according to Kuhn, the successful counter-arguments were often quite weak, and gave the theory permission to remain in force to some extent. For the propagandist, the message is that people are generally vulnerable to propaganda: perpetuate an error and it can remain in perpetuity, and Kuhn's research illuminates yet again the importance of teaching analytical thought processes as a defence against the propagandising of society.

Kuhn argues that if people use theories without thinking about them, they have little real understanding of the theory. In evaluating as well as seeking evidence, subjects are biased by their own initial beliefs or hypotheses. If evidence is simply assimilated to existing theories, any ability to evaluate the bearing the evidence has on the theory is lost. People's beliefs persist long after the evidence that provided the initial basis for the belief has been discredited. This would explain the resonance of stereotypes – Colonel Blimp, and the kind of bank manager who disappeared years ago. All this would tend to favour a propaganda that does not change, but simply feeds popular prejudice. For the propagandists, the lesson is to position and express ideas in accord with prejudices, since there are parameters outside which people will not think. According to Kuhn, other studies such as Perkins and Alan (1983) have shown that people tend to generate reasons that support only their point of view, without considering any other side of the issue. As a consequence, today we sometimes seem to have replaced dialogue and debate with polemical declamation.

Metaphor

Great rhetoric is primarily metaphorical: 'in particular, the English language is full of metaphors so concealed it is forgotten that they are metaphors. Metaphors defamiliarise the familiar to reorient thinking' (Gibbs 1994).

The customary differentiation made between rhetoric and philosophy, that rhetoric aspires to delight while philosophy drives at truth, is meant to illuminate the difference between decoration and content. Yet Plato's Socrates is also a doyen of rhetoric, since powerful imagery and metaphor are necessary to fragment entrenched ideas. A metaphor compares diverse, apparently irreconcilable entities, so posing a conundrum to excite our curiosity; the metaphor provides the possibility of resolving such a conundrum; it typically employs vivid language, and its ambivalence invites us to search out what is dimly apprehended; 'in bringing together different terms, a metaphor creates broader conceptual wholes'; we even think principally in imagistic terms, our thoughts being in the main figurative – 'metaphoric, metonymic and ironic' (Gibbs 1994). Without metaphors, persuasion would be toothless. Metaphors involve: the listener will embroider. They influence how we see and how we interpret, they affect therefore not only our intellectual but also our emotional response. As Klein (1998) says, while metaphors structure our thinking and condition our sympathies and emotional reactions, they may also seriously deceive by embedding a false analogy of an actual process, as for example the image of mind as a computer, with its consequent notion of a rational calculus in our decision making.

In rhetoric today the image is as likely to be an electronic one as a pictographic or literary one: in history, words alone and the images they evoked often sufficed. The events and technical advances of the twentieth century renewed and expanded our sources of metaphor, from phrases or words like 'hard-wired' or 'default programme', or history-derived words such as 'blitz' – but Mason (1989) warns that once connections have been made 'and everyone is familiar with the relations involved, the metaphor dies and loses interest'. Daily communication lives through metaphors, but behind the metaphor lies the ideology; 'harnessing the environment' may be welcomed by technocrats but resented by Greens.

Several studies examine the effect of metaphors on responses to political communications. They conclude that using an appropriate metaphor in a speech can lead to better memory for the arguments and can significantly influence the inferences people draw from that speech. Choice of appropriate metaphors therefore really does become the key to effective rhetoric: metaphors 'can resolve ethical ambiguity or confusion by pointing up a "moral" through semantic incongruities' (Mason 1989). The merit of vivid images is that they break with previous modes of thought; an outstanding (i.e. novel, appropriate) image can cause us to see a situation in a revolutionary new light, in a way that mere argument never can. Rhetorical devices, according to Mason, invite new interpretative schemata, but the rhetoric of persuasion is good only if it is appreciated from a particular perspective. Nevertheless after an effective rhetorical treatment the world may look different from before and move people in a direction they would not choose themselves.

Metaphor was one of the principal rhetorical devices used by Adolf Hitler. Metaphor is critical in Hitlerite rhetoric. Thus *Mein Kampf* is 'organised round a metaphor of a medical diagnosis and cure, the religious rite of guilt and redemption, and the drama of murder–revenge' (Blain 1988). We note that one of the central properties of metaphors is their capacity for extensive elaboration. Hitler's presentations were allegorical, his discourse structured round the metaphor of murder and revenge. Other images in Hitlerite rhetoric include 'the notion of blood contamination as a central motif. Since the Aryan–non-Aryan differentiation is a racial one, "blood" is a loaded term. It condenses racial, biological, medical, religious, moral and murderous chains of association' (Blain 1988).

Courtroom advocacy is perhaps the most eminent theatre of rhetoric. The mobilising power of words and images to direct perception is part of the art of the advocate, but it can be done so effectively that their memory saturates and stains our judgement. We simply cannot forget a memorable image and the perspective it embodies: it lives and breathes in our consciousness no matter how far we would deny it oxygen. Having read the phrase 'A sleazy woman with big hair from a trailer park' we can never think in quite the same way about Bill Clinton. But consider this criminal justice case, an ugly one about the abuse of boys (*Daily Telegraph*, 15 January 1997). The prosecutor, Alec Carlisle, QC, chose the brilliant metaphor of Captain Hook to describe the defendant: 'Mr Laverack presented himself to his young charges as a man of distinction and elegance who impressed his victims even, as it were, when prodding them along the plank.' This image and its appropriateness to the case was further elaborated by Mr Carlisle. In the end we begin to see the defendant as Captain Hook, no matter how far we try not to, such is the resonance of the image – and, unable to see him as other than Captain Hook, it is difficult to see how an objective decision could be made. Laverack, apparently, wore a silky dressing gown and cravat, and had an MGB, an elkhound and smart clothes: he was a 'persistent and menacing paedophile'. Carlisle continued, '*Peter Pan* is really a story about children whose parents have rejected them. They are called the lost boys'. And he then quoted J. M. Barrie's description of Hook: 'He is never more sinister than when he is at his most polite, and the elegance of his diction, the distinction of his demeanour show him one of a different class from his crew. The courtliness impresses even his victims on the high seas, who note that he always says sorry when prodding them along the plank.'

Thus the key to rhetorical persuasion is the manufacture of visual images. For Schopenhauer (Mason 1989) the visual image remains long after the argument is forgotten. Through reflection, images accumulate meaning. For Mason (1989) a live metaphor is a switchboard 'hopping with signals': important issues are up for grabs via such rhetorical devices because they are the ones with inherent indeterminacy, an absence of analytical proof. Potentially metaphors can fracture existing paradigms of thought and introduce new ones because their very vividness assaults our attention and lives on in our memory, and in this they are special, since subverting existing and often culturally determined ideologies is the hardest thing for a propagandist to do.

Labels

Another method is to pay the most careful attention to language but, in particular, labels. Under Reagan the Republicans even had a rhetoric committee, but judicious choice of label is the most important rhetorical choice of all. The pay-off for getting it right is considerable: the label adheres and over time it is naturalised so that people do not perceive it as a label at all. Labels are viewed as objective descriptions when very often they represent merely social judgements. They can be damning or they can be laudatory: but an ideology or perspective is inscribed within them. Thus euthanasia becomes 'mercy killing' and abortion becomes 'pro-choice'. The supreme art is to make the label enter common parlance so that every time it is used it becomes an unconscious act of propaganda, as with the 'Right to Life' movement: 'words are always important since learning new words or concepts may result in seeing new classes of objects or ideas that change perspective' (O'Shaughnessy and O'Shaughnessy 2004).

A fine example of this is the term 'political correctness', which implicitly associates liberalism with the coercion of the Soviet state. This is not to deny the possibility of liberal/left excess, merely that the left's opponents' success in choosing a label and getting liberals to use it was a triumph of some magnitude. Words describe, but they also judge. Different words will encircle the same reality but embody divergent judgements about that reality: 'whore', 'prostitute', 'harlot' and 'courtesan' reference the same activity but give it a different meaning; opium, heroin and morphine are refinements of the same drug but their cultural signification is entirely different.

Words get us to see something in a new light. Or they may be combined into a metaphor which catches on, even if there is little logic behind the transference. The idea of a 'trickle-down effect' became so popular because it was such an excellent riposte to socialist confiscation, not because it was a particularly true description of economic reality. Another (shopworn) example of the power of labels lies in the rhetorical terms 'terrorist' and 'freedom fighter' and 'guerrilla', since they illustrate the extent to which words describing the same reality can contain contrary judgements. Words thus do duty as sensitising concepts, such that if we have no word for something we are often actually blind to the existence of the phenomenon.

An important function of rhetoric today is the seeking to replace the old culture of rhetorical denigration with a new one of rhetorical uplift; the spastics and cripples of yesteryear, along with the mendicant plastic figurines that dramatised their claimed enfeeblement, are banished to rhetorical Siberia. New terms emerge in their place, so that 'backward' children become 'special needs', with the hope that we will see them as such in a new way. And terms may be deliberately chosen to limit our vision, language systems are a way of seeing but also of not seeing, and in modern warfare the importance of persuasion has given rise to a miasma of pseudo-technicalia ('collateral damage', 'target-rich environment') to veil the reality of what is being done: so different from the reply allegedly given in World War II by Air Marshal Harris to a policeman enquiring about the nature of his profession ('killing people'). We have become 'masters of duplicitous rhetoric' – or hypocrisy.

Rhetorical tactics[1]

One rhetorical device traditionally employed has been the *vox populi* method, to find a particularly striking phrase or dramatic moment to express what all are thinking. Thus Leo Amery's cry in the House of Commons to Arthur Greenwood, in 1939 'Speak for England, Arthur', achieved this criterion of

---

1 These well known sayings and aphorisms of the eminent can be gleaned from their numerous biographies and other historical works as well as from such reference sources as *The Oxford Dictionary of Literary Quotations* (ed. Peter Kemp), *The Oxford Dictionary of Quotations* (ed. Angela Partington), *The Oxford Dictionary of Twentieth Century Quotations* (ed. Elizabeth Knowles), *The (Bloomsbury) Biographical Dictionary of Quotations* (ed. John Daintith).

memorability. England personified: a silent, angry witness. Effective literary devices can be best summed up by Alexander Pope: 'What oft was thought but ne'er so well expressed.'

Great phrase making is made possible by the great historical moment, it rises to that historicity with exalted language. At such moments Roosevelt used the device of personification: 'We have nothing to fear but fear', 'Rendezvous with destiny', 'A day that shall live in infamy'. Others chose satire, as with Churchill's response to Goering's statement that Britain was like a chicken that Germany would strangle by the neck, 'Some chicken, some neck.' Analogy is another important device in rhetorical propaganda, as when for example Lloyd George told his audience that an English duke cost as much as a new Dreadnought – a satisfying piece of class invective.

Sometimes rhetoric involves repositioning some literary or classical quote, as with Chamberlain before Munich quoting *Henry IV* Part I ('Out of this nettle danger we pluck this flower safety') or Mao letting 'a hundred flowers blossom and a hundred schools of thought contend'. Sometimes rhetorical effect is gained by slightly perverting a quotation, as with Margaret Thatcher's 'The lady's not for turning'. Brutality is of course frequently a characteristic of rhetoric – the brilliant insult, as James Maxton MP to Prime Minister Ramsay MacDonald ('Sit down, man. You're a bloody tragedy') or Churchill to the same victim ('When I was a child . . . have waited fifty years to see the Boneless Wonder sitting on the Treasury bench'). Good rhetoric has a great merit, of course, of being recyclable: 'Peace with honour' was first used by Disraeli at the Congress of Berlin, thence graduated via Neville Chamberlain to Richard Nixon. 'One nation' is another phrase of Disraeli's which ended on many lips, included Nixon's.

Imagery – the choosing of the most vivid and appropriate image – is critical to all rhetorical persuasion. Thus Maynard Keynes's description of David Lloyd George ('This extraordinary figure of our time, this siren, this goat-footed bard, this half-human visitor to our age from the hag-ridden magic and enchanted woods of Celtic antiquity') is memorable for the associations it gives to the dominant feature of his protagonist's personality, his Welsh eloquence: Keynes connects it with an ancient and darkly brooding world. Images can be passionate. 'The workers have nothing to lose but their chains. They have a world to gain. Workers of the world, unite', or banal, as Mao's Great Leap Forward (with its 20 million dead), derisive (Lenin's 'garbage bin of history') or violent (Bismarck's 'iron and blood'). Even an essentially banal image, like Prime Minister Harold Macmillan's 'wind of change', can somehow catch on, as for example with Labourite Aneurin Bevan's 'naked into the conference chamber'. Frequently in political communication the images chosen are perhaps necessarily those of embattlement. Thatcherite rhetoric was saturated with aggressive imagery, and

Labour leader Hugh Gaitskell's famous 'Fight and fight and fight again' (against unilateral disarmament) shows liberals are hardly immunised against such images. Sacrificial imagery is another alternative – 'All I have to offer you is blood, toil, sweat and tears' etc.

Much great rhetoric is in fact a simple idea simply expressed but elevated by the grandeur of its context. Thus martyrdom is a particularly frequent setting for such utterances. But war is perhaps the primary context and here the examples are legion – whether General Pétain's 'Ils ne passeront pas' at Verdun or Earl Haig's 1918 'With our backs to a wall, and believing in the justice of our cause, we will fight on to the end', the rhetoric of stubbornness. Or Sir Edward Grey's plangent 1914 'The lamps are going out all over Europe'. Great moments in the life of a democracy can propel even the more mediocre to rise to the occasion, thus an otherwise dull Speaker of the House of Commons to the captain of King Charles's guard: 'I have neither eyes to see nor lips to speak, except as this House gives me leave.' And Jawaharlal Nehru at Indian independence: 'At the stroke of the midnight hour, while the world sleeps, India will awake to life and freedom.' Great events are remembered by language unremarkable as language but exalted by the occasion it articulated. Thus Nurse Edith Cavell on the eve of her execution in 1915: 'I realise that patriotism is not enough. I must have no hatred or bitterness towards anyone.' The power of rhetoric is hence often contextual, it might sound banal or ridiculous in another setting: 'I am just going outside and may be away for some time' is simple, yet the words of Captain Oates (as he left the tent for certain death in the hope that his colleagues on Scott's polar expedition could live) inspired a generation of Englishmen.

Rhetoric creates meaning

Rhetorical devices induce the reader to apply particular interpretative schemata to the text, the grain of the rhetoric will invite the reader to adopt a certain stance and attitude from which the world looks different from how it did before.

Language is not merely the vehicle for articulating our thoughts, it does in itself create meaning, an active agent for the creation of perception. If language was merely a vehicle for communication, there would be less interest in it, but, in the words of Umberson and Henderson (1992), 'language does more than merely express reality; it actively structures experience . . . language and linguistic devices structure how we think about things'. If language is power, then the control of language is the key to that power. Thus the hypothesis holds that language does not reflect reality but rather creates it according to the structures and limits permitted by the language of a given culture: Foulkes (1983) claimed that 'the rejection of the Indian-killer as cultural hero can produce a rejection of the US marine in Vietnam as national hero'. Names and words are not neutral, objective tools: they may contain, to a greater or lesser extent, some implicit ideology and their use helps bias perception, and (within limits) the more vivid and resonant the word the greater potentially the bias introduced.

The current stock of words in common circulation influences our thinking significantly, and when words cease to circulate, people may tend to think less in certain ways (though what is cause here and what is effect is unclear). For example, when Dickens was writing, the English language possessed a word 'enterpriser' (see *Little Dorrit*) which was the equivalent of the French *entrepreneur* (an earlier generation had used the word 'projector', but that was more with connotations of speculation). In the 1970s and after, when a newly minted image of the risk-taking businessman re-entered popular currency, the language had to turn to the French for a single word to express that concept, since the English equivalent had atrophied: the social reality it signified had again come to be esteemed. For Foulkes (1983) even the dictionary may function as propaganda – 'it may be part of a dominant group's attempt to control recorded knowledge and prescribe linguistic behaviour'; he is concerned that 'language in its social context reflects and transmits ideology without seeming to do so'. He adds that:

> an obvious example is the way in which modern English is pervaded by the buried metaphors of capitalism: we exploit opportunities, profit from experiences, cash in on situations once we have assessed the debit and credit side; we sell good ideas and refuse to buy the opinions of those with whom we disagree; pop singers and politicians may become hot properties once they have been taught to capitalise on their talents.

Power

Language is of course a weapon of thought control, the great theme of George Orwell's *Nineteen eighty-four*. Nor were his fears without foundation. One of the disturbing curiosities of the Third Reich, which Grunberger (1991) described and Klemperer (1998) reports in his *Diaries*, is how ways of looking at reality as embodied in particular words and phrases became general currency. The Reich propagated a linguistic style which condensed elements of its world, thus making formal persuasion less necessary; a new rhetoric of the everyday permeated the Nazi vocabulary and even that of the Nazis' opponents.

Hitler himself was a convinced believer in the raw power of the spoken word over literary exposition, criticising academic emphasis on the written word: 'the power which has always started the greatest religious and political avalanches in history rolling has from time immemorial been the magic of the spoken word, and that alone'. Bolshevik literature contained nothing in comparison with 'the glittering heaven which thousands of agitators, themselves, to be sure, all in the service of an idea, talked into people' (Blain 1988).

Perspective

To persuade a target group to identify with us, it is essential that we speak to them in their own language. Rhetoric, as has been already suggested, is necessarily rooted in particular cultural paradigms that are shared with the target audience. Another technique was to appropriate the vocabulary of socialism and – like any propagandist – draw from the cultural stock bank of languages, myths, forms and images: thus Hitler 'concocted an insider discourse from cultural resources familiar to his German audience' (Blain 1988) and from religion in particular. Burke (Blain 1988) argued that Hitler's use of dramatic form represented a political perversion of the religious notion of the struggle of good against evil.

The revival in the study of rhetoric owes much to the recognition that people, rather than being mere information processors, embody fixed and different social and ideological perspectives, so that the skills of persuasion are necessary if enlightenment is to be achieved. Certainly it cannot be gained by mere logic alone. Successful persuasive advocacy thus occurs within a *perspective* and not outside it, and the 'correct' perceptions follow on from this. A perspective exerts its own tyranny, it is a set of values to which we have an emotional adherence, so that our decisions must adequately cohere with that perspective. The consequence is that advocates are best advised to interpret their cause in line with the audience's existing ideological predispositions.

Perspectives are changed by rhetoric; sometimes by little else, and the recognition of this point has brought with it a new respectability for the study of rhetoric, as in the work of Chaim Perelman (1982) and Brian Vickers (1988). One element in changing perspectives is getting our partisan language accepted in the cultural mainstream, i.e. the ideological is concealed in the 'normal'.

Rhetorical ambivalence

Many have persuasively if not conclusively claimed that the most effective arguments are essentially co-productions. In this view an argument is all the more convincing if the audience is led to draw the conclusion for itself, since meaning is most persuasive when it is a co-production and the force of an argument varies directly with the freedom left to the addressed individual. Those that seem to be imposed seldom convince; an argument is all the stronger when the addressee is free to reject it. This could certainly be a definitive characteristic of sophisticated forms of propaganda – it negotiates effectively between autonomy and didacticism, and meaning is invited, not imposed. All this is true, of course, if the audience is capable of drawing the right conclusions: the problem is that the propaganda value may sometimes be lost in layers of subtlety, such as the Tory 'bleeding lion' poster in the 1997 British general election campaign. (Its meaning was not widely understood.)

The co-production of the argument is helped by the very ambivalence of language itself. 'The problematological view assumes language is referential and unequivocally so, whereas in practice language is ambiguous to the extent that most terms can receive multiple meanings according to the context' (Meyer 1994). Ambiguity is often deliberate and you extract your own understandings: was Tony Blair's 'tough on crime and tough on the causes of crime' actually a phrase without a meaning, and similarly with his 'education, education, education'? Simply asking what they mean exposes their vacuity.

The mechanism of rhetoric

Rhetorical tropes (figures of style, analogies, metaphors) are necessary for any significant act of persuasion. The importance of rhetoric is that it persuades because it gives vivid definition – to fluid situations, to what would otherwise be vague or abstract, since on so many matters individual opinion is tentative or confused. Rhetoric provides something for thought to get hold of, something concrete, an image, a scrap of language or feeling (Mason 1989). The power of rhetoric in a democracy lies, essentially, in the hands of others: for rhetoric is an unguided missile whose creators have no necessary control of how it is conscripted and duplicated. The press and media are of course supreme among these powerful others, and the primary target for modern oratory, hopefully circulating and amplifying the rhetorical imagery we have persuaded them to project for our selfish ends.

To achieve this degree of circulation and memorability, the rhetoric might be a simple and easily remembered phrase such as Cicero's 'Delenda est Carthagine.' Great rhetoric – or at least, that which seeks duplication – resides primarily in the choice of an especially appropriate image. The idea of 'resonance' (Schwartz 1973) is particularly apposite here, for good rhetoric fizzes, it 'smoulders in the mind', since often such imagery is open-ended and its plasticity invites curiosity and review: we turn it over in our minds, perhaps many times. Words are never neutral. They are association-rich. There is, for example, no such thing as choosing a brand name that has no association.

Any oral or written discourse carries a tone as well as a content, and meaning and persuasive power can be as much a function of tone as of message: as O'Shaughnessy and O'Shaughnessy (2003) remark, 'the choice of words conjures up a fresh perspective but the choice of words may also be designed to give a certain tone, say, of professionalism by the use of Latin or scientific jargon as occurs in advertising medicines to establish credibility'. They add:

> There are some words that are essentially feeling words, like 'annoyed', 'burdened', 'crushed', 'distraught', 'exasperated', 'fearful', 'hurt', 'pressured', 'sympathetic', 'tired', 'worried' and so on. There are some words that have highly positive connotations like 'progress', 'new', 'safe', 'security', 'low-calorie', 'fat-free', and some words with negative connotation like 'old-fashioned', 'artificial ingredients', 'non-user friendly', 'gas guzzler' and so on. Even ostensibly meaningless words have some kind of meaning; they may lack a concrete reference but still embody a sense-meaning. Invented literary words and names, such as Dean Swift's Yahoos in *Gulliver's Travels*, do precisely this.

We tend, perhaps, to see rhetoric as something valued – the pleasing metaphor, the exploding image, the cascade of words – and in its colloquial sense that is so. Rhetoric is the strategic and tactical use of language to persuade; as such, far from language being full of personality, effective persuasion may lie in deracinated language. According to Boardman (1978), the speaker can muddy issues under the pretence of providing information, the 'language of obscurity and deviation'. This language is unremarkable and with little apparent content, associated with bureaucracy and jargon. Another example is of words 'so carefully chosen as to imply more by what they didn't say than by what they do say', the illustration chosen is a denial by President Nixon: 'none of these [illegal activities] took place with my specific approval or knowledge' – note the rhetorical activity of that word 'specific'. Boardman also gives the example of Nixon on Cambodia – he used the device of dividing and defining: 'What American would choose to do nothing when he could go to the heart of the trouble?' Rhetoric can be low-key or even 'bureaucratic', with ideas and ideologies 'naturalised' as everyday speech. Everyday speech is not value-neutral, in it are buried the core ideas of the culture.

There is no one formula for effective rhetoric – different practitioners have mastered different aspects of the art, and different parts of it suit different occasions and different audiences. Is, for example, the audience some general public, or is it segmented in some important way – a professional audience, perhaps? With general audiences, such as for example a jury, the confectionery of image counts. A good image has an adhesive quality and we cannot forget it, a dweller in our half-consciousness flitting in and out of a mind's twilight zone. Framing and anchoring also matter – the way a choice or decision is framed can influence the way it is interpreted and judged, for example: 'voters are worried about . . . ' versus 'voters have not been worried about . . .'.

We might properly suggest that there exist elemental appeals in rhetoric that have been made by rhetoricians since the very beginnings of public argument. For example, loss (of status, cultural totems, material wealth, etc.) is one of the most effective themes in the history of rhetoric, one entombed in the very word 'conservative', and it is this that Hirschman explores in *The Rhetoric of Reaction* (1991), focusing on three fallacies which such a rhetoric is seen to embody:

1 The perversity thesis: 'improvement' will make things worse, not better.
2 The futility thesis: it will change nothing, but will waste money.
3 The jeopardy thesis: the cost is too high in relation to the benefits, or we risk the loss of what we already have.

Effective rhetoric has also frequently been grounded in appeals to authority sources. American rhetoricians, for example, have often been at their most effective when referring to the words of the Founding Fathers, Hamilton, Jefferson and so on. Other cultures have sought rhetorical homage to other, more peculiar figures. Thus Mazrui (1976) has shown the influences both of the classics and of Marx on African political discourse. Post-independence African politics saw the transition from a rhetoric with shades of Kipling and other literary figures to that of Lenin and other leftist thinkers. The confrontation between the Kiplingesque and Leninist traditions continues, with a marked cultural schizophrenia in the political conduct of postcolonial Africans. A good example was Nkrumah, who began by quoting Tennyson in his early works and ended saturating his last books with Marxist expressions and symbols. Another case of ambiguity was Tanzania's Julius Nyerere, whose rhetoric alternated between Shakespeare and Marx.

The end of language is not simply to communicate, as Austin points out (Mason 1989): there are statements that can be true or false ('constative') but there are also what he calls performatives or performance utterances to which the question of truth or falsehood is irrelevant because they are dramaturgic. When Disraeli called Gladstone 'a sophisticated rhetorician, inebriated with the sheer exuberance of his own verbosity' he was enacting a performance utterance, not asserting something that was true or false.

It is of course important to remember that a function of rhetoric has been to facilitate the killing of man by man – people one has never met and with whom one has no personal quarrel. Umberson and Henderson (1992) conducted a very timely content analysis of war-related stories in the *New York Times* for the duration of the first Gulf War, giving special attention to direct and indirect references to death and killing. This analysis revealed four major themes: (1) the existence of rhetorical devices that distanced the reader from death and encouraged denial of death in the war; (2) official denial of responsibility for war-related deaths and reassurance to the public that they would be minimal; (3) rhetorics that prepared the public for death in war and to view the deaths to come as just; (4) ambiguity and uncertainty about the actual death toll. Certain memorable phrases came about as a result of this war – 'collateral damage' famously being one: war was described in the new pseudo-science argot of the military. And speaking of Operation Iraqi Freedom and its secondary label, Shock and Awe, Rampton and Stauber (2003) argue that this sub-brand 'enables its users to symbolically reconcile two contradictory ideas. On the one hand, its theorists use the term to plan massive uses of deadly force. On the other hand, its focus on the psychological effect of that force makes it possible to use the term while distancing audiences from direct contemplation of the human suffering which that force creates'.

A new rhetoric

Visual rhetoric is the telegraphy of meaning via a significant background or foreground. Has visual rhetoric replaced verbal rhetoric? This is an age where 'visual literacy' is often described as replacing the articulative skills. Reagan's use of visual assertion accorded well with this new lingua franca of popular culture. For visuality is a universal language. In *Eloquence in the Electronic Age* (1988) Kathleen Hall Jamieson discusses how the nature of rhetoric has changed under the impact of television. In television eloquence, visual moments have replaced words: such visualities bypass the critical faculty and we should not in fact look to television for much by way of explanation.

Reagan, of course, gave a good example of this in his (1980) inaugural address, which he turned into a travelogue of Washington and its great monuments, the cameras following as his words directed. Symbolic forms of discourse have particular value for a general audience, they resonate and they avoid the kind of categoric articulation of values which in a heterogeneous society can alienate. In Reaganite rhetoric, these symbolic devices took the form of visual parables, or moral stories, and more generally a visual rhetoric which would use the actual imagery around him – say, the Normandy beaches, or images common to him and his audience. Jamieson describes Reagan as being the pastmaster of electronic forms of rhetoric, and she provides a close and sustained analysis of his rhetorical style. Thus frequently he employed physical props to signify and symbolise. His communication strategies engaged the use of ordinary citizens who would purvey some form of parabolic function – a youth, for example, who had shown conspicuous initiative in the fight against homelessness.

Reagan would commandeer shared visual memory, he would build from visual scenes that he and the nation had recently experienced, but, to succeed, such devices must represent some larger universe of meaning. His persuasion style therefore used a great deal of non-verbal communication: the verbal components were essentially colloquial and conversational. They were often framed by a dramatic narrative, a favourite Reaganite device, with Ronald Reagan cast in the role of storyteller. In this, of course, he is close to rhetoricians throughout history, for narrative is the primordial mode of communication, which Reagan simply adapted and effeminised for political persuasion in a Television Age.

There is, however, a fraudulence implicit in the visual bias of the medium, for a visual symbol enables the avoidance of rebuttal. Jamieson (1988) describes a Hubert Humphrey advertisement which, if it had been expressed verbally and not visually, would have invited derision. This imprecision is a gift to the rhetorician, as the new propaganda of the visual drives out the verbal. Electoral advertising spot ads in particular are non-nuanced, they telegraph meaning, they do not explain or imply (Jamieson 1988). This contrasts with earlier forms for rhetoric – Aristotle's *enthymemes*, for example, achieved their power from reliance on unexpressed beliefs and information. But, with a decline in shared cultural information, the ability to do this decreases.

Jamieson also argues for the 'feminisation' of rhetoric. According to Jamieson, television has rendered the old manly style of rhetoric redundant – it is a medium that mandates the articulation of feeling, and manly style is a noose. In the ancient world, the metaphors employed by rhetoricians were drawn from battle, but now a rhetoric of courtship is employed and public discourse has been personalised, as for example with Ronald Reagan's self-disclosive moments. Traditional rhetoric, in contrast, depended for its force on the physical aspects of performance – the drama, more than content; on the use of voice, the mesmeric interplay of facial expression, words and gesture. It was a physical rhetoric, demanding the rigorous, choreographed gesture. Rhetoric was physical articulation and seldom linguistic content alone, though powerful rhetoric could transcend this: Lincoln's Gettysburg address was in fact inaudible to his immediate audience, and may even have had more impact in World War II. Leathers (1986) gives a list of non-verbal channels for conveying messages. Facial expressions, for example, include smiles, frowns, eyebrows raised or lowered, eyes closed or widened, nose curled, lip pursed, teeth bared, jaw dropped, forehead knitted or relaxed.

Not all media with specific rhetorical applications are new, and nor are the old 'manly' rhetorical forms extinguished. Far from it. One of the phenomena of US politics over the 1990s was the invention of radio as a political medium – reinvention, in fact, since Charles Coughlin was the first and most spectacular exponent seventy years ago. Talk-radio hosts, along with single-issue groups, have become among the most important politicians in the United States today. What they offer is pure propaganda. This is a medium of reinforcement, not gaining new recruits but speaking to the provincial white male (he has the highest voter registration of all) in his own language, articulating his anger and ministering to his self-pity: there are 1,000 talk radio programmes, and Rush Limbaugh himself had an audience of 20 million. In Kurtz's words, 'Imus, Howard Stern and other loudmouths reflect a high-decibel society in which journalists insult each other on talk shows, pathetic souls denounce their relatives on daytime TV and politicians slam each other in attack ads' (Thomas Install, *New York Review*, 6 October 1994). Every day Limbaugh took events in the day's news

> and misinterpreted them as part of his larger indignation over the state of American culture, individual and group rights, sexual mores, and the ground rules of capitalism and democracy. He presented the discussions over each of these issues as part of a continuing partisan struggle between a demonised democratic liberalism and an idealised Republican conservatism . . . he took it as an obligation and higher duty to examine every action or pronouncement to show its deceptive purpose. . . . . . . :
>
> "I'm sick and tired of turning on my TV and being told that the Aids crisis is my fault too, because I don't care enough. . . . In this 500 anniversary year of Columbus's voyage, I'm tired of hearing him trashed. I don't give a hoot that he gave some Indians a disease that they didn't have immunity against. We can't change that, we're here. I'm sick and tired of hearing Western culture constantly disparaged. Hey, ho, Hey ho, Western culture's got to go, is the chant at Stanford University. What would Stanford be if the pioneers that are so reviled today as imperialists, racists, sexists, bigots and homophobes hadn't fought their way across a continent to California?"

While segmenting radio audiences by ideology is a gift to the propagandist, such channels represent a rejection of pluralism and the idea of political exchange. The United States may be a democracy but its airwaves became a one-party state?

Impact of rhetoric

Rhetoric is power. Commercial rhetoric can make the difference between success and failure for a company. Branding, for example: the right name can easily justify a 20 per cent, or even 50 per cent, price premium. Thus in business the power of rhetoric can be measured in monetary terms. The power of rhetoric is illustrated by the extent to which a well chosen image, possessing traits of vividness and appropriateness, not merely 'sticks', but hangs around for generations – such as Turkey as the 'sick man of Europe'. We also remember the past through its rhetoric. Thus the wartime British, despite the qualifications inscribed in such works as Angus Calder's *The Myth of the Blitz* (1991), are to most people as Churchill presented them, fighting on the beaches, in the hills and never surrendering: the rhetoric continues to do its duty in a later age.

Historically the power and influence of any author, preacher, politician (even scholar) has been – partly, mainly or even exclusively – rhetorical, they have lain in the command of rhetoric, as for example in the case of perhaps the greatest environmentalist messiah, Rachel Carson, whose mastery of metaphor gave her work a level of impact that mere rational exposition never could have found, calling, for example, the chemicals used for wood preservation and insect control 'elixirs of death' (Kevles 1994). Churchill's success lay principally as a rhetorician (certainly not for example as a military strategist). What we mean by his 'greatness' refers certainly to his moral character, but also to his powers of articulation, metaphor and personification: thus on Bolshevik Russia 'self-outcast, sharpens her bayonets in her Arctic night, and mechanically proclaims through self-starved lips her philosophy of hatred and death' (Keynes 1985).

Rhetoric and ideas

For one writer, Geoff Mason (1989), rhetoric can only ever flourish in the realms of opinion, for the activity of persuasion never ceases permanently. Only if certainty is demanded does rhetoric fail, but where a final conclusion cannot be reached, rhetorical argument is all we have. Argumentation is often defined as the endeavour to convince. One argues only because reasons do not follow on from each other with the absolute necessity of mathematics, leaving room for possible disagreement. Even here there is nothing preventing people disputing the rigour of some mathematical proof, so every discourse in practice is concerned with persuasion. Choice of rhetoric has been absolutely critical in the propagation of ideas, and in the twentieth century the intellectual ideologies that have flourished most have (arguably) done so because their sponsors were the most eloquent. Their proponents understood the need for rhetorical devices to command and sustain attention, they had an intuitive feel for the power of language to pierce the introversion of mankind and burn its meaning on to their conscious thoughts.

Rachel Carson was one such (Kevles 1994). Her great polemic, *The Silent Spring*, did more than any other work to bring about the modern environmental movement. She achieved this by literary power. Carson's description of her writing might stand as a definition of the more sophisticated forms of propaganda: she liked in writing 'this magic combination of factual knowledge and deeply felt emotional response'. In such propaganda the facts themselves are both correct and used generously. In this sense, it is not dishonest writing, but it remains manipulative, since facts are selected according to the guidance of an interpretative framework, and decorated with imagery and metaphor that lead the reader to the right emotional response. This is not 'mere' polemic, but neither is it rational analysis.

One such device was personification. She writes of her 'realization that, despite our own utter dependence on the earth, this same earth and sea have no need of us'. In this way she personifies nature, and nature becomes a real person whom we need but who doesn't need us. Thus both our dependence and our littleness are emphasised, an important part of the Carson project; 'she left government service increasingly despairing over the future of nature'. Carson often anthropomorphised nature, attributing human feelings to fish and animals in order to explain their behaviour to readers who know little about them: 'we must not depart too far from analogy with human conduct if a fish, shrimp, comb jelly, or bird is to seem real to us' or 'I have spoken of a fish "fearing" his enemies, for example, not because I suppose a fish experiences fear in the same way that we do, but because I think he behaves as though he were frightened'.

Any form of communication involves some rhetoric – there is a rhetoric of science (Prelli 1989), though it is much less overt than political rhetoric, since science has a deep- embedded ideology of truth seeking and objectivity in which persuasion should be irrelevant. This, of course, assumes that there is only one single interpretation of the facts: where multiple views are possible, persuasion and therefore rhetoric creep in. Even more is this the case on the fringes of science or in those areas which claim to be science while embracing a much more subjective methodology. This is true, for example, of socio-biology and true, in particular, of psychoanalytical psychology. The neo-scientist can avoid the rigours of the scientific demand for evidence and analysis by the employment of rhetorical devices, just as the politician does. Context and audience make it a more discreet and circumlocutory form, as with Sigmund Freud, for example in his 1909 Clark lectures (Patterson 1990). Behind his discourse lies the concept of the unconscious, but he does not explain it, merely offers analogy. Freud 'treated as proven the premises on which the analogy is based'.

Thus the main rhetorical form Freud used in these lectures was the device of analogy. 'His aim was to present an all-inclusive theory of the mind.' He began with the case of Emma O., claiming it 'typified hysterical patients': 'the woman's symptoms vanished when she traced their origin to the distant past. . . . Symptoms originate in experiences that occur in the past and are forgotten.' Freud describes the analogy of Charing Cross. This is an ingenious story that is told and elaborated at length, with descriptions of London scenery. Charing Cross is a monument to the Plantagenet Queen Eleanor. The lachrymose Londoner, claims Freud, is the correct analogy for neurosis 'but what should we think of a Londoner who passed today in deep melancholy before the memorial of Queen Eleanor's funeral instead of going about his business in the hurry that modern working conditions demand or instead of feeling joy over the youthful queen of his own heart?'

Patterson comments: 'does the hysteric and unpractical Londoner suffer from symbolic disorders?' Each has failed to establish a balanced relationship with the past. . . . Health lies in establishing a direct relationship between past and present.' But Patterson argues that 'by using analogy, Freud spared himself the responsibility for presenting a logical demonstration'. There is also Freud's analogy to describe repression – that of a person trying to interrupt the lecture. (The anarchist Emma Goldman was present in the audiences, lending the analogy intense dramatic relevance.) In the analogy the person is taken out and people have to hold the door shut, but then there is banging on the door. The chairman talks to him reasonably, and he is persuaded to resume his attendance at the lecture quietly. This analogy describes the mechanism and the treatment, and 'it was not an accident that he chose an analogy that allowed him to portray himself and his audience as being one'.

Freud was very concerned to project an image of credibility by stressing his own non-credulity. Moreover, he portrays himself as a slow and reluctant convert to psychoanalysis, for example to the notion of infantile sexuality. He 'began by disbelieving'. Then he flatters his audience. He compliments their attentiveness. He uses the metaphor of a journey to integrate the lectures and to present himself as an equal – merely an intellectual fellow traveller: others doubting could also follow the same journey as he did, a scientific guide who merely describes his private journey to psychoanalysis – 'it is with novel and bewildering feelings that I find myself in the New World before an audience of expectant enquirers'. This flattery and ostensible equality remove any fear of didacticism, condescension or intellectual bullying. They also establish Freud as a disinterested seeker of truth, not status. Self-denigration is another device by which he projects this ('I had no share in its earliest beginnings') and the denial that he was actually trying to persuade his listeners. Time and again he articulates an objection to his ideas, then answers it: 'it is not always easy to tell the truth, especially when one has to be concise: and I am thus today obliged to correct the wrong statement that I made in the last lectures'. Patterson remarks, 'in fact he strengthened his case. First, his willingness to entertain objections reinforced his audience's faith in his openness. Second, in raising the objection, it gave himself the opportunity to present more evidence in support of his position.'

Freud's public relations success in the Clark lectures is a tribute to the power of rhetoric. His lectures were extensively described in newspaper reports, often with enthusiasm: thus the *Boston Transcript* described him 'wearing the kindly face that age would never suffer'. The *Transcript* claimed that the lectures had won the adherence of many of the scientists there. The lectures 'marked an important element in the history of psychoanalysis and appeared in English within a year: by 1915, psychoanalysis had moved from being a topic whose merit was debated by only a handful of American intellectuals to a subject that was discussed in *Good Housekeeping* and other popular magazines. After the Clarke lectures Freud was awarded an honorary degree, which, he noted, was 'the first official recognition of our endeavours' (Patterson 1990).

Thus rhetoric also plays a crucial role in academic discourse. For one thing, it is rich in metaphors, and even scientists are forced to use imagistic rhetoric as their public language, since their private language of mathematics is accessible only to the few. Scientific metaphor is not merely a way of interacting with external constituencies, it affects the way that scientists themselves perceive their realities: in fact a metaphor created for the purpose of public communication can, perversely, spring back and affect the thinking of its creators as well. Metaphors help structure and limit disciplines, and give them a unity – the astrophysicist, for example, speaking of 'black holes' – but they can also illuminate the values of their creators and influence their further evaluations. In the social sciences this is particularly true – is man tribal, a herd animal, a robot, etc.? Different metaphors underpin different social science paradigms. Economists in particular have traditionally conceived of man as a self-seeking, rational decision maker with a clear, hierarchical conception of his needs and priorities, and much of their language is a rhetoric that embodies this, and as McCloskey (1990) has shown, economists actually use rhetoric to persuade even their professional peers.

Myth and propaganda

Myth making may not be part of any core or theoretic definition of propaganda, but most propaganda is concerned among other things with the confection of myths: mythology is thus, almost, a part of its working definition. A myth is a paradigm and shorthand. It surfaces the human interest and narrative quality that make it memorable in the sense that the abstract lecture or mere eloquence could never be. Propaganda makes continual use of myths: they are always a point of reference, implicit or explicit, in the propaganda texts. Myths provide a common cultural vocabulary, they unite, they flatter, they elevate the argument or group that claims association with them. They avoid the need for complex verbal exposition; they can be incorporated by minimal pictorial reference, or they can be rendered by a symbol: 'in simple terms, myth is the narrative, the set of ideas, whereas ritual is the acting out, the articulation of myth; symbols are the building blocks of myth and the acceptance or veneration of symbols is a significant aspect of ritual. A ritual generally observes the procedures with which a symbol is invested, which a symbol compels. Thus myths are encoded in rituals, liturgies and symbols, and reference to a symbol can be quite sufficient to recall the myth for the members of the community without need to return to ritual' (Schöpflin 1997).

Myths are universal, in democratic regimes as well as autocracies seeking to gain legitimacy. They are also a constant fact in history and have from deep antiquity been part of the political panoply of all regimes, at all times.

The definition of a myth

A myth may be described as a story or event that illuminates the key values of some society or association: the events can be real or imaginary, but, almost certainly, imagination will have embroidered them. The propagandist thus draws from the existing stock of social mythologies as well as adding to them. These core myths of a society are its foundation ideals – such as Governor Winthrop's 'City on a Hill' – and their undermining creates social upheaval.

Myth is a conceptual lynchpin of propaganda and it is impossible to imagine the propagandised without their myths. Myths are a feature of all human societies everywhere. A myth is a story, the story a culture tells about itself to perpetuate itself, the sound of a culture's internal dialogue. The gods of the Greeks and Romans, for example, were just like us humans, in all our weakness and triviality, they are a commentary on our foibles, our play of emotions and petty jealousies. 'Myth' in popular language means invention or untruth, but that is not the academic meaning of the term. Thus Calder's *The Myth of the Blitz* (1991) is not claiming that the historical memory of the blitz is untrue, merely that there are important qualifications to be made. The fact, for example, that looting took place after the bombing of the Café de Paris in the West End does not alter the core truth of nobility, community and sacrifice (and neither does Calder claim that it does).

Myths are exhortatory, exemplars of approved patterns of behaviour: the key problem for the myth maker 'is to find the set of values, paradigm scenarios or experiences that have wide appeal among the target audience. One way to do this is to look at the changing values of a culture or subculture in contrast to traditional values, and beliefs . . . ' (O'Shaughnessy and O'Shaughnessy 2004). For Schöpflin (1997) culture itself may be defined as 'a system of collectively held notions, beliefs, premises, ideas, dispositions, and understandings, to which myth gives a structure'. We have argued that 'what they share is the attempt to identify a basic level of cultural experience, manifested in words and deeds throughout history, and concerned principally with the articulation of the core concerns and preoccupations of their host culture' (O'Shaughnessy and O'Shaughnessy 2003). For Overing (1997) the myth is an exemplar of the work of unconscious logical processes:

> it serves as a symbolic statement about the social order, and as such it reinforces social cohesion and functional unity by presenting and justifying the traditional order. Mythic Discourse reminds a community of its own identity through the public process of specifying and defining for that community its distinctive social norms. Whether or not people believe in the irrational content of myth is irrelevant, for the symbols of myth have metaphoric value and serve a crucial social function in maintaining the given social order.

Eliade (1991) defines myth as 'an account of the events which took place *in principio*, that is, in the beginning, in a primordial and non-temporal instant, a moment of sacred time'. He says an important property of myths has been that they can change people, that is, they have a redemptive function: 'we may even wonder whether the accessibility of Christianity may not be attributable in great measure to its symbolism, whether the universal images that it takes up in its turn have not considerably facilitated the diffusion of its message'. Culture may be defined as a system of collectively held notions, beliefs, premises, ideas, dispositions and understandings to which myth gives a structure.

Social myths are perpetuated by propaganda, celebrated in film, ritual and print, and this has been a ceaseless activity. A myth can be manifested as a non-specific image perpetuated through time – that, for example, big business is amoral, or government is incompetent. (Nor, of course, do such myths have – as the vernacular sense would imply – to be untrue!) Or it can be a highly specific idea (as Keynes said, 'Practical men, who believe themselves to be quite exempt from any intellectual influences, are usually the slaves of some defunct economist. Madmen in authority, who hear voices in the air, are distilling their frenzy from some academic scribbler of a few years back'). Or it can be a generic myth, recurrent throughout many societies and periods of history, such as myths of a Golden Age or of an ascetic and uncorrupted past. Romans imagined an earlier and virtuous polity that was well embodied in the figure of Cincinnatus, the farmer called from his plough to serve as consul to save the republic from its enemies who, having done so, returned to his plough.

Why we have myths

In *The Marketing Power of Emotion* (2003) O'Shaughnessy and O'Shaughnessy argue that 'every culture is a storehouse of myths which, though
questionably accurate, suggest the origins of the culture's preference for
certain beliefs and values and in the process reaffirm a set of preferences'.
For Schöpflin (1997) 'myths are about the ways in which communities
regard certain propositions as normal and natural and others as perverse
and alien'. In *Athenian Myths and Institutions* W. Blake Tyrrell (Tyrrell and
Brown 1991) examines how myth makers reflect, define and defend the
status quo. For Tyrrell, myths refer to relations inherent in the culture's
value system, they depict in imaginary form a model to be emulated, as well
as the destructive forces active in society, which, left unattended, could rup-
ture the social bond. By telling what happens when core values are lost,
myths teach what is culturally valued, they act to assert the *status quo* – in
the case of Greece, a warlike, imperialistic society of aristocrats. They
become a kind of universal perceptual lens; in Schöpflin's words (1997)
'myth creates an intellectual and cognitive monopoly in that it seeks to
establish the sole way of ordering the world and defining world views'.
According to Tyrrell, heroes are particularly important in myths and establish model behaviours.

Those who would expose mythologies should do so with care. Any society needs its myths, and if we aggressively and systematically demolish
them we may be doing real damage, for myths are intimately bound up with
a society's identity, its ability to transmit a coherent culture and moral code
to cadet generations and to inspire pride and a sense of community. Moreover a society whose government cavalierly neglects its core myths faces
trouble. One reason for the terrible alienation of youth during the Vietnam
War was that US actions contradicted the myths of stainless American
decency that had been projected by film and popular culture in the ideological cocoon of the 1950s. It is necessary for a regime to keep myths in being
to guarantee its survival – the Roman emperors, for example, having to sustain the pretence that Rome was still ruled by people and Senate, perpetuated in the slogan 'Senatus Populusque Romanus', the SPQR of the
legionnaires' banner. Much of the intellectual and artistic energy of the
'1960s generation' has lain subsequently in the gleeful demolition of myths
– for example, a British television series, *Real Lives*, concerned itself with
taking famous national figures and posthumously outing them as gay
(Baden-Powell, on no real evidence, *Daily Telegraph*, 7 December 1996),
bastards (Group Captain Douglas Bader) and so forth. The pantheon of
national heroica was serially assaulted on its plinths.

News, especially, deals in myth. As Bird and Dardenne (1988) explain,
news narratives are constructed not through neutral techniques but

via symbolic devices and the confection of myths and manifest in simple explanations, reassurance and so forth; in fact the myths endemic in a culture constitute a form of selective perception of the world. Selective perception, common to members of a given culture, has the effect of importing a characteristic interpretation to phenomena.

Myth and story

Myths work because they are structured as stories, as elided stories that integrate meaningful facts into a persuasive framework. Thus Pennington and Hastie (1993) showed how jurors dealt with their inability to remember numerous details by imposing a story framework through which they could make sense of the facts, and they used this master narrative as a template to evaluate the narrative of prosecution and defence: acceptance or rejection of advocacy was determined by its cohesion with the master narrative. We identify people's perspectives by the stories they tell. Christianity succeeded not through the exposition of abstract ethical rules alone: its ethos and belief system gained inspiration from stories which carried the reader through from a beginning to a middle and an end and a message. The Prodigal Son, the Good Samaritan, Dives and Lazarus, the Labourers in the Vineyard and so forth were simple tales which could be instantly recognised in any culture. The narrative superstructure of the Gospels, which accords primacy to sacrifice and rebirth, constitutes a primordial myth system that can thereby usurp other sacrifice-based systems such as the Aztec. The figures of Christian scripture and tradition could absorb the pantheon of pagan deities via a manufactured resemblance, as when in Mexico the (pregnant) Virgin of Guadalupe replaced a (pregnant) Aztec female deity, or where the cross lies within a circle representing the sun god, as with the Celtic cross.

The impact of myths

Myths have had a real impact on the course of history, and since the creation of myths is a permanent activity, myths continue to be important even though some die out. They are merely replaced. The progress of our lives is festooned with myths. There are myths round every corner. Myths, their tissues of truth, falsehood and fantasy, are the context we inhabit and the atmosphere we breathe. Shopping behaviour is inspired by mythological structures – diamonds, for example, are a rather common little rock, but they are also a girl's best friend, and the success of the de Beers cartel in pouring meaning and exclusivity into this stone ranks as one of the greatest myth-making enterprises of all time.

Myth is thus impactful. The exculpatory myth fabricated by the German general staff in 1918 – the myth of the stab in the back – had horrendous consequences as a result of its acceptance by German public opinion. In the United States so powerful has been the 'log cabin to White House' myth that one candidate, Benjamin Harrison, ordered little wooden model cabins for his supporters to carry around (Melder 1992), even though he was the cousin of an English lord. Politically created myths have performed sterling service for their manufacturers, for example the myth of the 'winter of discontent' was endlessly promulgated by the Conservative Party throughout the 1980s, and it served them well.

Myths can be destructive. They can affirm our current sense of inferiority by reference to a more glorious past. They can perpetuate untruths, and the social iniquities which flow from this, such as the mythology of the Indian 'martial races' which grew up under the Moghul dynasties and was inherited by the British. It took World War II to make people realise that all Indians, not merely the splendid tribes, Jats, Dogras, Hazaras and so on, could fight well (Cohen 1990). Military myths are extremely important, establishing a powerful masculine identity for a nation or fortifying its wish to hold and conquer. France, for example, had the myth of *la gloire*, the belief that military success was a function solely of *élan* or spirit. ('Le pantalon rouge, c'est La France.')

And myths endure. Their long shelf life illustrates both their convenience as a shorthand for talking about one's culture and our failure to interrogate them. That Britain is 'strangled by the old school tie' is still a widely believed myth even though the social reality that underpinned it has faded. Such myths are convenient, they save us from new learning and thinking. The press deals constantly in one particular type of myth, stereotype, and one should never underestimate the after-life of a long-defunct stereotype: professors remain 'mad', colonels 'blimpish', long after the age of such characters has passed. Sometimes in persuasion we attempt to confront myth stereotypes head-on, as in an army recruitment advertisement entitled 'Spot the colonel' where pictures of 'real' – i.e. modern-looking – colonels were placed alongside a pukka silver-moustached actor representing the presumed anachronism. Myths can endure and have powerful impact even though they are factually wrong. The belief long persisted in Ireland that the practice of Roman Catholicism had once been illegal:

> O, Paddy, dear, did you hear
> The news that's going round?
> The Shamrock is by law forbid
> To grow on Irish ground.

In Kevin Myers's words, 'To enter a modern conspiracy against British rule merely repeats the earlier – albeit mythical – conspiracy required simply to practise one's religion' (*Spectator*, 18 March 1995). To Schöpflin (1997) 'myth is a way of offering explanations for the fate of a community and failure of particular strategies. Myth creates solidarity in adversity by offering answers that can be probed no further.'

Truth and falsehood

To be successful a propaganda myth must have intuitive plausibility: the myth spread by the Chinese communists, that a public park sign in Hong Kong said 'No dogs or Chinese allowed' was a distortion, but people could, just about, believe it of the British. This is significant because it underpins the proposition that myth 'cannot be constructed purely out of false material; it has to have some relationship with the memory of the collectivity that has fashioned it' (Schöpflin 1997). Truth is often irrelevant, it is a matter of what is believed. The charge of the Light Brigade, for example, has been since the mid-nineteenth century a key British myth of heroic but glorious failure, immortalised by the diverse epic talents of Tennyson and Hollywood. But the myth is sustainable only if we actually believe that many of the soldiers were killed, a prerequisite of the charge attaining its epic notes of glory and blunder. Modern researchers claim that over 80 per cent of the men survived, which makes the myth and its significance meaningless (www.factindex.com/c/ch/charge_of_the_light_brigade). Myths are in fact often disputed by historians because of their significance: but did they actually happen? For example, did soldiers really fire on striking miners at Tonypandy, or is it a Labour Party myth? According to Lord Jenkins (2001) it is. Much of modern historical endeavour is in fact, quite literally, demythologising. One example would be the notorious events at the commencement of the siege of the Alcazar of Toledo. According to Professor Hugh Thomas (1986), the leading British authority on the Spanish Civil War:

> Finally, on 23 July, Candido Cabello, a republican barrister in Toledo, telephoned Moscardo to say that if Moscardo did not surrender the Alcazar within ten minutes, he would shoot Luis Moscardo, the Colonel's 24-year-old son, whom he had captured that morning. 'So that you can see that's true, he will speak to you,' added Cabello. 'What is happening, my boy?' asked the Colonel. 'Nothing,' answered the son. 'They say they will shoot me if the Alcazar does not surrender.' 'If it be true,' replied Moscardo, 'commend your soul to God, shout Viva España and die like a hero. Goodbye, my son. A last kiss?' 'Goodbye, Father,' answered Luis. 'A very big kiss.'

The equally distinguished Professor Paul Preston (1995) is, however, curtly dismissive:

> However, the resistance of the Alcazar was being turned into the great symbol of Nationalist heroism. Subsequently the reality of the siege would be embroidered beyond recognition, in particular through the famous, and almost

certainly apocryphal, story that Moscardo was telephoned and told that, unless he surrendered, his son would be shot.

Myth manufacture

Myth entrepreneurship is the insightful seizure of material from a mass of cultural properties. The serious propagandists will think through their myths very carefully: 'for a myth to be effective in organising and mobilising opinion, it must however resonate. The myth that fails to elicit response is alien or inappropriate' (Schöpflin 1997). Propaganda thus becomes the judicious refurbishment of old myths but it is also the manufacture of new ones (for example, the Australian film *Breaker Morant* re-engineered the folk memory of the past to create a new Australian hero to add to its traditional ones). The insight, effectiveness and creativity with which this is done are a test of the skill of the propagandist. Myth has an inherent plasticity that can be recast for modern purposes. Film and television do this frequently as novel and history are reinterpreted in the light of contemporary obsessions and prejudices – as, for example, Walt Disney's politically correct version of Kipling's *Jungle Book* or the latest (it is the fourth) version of *The Four Feathers*. So a seemingly traditional myth can be invoked and recast for an entirely different purpose. Thus the 1936 (Warner Brothers) version of the film *The Charge of the Light Brigade* was essentially about the supremacy of the Anglo-Saxon race, with two events in historical time (the Cawnpore massacre of 1857 and the charge in 1854) reversed; the 1968 version focused on the iniquities of the British class system, each film ministering to the ideological needs of its era (Carnes 1996). For Webster (1988) 'it is important to see the populists' rhetoric as a strategic mobilisation of the past rather than nostalgia'. The past is not therefore an escape from the present but legitimates it by showing the ostensibly unchanging nature of people and by illuminating antecedent causes.

From our perspective the point about myths in propaganda is that they are not merely refurbished and recreated but actively manufactured. The great masters of propaganda have deliberately sought to construct them. Goebbels invented myths. Horst Wessel, a Nazi student probably killed by communists (Snyder 1976), was turned into a kind of Nazi saint. He also created the myths of an 'Era of Struggle', the Old Comrades and so on – magnifying the political obstacles and Communist violence the Nazis had to overcome in their rise to power, and all laced with maudlin sentimentality. Goebbels may have been the most influential myth inventor of the twentieth century but he was far from being the only one, and the impact of invented or amplified myths is everywhere. The extent and vigour of their manufacture or elaboration are highly visible in the history of totalitarian regimes such as the March on Rome and communism's similar litany with its *Battleship Potemkin*, *Long March* and so on.

Myth making can become a high art in itself, especially when entrusted to such as Edmund Burke, whose mythologising of the ludicrous Queen Marie Antoinette of France must rank as one of the most luminous examples of the genre: 'I thought ten thousand swords must have leaped from their scabbards to avenge even a look that threatened her with insult. But the Age of Chivalry is gone; that of sophisters, economists, and calculators has succeeded; and the glory of Europe is extinguished for ever' (Goodrich 1884).

Thus myths can be instantly fabricated to change perceptions, an aspect perhaps of what we nowadays call 'spin'. Propaganda is the imposition of an interpretation and myths are an important part of that; since there are few situations that permit only one fixed and unchallengeable interpretation, the possibility of persuasion succeeding, even if the perception is an unorthodox one, always exists. Defeat can be turned into victory, and the genius is to succeed here where logic would ordain otherwise. Dunkirk is such a case. The salvation of a routed and surrounded army, saved only by the inertia (or sufferance) of its conquerors, was turned by the masterful myth-confectionery skills of Winston Churchill into just possibly the greatest of all the British myths, an eminence it has occupied ever since. It was the best 'spin' of all time.

Myth, nation and race

The myth maker may be juxtaposed with the 'rational' persuader who favours a more rigorous discourse drawn more from scientific empiricism. That great political bout of British history, between Gladstone and Disraeli, was not about mere ideology alone or even ideology at all, but the application of analytical reason to politics energised by the idea of an essential fraternity of the human race, versus a deep faith in unreasoning instinct and the sacrosanctity of custom, inherited folkways and the ancestral calls of race and blood. Disraeli ironically was quoted on his view that 'race is all' by Adolf Hitler during a speech at the Sports Palace in Berlin. There are degrees in how literally a nation may take its myths. Myths may be popularly viewed as containing rhetorical truths, such as the US myth of national benevolence, or they may, more dangerously, be seen as portraying the objective truth, as with the Nazi belief in the existence from ancient times of an Aryan race. Perhaps nationalism, like race, is a utopian myth of purification, and nationalist expressions of propaganda share commonalities of mythic structure: in Smetana's *Blanik* the hero sleeps in the halls, one day to reawake with the nation. Sleeping, also, is Wagner's Kaiser Frederick Barbarossa, an anticipation of the Führer concept (Perris 1985).

Many propaganda myths focus on the superiority of tribe, or race (that mass society, mass media-amplified sense of tribe). Race myths are valuable since they make everyone within the master race, the chosen people, or whatever, feel superior, however plebeian their pre-existing status. For the First World War British, for example, *Punch* magazine invented a 'Professor of German Frightfulness' to remind them of the Germans' moral inferiority. Race myths – using race in the sense of a socially constructed category, which is not, of course, how believers regard it – were almost universally accepted in the nineteenth century. The impact and propaganda value of race myths endured long after they had become discredited among the intelligentsia who had once embraced them. Thus the notion of 'black Aryans', i.e. Tutsis, took hold in Rwanda during the colonial period and, since it was also a basis of preferment, further polarised the people, its legacy grimly apparent in the massacres of the early 1990s (Robert Block 1994).

Some race myths are almost too well known to merit discussion. The notion of a pure northern 'Aryan' race, uniquely superior, had been propagated by the Count de Gobineau in the nineteenth century and popularised in Wilhelmine Germany by Huston Stewart Chamberlain and sundry pamphleteers (Snyder 1976). From such sources the party ideologue Alfred Rosenberg constructed his gimcrack *Mythos*. These formative influences on the young Hitler and subsequently on Hess, Himmler and others were strong. They sanctified instinctual bigotry with the liturgies of scientism. The race myth was not only handed to the Nazis through the nineteenth-century pseudo-intelligentsia, there were also artistic sources, pre-eminently Wagner, whose Nibelungs, the dark and scavenger race, were deliberately likened by him to the Jewish people. In the twentieth century the ancient libels against the Jews – that they had, for example, engaged in the ritual murder of children – were supplemented by freshly manufactured libels such as the French forgery the 'Protocols of the Elders of Zion' elaborated and propagated by the Tsarist secret police. The Tsar had sought to combat Bolshevism by fomenting Russian nationalism, and this demanded the fabrication of an alien threat – as ever, the Jews. The 'protocols' were found among Nicholas's last few possessions (Figes 1997), but their influence upon European fascism, on characters like Archibald Maule Ramsay MP and his 'Right Club', were considerable (R. Griffiths 1983).

US myths

Now most propaganda is deeply embedded in myth. Propaganda creates new myths, of course (Horst Wessel), but more often it draws from or reinterprets old ones. Both sides in a dispute can, and do, pick from the same stock of myths and give them a different interpretation, thus 'Log cabin to

White House' is a common integrating myth of US culture which all parties exploited. Elements of US myths – the frontier, cowboys versus Indians, etc. – recur time and again in its cultural products. The family farm is another: thus when Midwestern viewers saw images of a deserted farm and the phrase 'It wasn't just a farm. It was a family. Vote Democrat' (Webster 1988) their manipulators were tapping into a key myth of the American heartland. It is difficult to imagine how a culture could exist without the myths that organise, reinforce and give it meaning. So myths celebrate the key values of a culture. The very language of a culture carries its core mythologies. These mythic appeals are used extensively in advertising. Thus Andy Rooney in *Sixty Minutes* (Tyrrell 1991) cited the ten most common words used in advertising. Such words evoke the dreams and aspirations promised by the US founding myth. 'Discover', 'fresh', 'new' and 'light' (that is, unburdened) evoke promise and opportunity; 'natural' and 'real' what the seeker may find here; 'extra', 'rich' and 'save' what accrues from initiative. The anthropologist Leymore (1975) argues that a role of advertising is to create modern myths, something that it is constantly doing.

Reich (1987) mentions various cultural myths that affect what Americans believe through the power of emotional resonance, such as the Horatio Alger story, which was even (according to Barbara Stern 1988) turned into a Budweiser commercial. Myths are the stuff of the United States, its cultural DNA. How many Hollywood movies, for example, tell and retell the story of the little guy battling the system or the big corporation or the bullies (such as Elia Kazan's *On the Waterfront*, 1954)? These are part of the traditional fabrics and fibres of Hollywood, yet they are also embedded US culture myths. Other redeployed myths include the damaged male (Bogart in *Casablanca*, Rambo and many others), authority figures such as soldiers, doctors, lawyers, policemen rebelling against authority, as with the *Dirty Harry* persona (reflecting Americans' ambivalence towards the official and the officious).

Some US myths – such as the notion of Americans as 'benevolent', which pre-date even the foundation of the republic itself – endure (the British by contrast being merely satisfied that they were Just!). Myths retail the story of the victors in historical conflicts. Our image, for example, of the foundation of the United States is that of the *Mayflower* and its austere cargo of black-clad Pilgrim Fathers; yet this is essentially a post-Civil War image, for the founding colony was of course Virginia, the heart of the Confederacy, and not New England.

Similarly the American War of Independence, as set forth in such films as *Revolution* (1985) with Al Pacino or *The Patriot* with Mel Gibson, is a narrative of the victors. Most Americans would be bemused to learn that the revolutionaries closed theatres and caused actors such as the American

Company of Comedians to emigrate (A.J. O'Shaughnessy 2000); that numbered among the causes of the revolution were resentment at the extension of civil rights to French Catholics of Quebec (the Quebec Act: Gardiner and Wenborn 1995) and the attempts by King George III's government to prevent colonists expanding westward into the territory of Native Americans, with whose leaders it had signed treaties. Myths are in essence victor myths: those of the vanquished either die out or lead a subterranean existence. Yet myths have remained critical to Americans, to how they interpret the present, throughout their history. Thus 'one of populism's key strategies has been the mobilization of history and tradition' (Webster 1988), yet in *Lies my Teacher told Me* James Loewen (1995) illuminates just how false the history we are taught so often is. Most probably believe – they have been told so often enough by the National Rifle Association – that they possess a constitutionally enshrined 'right to bear arms'. They have no such thing, otherwise of course cities like New York could not enforce their legal ban on gun ownership. The constitution lends them a right to bear arms only as members of a legally constituted militia, yet this myth continues to exert a baleful influence on the political beliefs of Americans, to the extent that the battle against the gun in public life has emigrated from the political arena, where the NRA has effectively sterilised most potential opposition (Anderson 1996), to the courts of law.

Myth and martyrdom

Deaths and martyrdom have always been fecund sources of myth making. Christ was the ultimate martyr, and all martyrdom has therefore the tincture of divinity. Irish Republican martyrology, for example, is an intricate subject in itself. Bobby Sands was the last of a great assemblage of Irish martyrs stretching way back in history well beyond Cardinal Plunkett, and prints, books, murals and, especially, song and ballad have celebrated martyrs such as Kevin Barry, the university student who participated in a terrorist act on his way to a lecture in 1920 and was subsequently executed by the British (Bennett 1995).

Martyrdom is a particularly persuasive way of inflating a sense of moral grandeur, and has been critical in the establishment of religious faiths and nation states. Foxe's *Book of Martyrs* (Ridley 2001), published in the reign of Queen Elizabeth I, gave the Anglican church the ethical pedigree it needed. Elizabeth herself ordained that a copy should be chained to each pulpit, and the book was carried on the ships fighting the Spanish Armada. The death by hunger strike of Terence MacSwiney, Mayor of Cork, was a critical propaganda blow against British rule in southern Ireland. The suicide bomber, of course, kills many others in the process of killing himself. But the act may still impress those who need most to be impressed, the tentative and the weakly partisan.

All nations, and all causes, seek and attain their martyrs. The martyr does not have to die, but death of course is desirable. The more gory the death, the better. The death of the heroine of French independence, Joan of Arc, by flame, created a permanent nation-building myth to be used by French patriots for all time, including de Gaulle. Events such as the death of Nelson and the assassination of Lincoln and Kennedy gave those men a martyr's crown: the manner of their death added retrospectively a sacerdotal glow to their high triumphs, and they became, as it were, Saints of the Nation. In some cases nations and groups have consciously sought to create a cult of death, and this was particularly powerful in all European fascist movements, Spanish nationalism, for example (Preston 2000). Nazi culture was permeated by a kind of death fixation; a movement which was responsible for the deaths of countless millions was itself animated by a bizarre death cult. *Triumph of the Will* is dominated by memorialist enactments, the rising to hail the memory of Field Marshal Hindenberg, the salutation to the dead of the First World War and the recitation of its battlefields, the solemn march of the Führer to the flaming plinths. This funereal quality of Nazi propaganda is one of its many curious aspects, but is made intelligible both in terms of the need for reconciliation with the enormous losses of the First World War and the need for preparation and acceptance of the great blood sacrifices that Hitler would now demand.

One successful fabricator of myths was Ronald Reagan. His achievement was to 'make the problems of the present disappear by flanking them with a reassuring vision of the past and a dream of a benign future' (Lule 1990). He did this by creating new myths that had resonance with the past, such as his 'production' of the *Challenger* disaster, where old myths (the conquest of the west) were used to manufacture new ones (the conquest of space). So the creation of myths has continued throughout history. They are simply too useful, to the advocate and to the propagandist.

Kenneth Burke (Lule 1990) asks 'whether human societies could possible cohere without symbolic victims which the individual members of the group share in common'. The question is not how the sacrificial motives revealed in the institutions of magic and religion might be eliminated 'but what new forms they take'. In the *Challenger* disaster Ronald Reagan deployed effective rhetorical strategies, using these reference points, to turn disaster into a heroic endeavour. Even a seemingly decisive event with an ostensibly unambiguous message – such as the poor leadership and mismanagement which disasters reveal – has plasticity, the territory of its meaning open to contest, and the function of rhetoric is to affix an interpretation which freezes it into the definitive paradigm of the event for all future discussion. Lule comments perceptively that:

> quite possibly, the *Challenger* Seven could have served as powerful symbols of failed policy and flawed leadership. Yet Reagan reconciled the failure of the shuttle and renewed US commitment to the space programme through enactment of the drama of victimage. He sanctified the crew and offered Americans consolation and purgation through sacrifice and redemption.

However, he 'referred to the deaths of the astronauts only twice and obliquely. . . . Reagan saw the deaths as giving meaning because the programme was going forward'.

And these questions of meaning are critical to explaining propaganda. Lule quotes Deetz:

> in tracing the metaphors that are used by the society, we trace the way people in that society experience things. . . . Reagan used the metaphors to structure the eulogy – astronauts and pioneers, space and the American west, death and life everlasting: Reagan implied that the shuttle crew was extending America's boundaries into space. . . . Near his conclusion Reagan spoke directly to the dead and he implied the seven earned eternal life through their sacrifice for the nation.

Lule also notes that 'the drama of the victimage effectively sidesteps questions of blame or responsibility', and adds:

> the astronauts had given their lives for the nation. Partisan bickering over their loss, as if their deaths had not been a sacrifice but a horrible mistake, would rob the deaths of dignity and meaning. In this way, Reagan's eulogy used the victims to effectively silence and dispel questions of responsibility. . . . By placing the space programme within hallowed, American pioneer tradition, debate on the programme's merits was cut off or limited to discussion of when and how the programme would proceed and the promise be fulfilled.

Propaganda and symbolism

If myths are the heart of propaganda, symbolism is its outer garment – indeed, to speak of a propaganda devoid of symbolism is really to be speaking about some other phenomenon, for a propaganda bereft of symbol structures would be unintelligible as propaganda. Symbols telegraph meaning, and life is a cacophony of symbols, since they are the mental heuristics or short cuts through which daily life is interpreted and organised. A key function of propaganda is to manufacture such recognition devices.

Propaganda texts are symbol-rich. Thus in *Battleship Potemkin* the firing of the ship's guns in response to the massacre are juxtaposed with shots of ponderously regal stone lions fronting a palatial edifice. They symbolise the *ancien régime*. Nor do we see the Tsarist guards killed: instead it is the stone lions that are smashed. Roman symbolism in particular became an idiom and symbolic grammar of various dictatorships, Napoleon, Mussolini and especially the Nazis. The propaganda of the Reich was encrusted with Roman imagery: it became, in the Roman salute, an adjunct to every day communication. The Nuremberg rallies themselves were gimcrack Roman triumphs, with flames atop columns, gigantic eagles, temple-like structures: the very word 'fascist' is of course derived from the Roman *fasces*, symbol of magisterial authority.

Commercial advertising also acknowledges symbolism. Much commercial signification celebrates the idea that material things are not an end in themselves but a means of expression, signifying affection, status. Gift giving is symbolic drama: symbols represent social meaning rather than point to something concrete. Products are means to social ends such as admiration, and the thrust of much advertising is that these things are attainable through the agency of some purchased symbol, that is, a commercial product. When this is understood we come finally to the view that the briefest, most comprehensive definition of a product is simply as 'meaning'.

The symbol has been described as a sign that incorporates something in addition to its direct references. A symbol, unlike an idea, is something visible, something into which communication has poured meaning, it is a dynamic referent that refers not only to itself but to the myriad associations that have been packed into it. For Douglas (1982) 'symbols are the only means of communication. They are the only means of expressing value; the main instruments of thought, the only regulators of experience.' For any communication to take place, the symbols must be structured. Symbols, often considered the most powerful and complex forms of comparison, are thus a class of representatives which stand for other things (Firth, in Stern 1988), without the explicit expression of comparison. They are commonly regarded as metaphors from which the first term has been omitted (Beeks and Warren, in Stern 1988). Symbols act as heuristics or cognitive short cuts: when relative choices are confusing and ambiguous we fall back on symbolism.

The value of symbolism

Symbols are effective because they save cognitive energy, but also because much appraisal is first emotional and only latterly a cognitive evaluation. Persuasion can resort to mere symbolism alone, rejecting any kind of rationale or rational construction of a case, and this has been described by

Mayhew (1997) as the rhetoric of presentation. A statue, for example, or a photograph without explanatory text can be doing simply this.

Symbols are an important aspect of propaganda and one which the extant literature on propaganda has tended to devalue. First, they are an immensely cheap form of propaganda: they attract public notice, they are remembered for decades or even centuries afterwards. A symbol speaks directly to the heart and does not tax the critical intellect. Commercial organisations have long grasped the importance of symbols. (Some service examples are Prudential Bach's rock, the Travellers' Insurance Company umbrella and Merrill Lynch's bull: Stern 1988). A brand is also a symbol, and branding is now a commercial science: corporate investment in brand designs, brand building and brand identity is really testimony to the enduring power of symbols. Brands resonate in ways that ultimately defy analysis. Advertising itself has been described as 'pouring meaning into the brand'.

A symbol is shorthand. Its essence is compression. For a symbol expresses, often in visible form, what might take ages to write down or debate. The French revolutionaries were 'great believers in the use of symbols as a means of transmitting complicated ideas in a simple form' (Taylor 1990), such as the Phrygian cap denoting equality, the fasces for fraternity and Marianne as the symbol of liberty. It is also economic. A memorable symbol such as the wartime 'V for Victory' campaign in occupied Europe is an extraordinary weapon, since it can be brief, ubiquitous and costless. In this case the V signature was daubed all over the lands the Nazis occupied and incessantly broadcast by the BBC as the opening bars of Beethoven's Ninth.

Symbols are attractive also to those with less capacity for abstract thought. To Pope Gregory the Great, for example, statues were 'books for the illiterate' (Taylor 1990). It is a paradox that, the more educated people seem to become, the less symbol-conscious they appear to be. Often what we mean by saying, for example, that academics are 'out of touch' is that they are unaware of symbolic values and the charge they carry, for reason is myopic when it confronts symbols, and the process of education is one of editing out symbolic awareness. This, perhaps, is why intellectuals become so perplexed when they look at situations where the issues are, or are in the main, symbolic. Northern Ireland in particular baffled them because everything was organised around symbolic issues where the core of political debate comprised such arcane matters as the kind of cap badge that police officers should wear. The symbol speaks, essentially, to simpler folk: academics are often so trained that they are immunised to the power symbols hold for ordinary people, and thus too often their analyses ignore them. The fact that the highly academically educated tend to be insensitive to non-verbal symbols and dull their meaning is central to the difficulties of Christianity today. For example, the Catholic church hierarchy failed to see the significance of Friday's abstinence to the Irish labourer in London. For him it symbolised allegiance to a humble home in Ireland and to a glorious tradition in Rome (Douglas 1982).

A ritual is an enacted symbol, and any ritual is propaganda of an authoritarian and inherited kind. Rituals act as a social adhesive, prescribing and proscribing the key concerns and values of a community. Recognising this, propagandists in times past, from the French revolutionaries to the Nazis and Stalin, have sought to create new rituals, ones plagiarised from the ritualistic performance of religious and monarchist institutions but celebrating new state ideologies. During the French revolution, ceremonies, Festivals of Freedom and Statues of Liberty helped 'to consolidate the Republican idea in a society familiar only with monarchical government' (Taylor 1990).

Today there is an attack on ritual and we speak often of 'empty' symbols and 'meaningless' ritual. Yet rituals are seldom meaningless and the astute propagandist will recognise their value. Douglas (1982) argues that one of the greatest problems of our day is our lack of commitment to common rituals, while more mysterious is a widespread, explicit rejection of rituals as such. Ritual has become a bad word signifying empty conformity. She also suggests that many sociologists, following Merton, use the term 'ritual' of one who performs gestures without inner commitment to the ideas and values expressed. This is a distractingly partisan use of the term, since anthropologists use 'ritual' to mean action and beliefs in the symbolic order without reference to the commitment or non-commitment of the actors.

Symbols in history

Symbolic acts have been the core of politics, almost since recorded history began. What is often regarded as great political leadership is in fact, and very often, the highest sensitivity to symbols and a mastery of their manipulation. Mahatma Gandhi, for example, was the supreme magician of symbolism: that of his dress and spinning wheel, with their message of ascetic simplicity and self-reliance, spoke both to his followers and to the British imperial rulers he wished to influence. His use of the fast was well contrived, and his great Salt March a masterpiece of symbolic propaganda – as great and significant in its way as the Boston Tea Party, with its message that India's natural bounty, sea salt, was being absurdly taxed by her colonial rulers.

Such is the strength of symbols that much of history, much, indeed, of war, has been spent quarrelling over them, seeking them out or exorcising them. In the Spanish Civil War the Alcazar, or fortress, of Toledo held no military or strategic value, but its heroic resistance, deep in republican territory, made it a symbol both of nationalist determination and of the struggle to control Spain. Franco's strategy was dominated by the need to capture this potent but militarily irrelevant symbol and the war itself was spun out needlessly. Again, the Irish Civil War (1922–24) was fought not, as is commonly imagined, over the integration of the north – General Michael Collins was in fact more radical on this issue than de Valera – but about a symbol, a mere oath of loyalty to the British king, to be taken by ambassadors, members of the Dail, and so on. Yet this symbol was sufficient to drive its antagonists to the sordid brutalities of civil war, even though the British government no longer exercised any political jurisdiction in the south (apart from the four treaty ports).

All political events have some symbolic aspect, ways in which their meaning is related to broader interpretations of the political *status quo*: they are construed not only as events in themselves, but as a statement about the larger trend or situation. Thus during the American War of Independence, the death of Jane McCrea, the fiancée of a Tory loyalist, was alleged by republican propagandists (see 'The death of Jane McCrea', painted by John Vanderlyn in 1804) to have been scalped by tribesmen in the employ of the British (Taylor 1990). This aroused more than mere rage, yet why should the death of one ordinary individual contribute to the outcome of a revolution? The answer is that the horrific event also carried an obvious symbolic construction, namely the opportunism and amorality of the British and their cynical belief that any means would justify the imperial end. The power of this event is comprehensible only if we realise the fear and contempt Americans then felt for the 'savage' original possessors of their soil. (In fact Miss McRea was probably shot by the revolutionaries themselves in error.)

Events thus become symbolic because they have a political meaning that describes a larger problem, and because the appropriateness of their symbolisation is accepted, interpreted and amplified through the media. They do not have to be 'great' or important events themselves. The refusal of striking undertakers to bury the dead in Britain's 1979 'winter of discontent' became symbolic of the surrender of control from government to unions, and it was endowed with a significance far beyond the inconvenience of a few mourners, while over the next decade or so this symbol was used time and again in Tory party propaganda to remind people of life under Labour. A symbol is not, of course, necessarily contrived – it can be spontaneous, but none the less strong: Alexander the Great, when confronted with the Gordian knot, was supposed to have simply slashed it with his sword, and William the Conqueror, stumbling on English land, reputedly arose and with handfuls of soil claimed to have taken the earth of England. Napoleon famously seized his new imperial crown for himself from the Pope's hands at his coronation.

Commerce and history are so encrusted with symbols that they are a way, and often *the* way, in which we remember, from the Marlboro cowboy to Mayor Giuliani at Ground Zero to Marian Anderson singing (9 April 1939) – and, later, Martin Luther King speaking – in front of the Lincoln Memorial. The random images which flood into our minds as we contemplate our collective past were, once, artfully contrived: in fact they are not random at all.

One particular form of symbol-rich propaganda, of high significance in the nineteenth century as well as in the twentieth, is terrorism in all its forms. In terrorism the symbol is the victim, and terrorists particularly seek out victims who are rich in symbolic meaning: 'the selection of victims is symbolic and instrumental . . . the victim is chosen because of whom she or he represents and because their victimisation will resonate with specific audiences' (Crelinston 1989). Crelinston argues that terrorism is 'a specific form of political violence, one that is characterised by its communication function . . . [T]he victims of terrorism function as signs in a propaganda war'. Much political violence, including war itself, focuses the attack on identifiable and specific targets that are deeply symbolic and whose defilement pleasures the partisans of a cause. Indeed, Blain (1988) concludes that 'human violence is not the fall into latent animality but rather an extreme expression of our symbol-mindedness. It is in the hyperbolic possibilities of linguistic symbolism that they should seek an answer to the question of why human beings fight wars.'

Symbols and meaning

Symbols are not universally decoded in the same kind of way and their meaning varies among groups. They also elude the kind of precise focus and content that might antagonise some of those whose loyalty we seek: a symbol has a flexibility of meaning to which the viewer can bring his or her own imagination, it carries an openness to interpretation. Symbols resonate. They convey multiple meanings, since images by their very structure are multivalent. Eliade (1991) argues that if the mind makes use of images to grasp the ultimate reality of things, it is just because reality manifests itself in contradictory ways and therefore cannot be expressed in concepts. To translate an image into concrete terminology by restricting it to any one of its frames of reference is to do worse than mutilate it, it is to annihilate, to annul it as an instrument of cognition.

An example of this multivalence is the symbol of the gun in Irish politics, particularly relevant now given that decommissioning has become such a significant issue. Kevin Myers (*Spectator*, 18 March 1995) has argued that it 'is not just some weapon of offence or defence in the history of Irish "republicanism". It is the grail which transmits the apostolic succession of Irish republicanism from one generation to the next.' The failure of John Major's peace process in Northern Ireland was due in part to his insistence on a Republican hand-over of weapons – something even David Lloyd George was willing to back down on in 1922. The British had simply failed to appreciate that the gun was more than a political bargaining tool to the IRA, it was an ancient and totemic symbol.

Symbols do not mean the same thing for everybody, and the astute propagandist will be aware of this. Symbols can divide or unite us: the baseball cap, for example, is now the headgear of global youth and symbolises Americanism and the associated ideas of hedonism, lack of deference and freedom. When the leader of the British Conservative Party assumed one for a photo opportunity he was attempting to embody a younger and more vibrant party, but the general derision with which this essay in self-conscious sartorial gaucherie was greeted indicates that his interpretation of the symbol was not universal: wearing it was felt to be jejune in the leader of a Great Party. For many, the baseball cap is a signifier of the crass and self-centred (especially when reversed!). Similarly, pictures of Bill Clinton, on a yacht, at Martha's Vineyard, with a rock star, expressed everything his advisers wished to leave unsaid: the collective elements of that tableau were repugnant to many Americans when associated with their head of state. According to Hodge and Kress (1988), the meta-signs of the elite who control high culture incorporate meanings of hostility towards the majority just as much as do meta-signs of punks or Mafiosi. Even such a significant cultural symbol as the American cowboy is not universally greeted warmly as a positive token of national identity. For one critic (Webster 1988) the cowboy image 'glorifies the male', it 'costumes him in unfeeling masculinity, [his horse] a kind of pedestal to display virility and hint at imminent violence'.

Meaning is also mediated by our cultural milieu and its patterns of signification. What something symbolises may be conventional within that culture, such as the images on a nation's currency, or universal throughout many cultures, as the colour red symbolising danger. But the meaning of a certain symbol to a certain individual may be unique, mediated by social context and individual experience: symbols have a plasticity and so are subject to multiple and even oppositional readings. Symbolic meaning can reside in a privatised code. Hitler's moustache was found merely comical by the British and US publics, but was a studied reminder that he is 'one of us' to the veterans of the Imperial German Army of World War I. (Moustaches were trimmed to reduce the problem of trench lice.) We can speak, with justice, of a 'powerful symbol', and those who reject our perception of its power may do so at their peril. Hence the Leeds United football fans who burned Turkish flags in Istanbul (*The Times*, 20 January 2004) may not have understood the enormity of the insult, but it certainly contributed to the murder of two of their members by inflaming Turkish supporters. That is the price of cultural deafness to symbolisation.

Nor is symbolism static. There can be creativity and initiative in seeking and developing effective symbol strategies, new symbols can be invented, and so the early Christians jettisoned their symbol, the fish, for that of the cross. Or old ones can be retrieved from the past and given new meaning, the swastika, for example, as in the almost surreal vistas of massed swastikas in *Triumph of the Will*. By what process of semiological transmography, for example, did the cross of Christ crucified become the cross of iron on Adolf Hitler's chest? A symbol thus embarks upon an historical journey, but symbols are also powerful in the cause of peace, as we speak of a dove of peace, an olive branch, an angel of mercy, a peace pipe. And symbols can continue as symbols long after the reality of the content they represented has changed. Hardly any prisoners were left in the Bastille in 1789 but, for the French revolutionaries, it was the most powerful of the symbols of the *ancien régime*, massive and darkly brooding.

Since political control of symbols is a crucial feature of political power, failures in political control of symbols are therefore political failures. Symbols can appear to take over and even usurp political authority, and one of the physical props in a situation can become its embodiment. Under appeasement, Neville Chamberlain's umbrella seemed to assume a life of its own as a symbol of supine British policy. The political intent underlying the creation of a symbol may not be 'read' by the audience: they may wilfully misconstrue, and a propaganda symbol can be conscripted into becoming a countersymbol. Thus, Prince Trubetskoy's statue of Tsar Alexander was 'read' by the enemies of the regime as a satire on it (and that might actually have been Trubetskoy's intent in making it so huge and menacing: Figes 1997). Indeed, it was subsequently conserved by the Bolsheviks, thus servicing the propaganda apparatus of both the Tsarist and the Soviet states.

Symbolism and the social sciences

What has characterised human advance has been the reliance on ever more sophisticated symbols – language, art, myths, rituals – for understanding the world, communication and social organisation. For Mircea Eliade (1991), all that essential and indescribable part of man that is called imagination dwells in realms of symbolism and still lives on in archaic myths and theologies. To have imagination is to enjoy a richness of interior life, an uninterrupted and spontaneous flow of images. He believes that the most commonplace existence swarms with images, the most realistic man lives by them. Margaret Mead (Taylor 1990) spoke of the significance of visual symbols in inter-tribe relations: the more politically immature the culture, the more reliance on symbols in political discourse. Thus a review of post-World War II political events in the Cameroon shows how problems of unemployment or agriculture are discussed in symbolic terms rather than by reference to a specific policy of substance (Stark 1980).

For Baudrillard (W. Lance Bennett 1996), 'hyper-reality' is a phenomenon of modern consumer societies wherein the difference between symbols and what they represent disintegrates. There remain only simulacra which have no reference meaning or nuance beyond their mere identity as signs. They are disconnected from the things signified: dynamic change has bleached out the original meanings of signs.

Symbols are condensed meaning, and many of the more interpretative social scientists claim that it is the meaning of things that defines, directs and governs our behaviour: symbols organise, focus and structure that meaning. A brand, for example, is a symbol, and the phenomenon of branding in the commercial world is a testament to the power of symbolism. Such areas as cultural anthropology and cultural sociology make interpretation their focus ('hermeneutics') and see people as motivated by meanings rather than rational calculation. Geertz (1984) sees the mind as entertaining symbolic models through which it interprets the external realm, and culture is above all a system of symbols; the task of the propagandist is to identify the symbol systems of a culture that underpin its rules.

Talcott Parsons was an advocate of the importance of symbolic rewards and not tangible objects in meeting people's deepest needs: he thought infants began by identifying objects and extending the analogy as they matured. This stress on symbolic, status-directed rewards chimes with the activities of many propagandists, from the inventors of the Mother Heroes of the Soviet Union to the Nazi presentation of the ceremonial dagger to the German 'pimpf' at the age of ten (Grunberger 1991), to the inflationary use of the title vice-president in American corporations. Titles in particular convey status and every social order produces them, and the entire Nazi enterprise could be seen as a status exercise: one was no longer part of the proletariat, the international brotherhood of workers, but something far more alluring. Another approach to the role of symbols in propaganda is via behaviourism (based on the concept of the conditioned response, see Chapter 2), that continuous exposure to repeated stimuli produces reflexes and these become both inevitable and predictable once the initial associations have been made. Certainly propaganda uses symbols to create reflexes (the British bulldog, deftly leased from the iconography of political reaction by Tony Blair in his 1997 campaign?). Indeed, there can be popular anger when a familiar symbol is dropped, as the Democrats attempted to do with their donkey.

Conclusion

Schöpflin (1997) goes further than other authorities in perceiving myth, symbol and ritual as constituting a language that lies deeper than language itself, an imagistic grammar which undergirds and transcends mere verbal exposition:

> it follows that what is not symbolised is either very difficult to communicate or cannot be communicated at all, because it is not a part of the fund of knowledge of the community. The language of symbols, rituals, myths and so on is, consequently, a part of the web of communication shared by any community and is, incidentally, more significant than language itself. Members of the community of shared symbols can continue to recognise one another and maintain communication even after they have abandoned their language in the philosophical sense.

Were these propositions true, then myth and symbol would not represent one among a number of creative possibilities for the propagandist. In fact there is no choice: strategies based on their use are not just useful, they are essential, and no propaganda can truly aspire to work that ignores them.

4

Integuments of propaganda

Key foundations of propaganda

This chapter explores key ideas which are generally associated with the concept of propaganda though they may not be integral to its definition. Propaganda, it argues, represents hyperbolic possibility and multiple exaggeration: it is emotional, deceitful and irrational; it does not ask for belief, rather it represents an invitation to share a fantasy. Above all, we identify the creation of enemies as a fundamental activity of propaganda (the Mary Douglas notion of how we structure our universe by knowing what we are against rather than what we are for). Since propaganda as the rhetoric of enmity aims to persuade people to kill other people, others must be demonised in a denial that we share a common humanity (atrocity propaganda).

Emotion

Propaganda has a highly emotional foundation to its appeal. For Aristotle, emotion is central to persuasion: Pathos, distinguished from Ethos and Logos, relied on putting the audience in a state of mind that stirred the emotions, for 'our judgements where we are pleased and friendly are not the same as when we are pained and hostile' (O'Shaughnessy 1995). The aim and content of Hitlerite rhetoric were pure emotion, logic could safely be ignored, reason simply jettisoned, thus contradictions were no problem, the Jew could be both capitalist and communist, and this was just further proof of Jewish cunning. For Hitler was a theorist on rhetoric and propaganda, and all his persuasion was constructed round the idea of the supremacy of the emotional appeal: 'the people in the overwhelming majority are so feminine by nature and attitude that sober reasoning determines their thoughts and actions far less than emotion or feeling'. Changing behaviour that has a basis in emotion involves changing an interpretation, and for this to be done the communication must relate to the values of the audience, and evoke the sort of emotional experiences that led to the values in the first place.

What then is the long-term impact of the emotionally driven messages characteristic of propaganda? They would tend, according to the Petty–Cacioppo Elaboration Likelihood Model, to lead only to superficial acceptance of the message via the peripheral route to persuasion (Petty and Cacioppo 1979). The central route, which supposedly involves the recipient of the message in intellectual engagement, is claimed to lead to long-lasting and rational attitude change. To accept this model would mean that we believe the consequences of propaganda to be short-term, but the model has been much criticised on the grounds that it devalues the power and significance of emotion: the deepest influences on behaviour – personal attitudes, religion, morality – are integrally linked to emotion. In contrast, other theoretical models have downgraded the significance of rational persuasion. Zajonc and Markus (1991), by way of contrast to Petty and Cacioppo, have argued that attitudes may have a strong emotional base, developed before any cognitive elaboration. Such attitudes, they claim, can be changed only by exercising emotional influence that bypasses the cognitive.

There are certainly many differences in the kinds of emotion propaganda exploits – for example, social propaganda under the auspices of non-profit organisations and government often seeks to exploit feelings of guilt. Many 'safe driving' appeals would fit into this category as well as some of the most famous social advertisements of all time, such as the Saatchi pregnant man – 'Wouldn't you be more careful if it was you that got pregnant?' – and the Salvation Army's grainy black-and-white images with the refrain 'For God's sake, care. Give us a pound.' Behind the guilt is cognitive dissonance. (In Festinger's 1957 theory this arises when a person holds at the same time inconsistent beliefs: people try to reduce the discomfort by reducing the conflict.)

Ideology

It is difficult to imagine propaganda without ideology. For ideology lends to propaganda both its structure and its clarity. A propaganda for a vague and timidly defended belief may still be classified as propaganda but it would be scarcely recognisable as such.

Propaganda feeds off ideology. At one level, of course, everything, all discourse and every text, can be viewed as 'ideological' but that perspective may not be particularly helpful in the analysis of propaganda. There are degrees. For example, some might even argue that all journalism is ideological and therefore propagandist, though journalists themselves frequently claim to represent free opinion or information rather than ideology and its economic base. According to Bird and Dardenne (1988), journalists have to assign meanings to new realities – this is how the ideological effect is perceived, since prevailing maps of meaning have come to be accepted as common sense, blinding us to the fact that even 'common sense' is culturally derived. (One example would be the frequent description of something as a 'problem' which can be 'solved' via some technical type of solution, usually the kind of quick fix that is the source of foreign-policy blunders.)

The point about propaganda is that it is not merely ideological but, in its historical manifestations, emphatically so, and it is this that for the general public would distinguish a propaganda text from other forms of persuasive advocacy such as, indeed, consumer marketing, where the attitudes of the consumer, not the producer, determine ideology. In other words it is not the mere fact of ideology alone, but that the ideology is both producer-driven and intensely felt, that distinguishes the propaganda text. The public image of propaganda is thus of an explicitly ideological media communication, in which the ideology lies on the surface: it does not court the viewer or listener, but confronts and even berates and assaults them. An example of this kind of propaganda would be the anti-colonialist film *The Battle of Algiers* or – a more modern example – the Michael Moore documentaries *Roger and Me* and *Bowling for Columbine*.

Many would, however, see such a propaganda style as anachronistic. Living in an age of sophisticated media consumers, of visual literacy in which constant viewing of media images is in itself an education in the consumption of media imagery, such a blatant style may not be as effective as more indirect propaganda forms: but it is not made thereby less ideological communication, merely more subtle. For example, there is the printed polemic, such as the sixteenth-century 'Little Treatise against the Muttering of some Papists in Corners' (Foulkes 1983), or the laudatory manifesto like that issued by Gustavus Adolphus in 1630 (Taylor 1990). Such items pretend to be nothing else; they seek to persuade by rhetorical power alone and court the rejection which their well advertised partisanship may arouse. They also risk falling into self-parody. *Roger and Me* is a diatribe against the chairman of General Motors, Roger Smith, whom it accuses of unfeelingly destroying the town of Flint, Michigan, and (by extension) the selfish irresponsibility of big business is laid bare: 'Michael Moore argues that the American dream is dead, corporations are disloyal and we are seeing a modern-day *Grapes of Wrath*' (Bateman *et al.* 1992). At Flint, General Motors lay-offs made some 30,000 workers redundant.

Clearly, then, there are media products whose identification as propaganda few would dispute. There is the documentary that declares its purpose openly, seeking no disguise – for example, the anti-nuclear propaganda genre that emerged with particular force during the 1980s (Diana Papademus 1989). Susumi Hani's *Prophecy* was a half-hour documentary concerning the victims of the US atomic attack on Japan based largely on footage of Nagasaki, Hiroshima and their inhabitants, photographed in the wake of the bombing. It thus exploited familiar imagery, that of atrocity propaganda. Even propaganda as entertainment can also eschew disguise, the 'committed' film, uncompromising in its beliefs, clear about its enemies and utopian in its aspirations. Such a film might, for example, be *Some Mother's Son*. But what is popularly imagined to be propaganda is actually one particular kind, namely the ideological, explicit propaganda that announces itself as such, and self-articulated in formats well known for their propaganda uses.

Values

Propaganda deals, obsessively, with values, and no discussion of propaganda would be intelligible without reference to their centrality.

Values embody the highest strivings of a civilisation, its wish to be just and to be free, as well as the non-material and self-centred concerns, to be in control, to enjoy high self-esteem, to be comfortably off. The gap between what we have and what we want always has the potential to cause powerful emotions and to be exploited by propaganda. Although Milton Rokeach (1971) speaks of terminal and instrumental values, they are better seen as the highest court of appeal, whose word on otherwise irreconcilable trade-offs is final. And all trade-offs invoke them. As Alastair MacIntyre (1981) says, questions of ultimate goals are questions of values, and on values reason is silent. Yet reason cannot arbiter values, cannot prescribe, it is a tool in the service of values and not their replacement.

Propaganda does not try to destroy values, it attempts to conscript them. Every advocate knows that values are almost impossible to change overnight, but move slowly over time as a result of exposure to rival arguments and mature reflection. This is because they are difficult to challenge since they are not vulnerable to factual revision. Values can be neither proved nor disproved. They are also part of a structure where to revise one is to revise the relationships of all the variables in the system, a potentially life-changing event. Ellul is wrong in suggesting that a propaganda of virtue would get nowhere. On the contrary, appeals to selflessness are one of the most powerful appeals that can be devised, with high cultural resonance not merely in Christianity, but in the more general enjoyment of expressions of group solidarity.

Political rhetoric, verbal and visual, is value-drenched ('Give me liberty or give me death' (Patrick Henry); 'The tree of liberty must be refreshed from time to time with the blood of patriots and tyrants' (Thomas

Jefferson). This element of appeal to values is especially strong when enlisted in controversy. Mussolf's (1991) analysis of congressional debates illuminates the role of value-referenced rhetorics. Opponents of bailing out giant businesses invoke free enterprise, and, fearing this appeal, supporters counter by defending their regard for this value and by asserting its positive relationship to the policy proposal: the same values are conscripted to suit the purposes of the rival partisans. Hence propagandists seek messages that resonate with values. Persuasion should speak to values, it should relive and reaffirm and revisit those emotional experiences that first gave them birth.

Hyperbole

An important function of propaganda is to stimulate, another is preachment to the converted. Propaganda is not dialogue but monologue. Hyperbole is another characteristic, and a technique (often associated with advertising) which carries the potential for self-parody. Hyperbole does not make the mistake of asking for belief, it is an illusion which we are exhorted to share, explicit and even paranoid. Our pet bigotries are dramatised and enlarged to surreal proportions, but the fantasy does nevertheless affect perceptions of the reality. Thompson (1979) claims that the media merely exploit prejudices, and this absolves our leaders. Others argue that propaganda is often a co-production and that people lend to it a suspension of their disbelief, and they have a need to see what they recognise as their own fantasies reflected in an equally fabulistic media, their own lies to themselves reflected and sustained by the larger lies of the public space. When critics claim that propaganda is 'manipulative', they perhaps envisage a passive recipient. While some propaganda exchanges may resemble this stimulus–response form, what is often going on in the propaganda process may be more subtle. The idea of people willingly misled strikes at the root of concepts of man as a rational decision maker, yet surely this is what occurred in Serbia, Rwanda and elsewhere.

   While the relation of journalism to propaganda is a complex and elusive one, there are certainly hyperbolic moments in the history of journalism whose status as propaganda few would dispute. The determination of the British press to package opposition Labour Party leader Neil Kinnock as an ignorant boor and an alarming leftist is an illustration of this. Tabloids instructed reporters to discover all manner of blunders committed by Kinnock on overseas trips, and the indiscretions were duly produced. The *Sun* capped this process with one of the most lurid fantasies in the history of journalism, the eight-page pre-election spread 'Nightmare on Kinnock Street'. The contents can be listed at some length (McKie 1995): 'Unions will expect

Neil to cough up', 'Labour's lukewarm start on immigration', 'Apologies to Neil for an earlier *Sun* claim that he had never held down a real job', 'Gays to rule on planning applications' (even loft conversions and garages would have to be approved by gay and lesbian groups), 'Baby Carl would not have lived but for Tory NHS reforms', 'Lest we forget' (pictures and story on the winter of discontent), 'Alan Sugar of Amstrad blasts Labour's con trick', 'Tory doc barred as Kinnock visits hospital', 'It's Mao or never, swore Neil'. Allegedly a psychic asked some famous dead people how they would vote in the election. Conservatives were Churchill, Montgomery, Elvis Presley, Sid James, Queen Victoria. Labour supporters were Marx, Stalin, Trotsky, Robert Maxwell, etc. (p. 7). The *Sun* also claimed that the first day of a Labour government would see shares drop billions in value. Uncommitted voters were more likely to choose the Tories if they read a conservative paper, and in the year up to the 1987 election there was a 5 per cent overall swing to the Conservatives; among persistent readers of Tory tabloids it was 12 per cent (McKie 1995).

The emotion-driven hyperbolical propaganda text is exemplified by a two-page advertisement placed in *The Times* (17 February 1992) by the International Fund for Animal Welfare. The caption – large white letters in an 8 in. red box – read, 'To show you what kind of animal your MP is, we're naming names.' The use of the word 'animal' is a rather laboured *double-entendre*: pro-hunting MPs are animals and in the advertisement their names are marked with red dots. This may be contrasted with another, scarcely better-mannered advertisement (pro-hunting) that pictured a screaming thug with the caption 'The voice of reason?' (*Daily Telegraph*, 10 February 1992). Clearly an advertisement which is configured in such a way does not, as social and commercial advertising so often does, invite several interpretations. Meaning here is not a matter of negotiation between text and reader. It is a fixed and highly political meaning where all dissent comes to be associated with an iconic representation of mindless proletarian violence that instantly surfaces other civic fears about out-of-control youths: implicitly here they represent the same phenomenon. Their aim is to motivate sympathisers to action and to identify hunting as part of conservative, property-owning values.

The partisan propaganda approach may fail on several criteria: does it get opponents to question the vehemence of their resolve, does it persuade neutrals? The task of inciting core loyalists to action should not be sought at the cost of alienating other constituencies whose support or neutrality could be solicited; more ambivalence permits supporters, the neutral and even the opposition a limited degree of latitude in affixing their own meanings.

The persistence of classical propaganda

Propaganda has a popular image, that of the polemical rant, an explicit and shameless diatribe fomenting war and revolution in exotic places. The currency of this idea of propaganda does certainly anaesthetise people to its more ubiquitous and less visible or more sophisticated forms, but it is important to remember that crude propaganda, propaganda in its popular understanding, is still offering its benediction for the indulgence of mankind's most miserable instincts.

The continuity of classic propaganda of agitation (in Ellul's terminology) remains not merely a political force but also a social threat. Tribal and ethnic tensions, successors to the dying imperialisms of the twentieth century, are irritated by a propaganda that galvanises hatred into violence. Events in Rwanda were precipitated and orchestrated via polemical radio broadcasts which stigmatised the Tutsis much as the Nazis did the Jews: those broadcasts, their content, number and impact, are a critical explanatory factor in the genocide of the 1 million Tutsis. Serb and Bosnian Serb television adopted much the same role in ex-Yugoslavia – chauvinist hyperbole which demonised the Bosnian Muslims as 'Turks' and so forth, nightly decanting the noxious bile of sectarian propaganda.

Unfortunately the role of 'classic' propaganda in precipitating and sustaining modern conflict tends to be under-reported. News reportage is responsive and crisis-driven: causation and antecedent events are analysed only retrospectively, often superficially, with the focus on personalities and moments of critical evolution but not on phenomena of persuasion. Communications tend to be neglected because analysis and objective measures of impact are difficult (we ignore what we can't measure) or they are seen as manifestations of discontent rather than causes. Depth research or long residence is thus beyond the opportunity of the average portable newsman, and, when academics finally come to excavate the significance of communications, the discovery is no longer newsworthy. Time has marched on. The signature of propaganda on events is missed.

Subversion

Much of propaganda works, essentially, by subversion. Never in fact was that word more appropriate, since propaganda will rarely succeed by directly challenging a deeply held belief or value, but rather proceeds by misrepresentation that insinuates the individual's ideological defences. Gaining agreement with a certain definition and the ideological perspective it illuminates is the key, then perfectly logical arguments can then be deployed (and this essentially is what the activity of spin-doctoring refers to). Techniques used to achieve these shifts in interpretation include:

1 *Redefining the situation.* Thus Philip Morris has consistently sought to have the cigarette issue defined as one of freedom of choice: no more, no less.
2 *The interrogative mode* is a way of getting people to rethink existing perspectives, which is why many propaganda slogans are framed as questions such as 'Who governs?' (Ted Heath), 'Whose finger on the trigger?' (*Daily Mirror* headline). An aspect of Hitler's rhetorical technique was to raise and answer the questions of critics at the beginning of his speeches (Blain 1988): rhetorical theorists argue that this is a highly effective method, since successful persuasion is when the persuader has answered all the questions raised by the audience, or those the audience had in mind.
3 *The use of language* to reposition in the mind of the target audience some concept that earlier language had made problematic, so that the disabled become differently abled.
4 *Social endorsement.* Demonstrating something to be socially appropriate eliminates the embarrassment connected with it. Alternatively, show public disapprobation. More generally, persuasion must identify not what is objectively most important but what is most meaningful to the target audience. Campaigns targeted at teenagers would thus emphasise the social rather than the health consequences of smoking, drugs and other high-risk behaviour. To show endorsement by someone's social milieu is a useful form of persuasion, and advertising does this all the time: 'people can be talked into an emotional state, talked into a more intense emotional state but also talked out of an emotional state' (O'Shaughnessy and O'Shaughnessy 2003).
5 *Framing the 'evidence', real or manufactured, in the most favourable way.* For example, the assertion that 10 per cent of the population are in a state of abject poverty is more emotionally charged and therefore persuasive than the more impressive claim that 90 per cent of the population are comfortable. Labels matter. People will still feel that beef labelled 75 per cent lean is superior to that labelled 25 per cent fat, even after they have actually tasted it. The model of utility-maximising economic man calculatedly measuring up alternative choices neglects the impact of persuasion on the way these choices are presented.
6 *Illusory correlation* involves seeing events or features as related when they are not. Propaganda is constantly creating illusory correlation, in particular advertising, for example between the product and social success.
7 The power of persuasion is augmented by an advocate who does not appear to hector but to make an offer of friendship, fraternity and affiliation. (In fact this would be an alternative exposition of Hall Jamieson's

feminisation of rhetoric thesis.) Hence the persuasive (perlocutionary) act uses indirect means.

It may be necessary to position a message away from its true, objective position. Thus the 1997 Hyde Park rally in favour of country, i.e blood, sports was ingeniously positioned as a 'countryside' rally and we were told that some of those attending had, in fact, no special fondness for hunting. Then there is 'political correctness'. An important distinction between modern propaganda and that of earlier historical epochs is that propaganda now often has to be more indirect and therefore relies on devices such as coded language and the subtext. People cannot today be addressed directly in the language of their prejudices, even if accessed in the specific media appropriated by their group. This is because the collective consciousness has become progressively more sensitive to the agenda of every kind of non-mainstream group. Governor George Wallace of Alabama, for example, offered, especially after he had formally eschewed his earlier racism, many of the same populist sentiments as Reagan. It was greater urbanity, not a different ideology, that made Reagan electable.

Deceit in propaganda

Forgery
While much propaganda can be said to involve exaggeration – that, almost, is its definition – and indeed active misrepresentation, undeniably it sometimes involves the manufacture of falsehood, even forgery. Here we are in the realms of active fabrication and deceit. Thus Bush's spring 2003 State of the Union speech 'cited alleged documents stating that Iraq had attempted to buy 500 tons of uranium from the country of Niger. However, officials of the International Atomic Energy Agency looked at the documents and concluded they were counterfeits' (Rampton and Stauber 2003). Deception, it should be added, is one of the constituents the Pentagon includes in its definition of 'perception management'. Propagandists can do this almost openly with the audience even conscious of the falsehood being perpetrated, becoming willing co-conspirators in an act wherein they themselves are in a sense the victims. Once again, the explanation is that they are really being invited to share a mutual charade of anger, a point missed by critics who too easily reach for words like 'gullible' and 'naive', assuming the audiences have no recognition of the techniques being used.

The fabrication may not be obvious at all and the audience really deceived, an increasing criticism of certain television productions. This is nothing new. *March of Time* used real footage but also staged scenes when describing the rising Nazi menace (with some footage being banned in Britain: Taylor 1990). Such methods, of course, always carry the risk of being nullified as propaganda when they are exposed. Rumour is another type of fabrication, though it has been more identified with wartime and black propaganda. Britain's black propaganda radio station Gustav Siegfried Eis circulated rumours among the German services, claiming to be run by a Nazi to the right of Hitler and specialising in the invention of stories about the private lives of the Nazi elite. Rumour was also a chosen instrument of the Nazis themselves, not least in the final days of the regime when claims were circulated that General Wenck and his army were poised to save Berlin, 'a false message spread right at the *Götterdämmerung* of the regime' (Herzstein 1978).

Deception has been described as an abuse of rational process, since it involves hindering in some way the passing along of information. Today in Western countries a more cynical and media-literate generation has shrunk the possibilities for classical or overt propaganda in that, to succeed, propaganda needs greater subtlety, even disguise. The incentives for it to become deceitful, which always existed, are now greater. One medium can through stylistic devices mimic another and more plausible form, as does the docu-drama, whose progenitors include *Citizen Kane* and *The Battle of Algiers*. Another method used quite openly is 'faction', giving assistance to the documentary exposition of a case by visually inventing part of it. This deliberate mixing of fact and fiction is a formula that could actually serve as a definition of propaganda itself. The Nazi newsreels represented an early variant of this: they were manufactured political consumer products, combining '*actualité* footage and propagandistic editing'. Television documentaries use this increasingly, such as the 'exposé' of the former Cabinet Minister Jonathan Aitken entitled 'Jonathan of Arabia', where actors dressed as pseudo-Arabs were filmed traversing the exotic sands of Morecambe Bay mounted on camels (*Daily Telegraph*, 15 April 1995). There were faked scenes in sex industry documentaries, fake guests on the Vanessa show (*Daily Telegraph*, 31 August 1999) and, notably, the faked Kerry–Fonda peacenik image (*Independent*, 18 February 2004). Another propaganda technique which has become a major influence in recent years is the propaganda video. This is an image-rich product retailed free to the mass media, whose intense need and *raison d'être* is the reproduction of images. The media thus feed off the propagandist, and the relationship is not parasitic but symbiotic, yet the public, their target, believe the images they consume transmit from an innocent source. Single-issue groups have been particularly noteworthy exponents of video propaganda, their tenacity enabling them to supply images that are more raw and authentic-seeming than those created by network television (see Chapter 7).

Propaganda does not have to create a text – an image, a symbol, a film, an article, a slogan. It can operate simply by a process of denial, by preventing an opposition text from ever emerging or by rinsing out any negative perspective that might contaminate the mainstream media. In apartheid South Africa (Tomaselli 1987) one form of censorship was of course the direct physical intimidation of film makers; with arrests and confiscations, including (in the case of Sven Peterson's *Land Apart*) intimidating MGM's head office in California. Control of distribution, specifying who precisely can watch the film, is a significant form of counter-propaganda. Whites could be trusted with more subversive material, since the state operated in their interests, and about one in three films passed for whites was banned for blacks, the most ridiculous example being the ban on black viewers seeing the film *Zulu* (1966). The Minister of the Interior said 'there are some films which can be exhibited much more safely to the white child of fourteen years than to an adult Bantu', but much depended on who the audience was. Negative and even socialist views could be allowed. Nor historically has government censorship been the exclusive province of reactionary regimes. For example, Gillo Pontecorvo's *The Battle of Algiers* (1966) was banned by France until 1971 (*New York Times*, 4 January 2004).

Thus propaganda can be made through creative use of the censor's scissors as well as specifically commissioned propaganda films. Tomaselli (1987) points out that film 'may have the meaning inverted through censorship directives'. One example is where the South African directorate ordered cuts and conditions so that, according to the Appeal Court, 'the emphasis is thus changed from a successful to an unsuccessful terrorist attack'. (In another incident the Minister of Information said that no African had asked to be included on the censorship committee.) Decisions in a commercial environment made under political pressure (though not direct government diktat) can have the same impact. The effectiveness as propaganda of Susumi Hani's *Prophecy* and Terry Nash's *If you Love this Planet* was emasculated by the reluctance of distribution agencies to show them (Papademus 1989).

Censorship is not the prerogative of governments alone. During the 2003 Iraq war Al-Jazeera 'became a target of hacker attacks that kept its English-language site unavailable throughout most of the war and kept down its Arabic language site for nearly a week' (Rampton and Stauber 2003). And the most effective form of control remains the intellectual self-policing of the media themselves. Peace groups were denied the purchase of air space by all major networks, including MTV; anti-war demonstrations in European capitals were ignored. Rampton and Stauber claim that 'the rest of the world did not experience the war as the clean, surgical operation that was presented on US television, where major media outlets cited reasons such as taste, news judgment or concern about offending viewers to explain why they are rarely showed images of dead and injured civilians'. They add that during the entire war the *Chicago Tribune*'s front page had 'fewer than six' pictures of 'dead or injured' bodies, while European and Australian publications were ten times more likely to mention cluster bombs than their American equivalents.

Propaganda may also critically pervert the political information system and hence the political agenda. An example of this is the Information Research Department of the Foreign Office, the focus of Lashmar and Oliver's *Britain's Secret Propaganda War, 1948–1977* (1998). We cannot really know the truth here until after 2020, when the relevant documents are declassified, but the impact of this group, founded in 1948 to 'expose the realities of communism and the lying communist propaganda', was apparently malign. It engaged, as it never should have done, in domestic campaigns, for example to discredit left-wing churchmen or anti-Common Market campaigners (a 'communist-inspired plot'). It supplied inaccurate information to diplomats and key political decision makers: according to Adams (1993) 'one report, for example, alleging the Cubans were in Guinea training Africans in guerrilla warfare, was questioned by King and eventually tracked down to a single, small German publication, in which it may well have been originally planted by the IRD, to lend credibility to its report', and only communism mattered: 'it could have survived doing work of value to this day, if only it had committed itself to promoting democracy . . . when a Labour Minister asked the IRD to produce a paper on South Africa it came back with one headed 'South Africa: the communist peril'. Propaganda can thus pollute the springs of information and fatally distort the policy agenda. There is a process of continually engaging in small deceits that lead inexorably to large deceits and the loss of moral perspective. The question of integrity is an interesting one: the inhabitants of the IRD were presumably blazing with moral zeal, loathing of sovietism and all its works. But this *idée fixe* blinded them to every other kind of abuse, their own included.

Bogus empiricism
Another device is empiricist or 'scientific' propaganda with its demand for 'proof'. Ultimately this is a utopian request, since the standards demanded of proof can be endlessly raised, but it places government's cause firmly under the auspices of science and makes them seem (and who would wish otherwise) to be on the side of reason, not emotion.

So 'proof' is often an argument deployed to conceal the sins of government, as with the December 1992 massacre of villagers in El Mozote, Salvador (Didion 1994). The US government at the time was seeking to certify Salvador as being still eligible for US aid and military assistance. A massacre was most inconvenient, and it therefore sought to discredit the reports on the grounds that there was 'no firm evidence', even though there were photographs of corpses. Here they were invoking the ideology of scientism by demanding the exacting standards of evidence needed in the scientific laboratory but unnecessary in political decision making where a balance of probabilities may well be evidence enough. The *New York Times* did not support the journalist who had written about eye-witness accounts of the bodies, who was also vilified by the *Wall Street Journal*, and the subsequent US effort in aid of homicidal bandits 'became the most expensive attempt to support a foreign government threatened by insurgency since Vietnam' (Didion 1994). The state invited the press to become co-conspirators via its exploitation of a cultural reflex that all decisions be made rationally on the basis of empirical evidence, and its success in apparently persuading Americans to reject the contextual information provided by others was a masterstroke. The finest propaganda always does resonate with the deepest reflexes of a culture, and here propaganda created a legalistic distinction employed to rhetorical advantage.

Science's ostensible monopoly of truth can be used or abused. There is science, and then there is pseudo-science, and the role played by pseudo-science in propaganda has been, and is now, a critical one. Science is seen as the antithesis of emotion, which is equated with disproportionate reaction, and those who use overt emotive appeals are making an open declaration of their intent to manipulate. The self-concept of highly educated societies is of reasoning individuals who make their decisions on the basis of evidence and analysis, not feelings. Scientific empiricism is the core of modern Western culture, underpinning its material achievements, conveniences and technical strengths, so evidence becomes the stock in trade of argument and exposition, fashion magazines, for example, reviewing the results of the latest medical investigation at length. Implicitly, all our problems are ultimately technical ones and amenable to technical solutions. Under this ideology, the evidence of experts carries great weight and problems can be elucidated via data. Questions of interpretation are given less attention because the belief is that they can be made irrelevant by sufficiently vigorous pursuit of the 'correct' data. What cannot be measured tends therefore to be excluded from the argument and dismissed as subjective.

How then can there be intuitive or interpretative standards of truth, since these are neither demonstrable nor empirically verifiable? Relevant 'evidence' can be manufactured. In the case of alar on apples, a shoddy account by an environmentalist group was expounded on *Sixty Minutes* and caused mayhem: sales of apples collapsed (Vanderwicken 1995). For Hewson (*Sunday Times*, 31 March 1995):

> most junk science started with the tobacco industry and revolves round that
> simple word 'proof'. The tobacco companies just adore proof. It lets them hand
> out the moolah to their tame professors and then come up with the startling
> claim that there is no causal link between tobacco and that cocktail of diseases

which millions of deaths seem to suggest are not unconnected with the dreaded weed.

He claims that Professor Richard Lacey, a member of the Ministry of Agriculture's own Veterinary Products Committee and an early whistleblower in the BSE (mad cow disease) crisis, was persecuted under the same logic: no proof to link BSE and Creutzfeldt-Jacob: 'never mind that a five-year-old can see that in matters of public health the burden of proof comes from a different direction to its legal cousin. We don't want scientists to prove that British beef is dangerous. We want them to prove it is safe'.

Since the US public places great reliance on data, a growing industry has developed to create the research to legitimise policy positions or marketing objectives. White bread won't precipitate the pounds, and it is nutritious, asserts a study from the people at Cooper Institute for Aerobic Research (its sponsors are the bakers of Wonder Bread) while Princeton Dental Resource Center assures us that chocolate may actually inhibit cavities; they are funded by Mars (Vanderwicken 1995). All this, of course, is a gift to the propagandists because it potentially offers what they most prize, concealment. 'Facts', the antithesis of emotion, can be allowed to 'speak for themselves'. The selection of some facts and the rejection of others, the choice of particular base years on which to draw figures, the claim that something must be a lie because there is 'no evidence', the privileging of some types of evidence over others – all these are famously part of the manipulative process, but unless exposed by the acuity of counter-analysis they are more successful than other forms of propaganda because the craftwork of manipulation is more submerged and the masses will give them the deference they have been trained to give impartial 'data' and expert scientific opinion. (There is also a technical component: very few have the relevant training to critique statistics and other analytic techniques.)

Why we need enemies

Propagandists invent their enemies. The creation of a despised 'other' is neither an essential part of all propaganda nor an integument of its definition. Nevertheless it is difficult to imagine a propaganda cleansed of victims: the creation of an internal or an external threat is achieved by seeking out blameworthy groups, domestic marginals such as Armenians or cosmopolitan threats such as the 'international' Jew. In psychology the 'granfallon technique', where groups cohere according to arbitrarily acquired labels, shows how easily 'otherness' can arise (Pratkanis and Aronson 1991). Schöpflin (1997) argues that thus 'the existence of community is preserved from pollution and thus its means of cultural reproduction kept safe from outsiders'. Such 'otherness' is not merely a phenomenon of tribal and ethnic dispute. Academic, religious and philosophic arguments abound with the serial creation of enemies, and apparently closely related sects seem to hate each other most: Sunni and Shiite, Trotskyite and communist. The essential triviality of such destructive differences was satirised by Jonathan Swift in *Gulliver's Travels*, where Big-endians and Little-endians are polarised over the issue of which way to crack an egg open.

People know, and know abundantly, what they hate: they are more ambivalent about their likings. As emotions our hatreds are more intense than our affections. This argument has been made by the social anthropologist Mary Douglas (1982): as discussed in Chapter 2, for her any choosing 'for' is a choosing 'against' because to choose *x* is a protest, with each choice a declaration of defiance against alternative lifestyles and a signal of allegiance to his or her opposing lifestyle. Much political behaviour is symbolic, and that symbol is of what we wish to be perceived as standing against. Lupia (1994) shows that less educated voters in California see any support for something from those they oppose, any endorsement, as negative symbols and they vote accordingly. The 'enemy' can also be more abstract, an idea perhaps, and the more sophisticated forms of propaganda may eschew a human enemy, though there is always a suggestion that only the less admirable human beings would associate with the discredited ideology. In the world of managerial propaganda, Oliver describes an evangelist for a new management theory thus: 'there was to be a discarded old order and a shining new order: the expression "cost world" was used to denote the old order and the "throughput world" to denote the new one, encompassing JIT, TOC and Total Quality. A large American was introduced' (Oliver 1995).

So propaganda usually needs an enemy, and if none exists it will create one – the social construction of enemies is one of the key defining characteristics of propaganda. The sense of superiority thus created is attractive to people at the bottom of some social pyramid, and they can be managed by creating a new people lower than they, upon whom they can look down. Those in the Middle East who are antagonistic to the West face an enemy that is richer and stronger but a sense of worth can still arise through recognition of the Westerner's moral deficiency and infidelity – their faith, and our faithlessness – convinced, in Samuel Huntington's words 'of the superiority of their culture, and obsessed with the inferiority of their power' (Huntington 1996). The absence of enemies sends us back, naggingly, introspectively, on ourselves – indeed, since the end of the cold war the United States has been seen by some as experiencing a problem of enemy deprivation. In this light, new enemies like Saddam Hussein are not just there but necessarily there.

We need enemies because we need someone to blame when things go wrong: the term 'witch hunt' is apposite and propaganda involves finding the appropriate victims. The qualifications for victimhood would include things like physical appearance, membership of some social subgroup, a tendency to look and feel intimidated: the key is separateness from the social mainstream. To Overing (1997) 'myths of alterity are not usually subtle, for they dwell upon the exaggerated excesses of the despised and threatening other'. Merely to be Afghan could have been enough, as in the case of the taxi driver paralysed in London, even though Afghans were themselves the first victims of the Taliban.

The social construction of an enemy fulfils several important functions. We define ourselves by reference to what we are not. This clarifies our values or where we stand, and gives us a coherent sense of selfhood. Second, it is only by reference to enemies that we became united, and the greater the internal discord within societies the more powerful will our need for enemies be: the propaganda construction of enemies is a source of social integration. Schöpflin (1997) argues that 'this process will frequently go together with the construction of mythic enemies who are attempting to destroy the collectivity in a demonic conspiracy'. According to Blain (1988), 'just as people can be talked into buying things they do not need, so the political leader can talk the desire for revenge into people. . . . The rhetoric of enemies is a potent means of gaining and sustaining social integration in modern society.' And Blain believes that 'political agents concoct a rhetoric of motives that they use to incite their followers to fight their enemies': he claims that the main effect of war rhetoric is social integration through the constitution of common enemies: 'a victim–villain hierarchy is necessary to the production of political incitement'.

Politicians, especially governments in trouble, look about for new enemies to manufacture. Hence in Britain New Labour's search for a 'reactionary' enemy (Blair's 'forces of conservatism') against which to define itself. It thought it had found one in the ancient universities of Oxford and Cambridge, and their failure to admit an undeniably bright state school student to study medicine (Stevens 2001). This served several purposes, including diverting attention from low state expenditure on education and the quality of state schooling. In totalitarian regimes, the creation of enemies is an important part of state activity. In Khomeini's Iran, for example, the figure of the author Salman Rushdie was a useful enemy because he could be presented as a blasphemer, thereby subject to a death sentence even though he lived in a Western country; some of his translators were in fact murdered. (It is difficult to imagine propaganda without enemies.)

Zimmerman (1995) had argued that when government assumes precisely the opposite role to that of protecting the competition of ideas, when it uses its power over the mass media to exhort people to hate, then citizens look to the press not for information but for emotional reassurance: they can take satisfaction in discharging their anger at their neighbours. 'When you realise that highly manipulated pictures of the maimed and the murdered, the cleansed and the condemned, are seen every night by nearly everybody in the former Yugoslavia, you can imagine the enduring effect they have.' Moreover, enemies stimulate and focus the energy of anger and hate, they are great motivators to action, and the more horrible they are made out to be the more energised our anger becomes. Horrible enemies also cause fear, propaganda leads our imagination to paint in lurid colours what will be done to us if our enemies succeed. Indeed, many of the very worst atrocities are carried out because their perpetrators are fearful. Thus in Rwanda the Tutsis 'not only refused to reject the leadership that urges them to kill but sincerely believe their own survival depends on killing' (Block 1994). Enemies also freeze our conscience and assuage our guilt, nothing we do to them can possible be bad enough. Pointing out that in Rwanda 'the killings were neither random nor spontaneous', Block adds, 'but almost everyone you meet in the camps does not see their ordeal as self-inflicted but as the fault of the Tutsis. There is no guilt.' And after Nine-eleven Anne Coulter had proclaimed, 'This is no time to be precious about locating the exact individuals directly involved in this particular terrorist attack. We should invade their countries, kill their leaders and convert them to Christianity.' Rampton and Stauber (2003) comment:

> Shortly after Coulter's column appeared, it resurfaced on the Web site of the Mujahidean Lashkar-e-Taiba – one of the largest militant Islamist groups in Pakistan – which works closely with Al-Qaeda . . . During the period when Coulter's article was featured, the site was decorated with an image that depicted a hairy, monstrous hand with claws in place of fingernails, from which blood dripped on to a burning globe of planet Earth. A star of David decorated the rest of the hairy hand, and behind it stood an American flag. The reproduction of Coulter's column used bold red letters to highlight the sentence that said 'Invade their countries, kill their leaders and convert them to Christianity.'

Yet, even here, there arise propaganda lessons relevant to our current circumstances. Particularly here: in the management of the current crises, a necessary condition of success is that the doctrine and practices of one billion Muslims are not subject to denigration. Conversely, we must recognise that terrorists and their apologists can perform those acts – and we now know that no imaginable outrage is beyond them – because they have been convinced. Terrorists are persuaded, not born, and their monstrosities arise out of a process of conviction. That rhetorical activity which arouses and sustains terror, and which in current conflicts we should seek ourselves to avoid, is the creation of the demonised 'other', a phenomenon which is historically the essential dynamic of propaganda, and whose key property – the conviction that some out-group does not share our common humanity – has been the preface of genocide throughout time. The terrorists have done what they have done because they have succeeded, first, in dehumanising us in their own minds. Conversely, the danger for us is that we generalise from errant individuals to the entirety of the population from which they were drawn.

Atrocity propaganda

Atrocity propaganda has been historically its most consistent feature and probably also its most effective. From Pope Urban II's 1095 sermon at Clermont mentioned in Chapter 2 (Taylor 1990), when the Saracens are described as pouring blood into baptismal fonts, to the Nazi film *Menschen in Sturm* with its depictions of Polish barbarities such as the wrecking of German schools, or films such as *Mein Leben für Ireland* (1941) (Herzstein 1978), propagandists have competed to depict steadily more dreadful images of the enemy. The reasons are not difficult to see: one of the most important aims in propaganda is to demonstrate, indeed, that the enemy is not like us, is a ruthless, amoral monster, in order to incite the mobilising emotion of anger. In *The Little American* (1917) Mary Pickford, the People's Darling, is torpedoed, gives information to the French and manages to escape a German firing squad. Nothing must threaten this illusion of enemy frightfulness (Taylor 1990).

We remember the enemy's atrocities and forget our own, and we commit further atrocities in retaliation, which may even be the intent of the atrocity propaganda. (In the *Baralong* incident, British sailors boarded a neutral American ship and murdered the German submariners who had taken refuge there.) When Nurse Edith Cavell was executed in 1915 British troops were told of the event and carried her picture into battle. In an incident soon afterwards German prisoners of war were massacred (Williams 1987) – ironic in the light of Nurse Cavell's final words. Atrocity propaganda is still effective, in spite of all that the twentieth century did to exploit the genre.

The 'other' can also function as an instrument of terror. During the Spanish Civil War General Queipo de Llano's nationalist propaganda broadcasts stressed the figure of the Moors, the colonial soldiers under Franco's command, their brutality and what they might do to Republican women, surfacing ancient Spanish fears (H. Thomas 1986). Of course there is the role of pure invention in atrocity propaganda (Knightley 1975). Subsequent exposures of organised collective fantasy after the Great War made people incredulous of atrocity rumours in World War II, though truth and fiction remain interwoven, for there were indeed Belgian atrocities, with 6,000 civilians murdered, even if they were not as extensive, or depraved, as the British claimed.

In *The First Casualty* (1995) Philip Knightley describes World War I portrayals of Germany thus:

> The war was made to appear one of defence against a menacing aggressor. The Kaiser was painted as a beast in human form. (In a single report on September 22, 1914, the *Daily Mail* succeeded in referring to him as a 'lunatic', a 'barbarian', a 'madman', a 'monster', a 'modern judas', and a 'criminal monarch'.) The Germans were portrayed as only slightly better than the hordes of Genghis Khan, rapers of nuns, mutilators of children, and destroyers of civilisation. Once the commitment to war had been made, an overwhelming majority of the nation's political and intellectual leaders joined this propaganda campaign. Prime Minister Asquith, using the technique of atrocity confirmation by sweeping generalisation, told the House of Commons, on April 27, 1915, 'We shall not forget this horrible record of calculated cruelty and crime.' British newspapers lent their prestige to the campaign. The *Financial News*, in what now seems an unbelievable editorial, said on June 10, 1915, that the Kaiser had ordered German airmen to make special efforts to kill King Albert's children, that double rewards were paid to German submarine crews for sinking ships carrying women and children, and that the Kaiser had personally ordered the torturing of three-year-old children, specifying the tortures to be inflicted. A committee of lawyers and historians under the chairmanship of Lord Bryce, a former ambassador to the United States, produced a report which was translated into thirty languages, in which it was stated that the Germans had systematically murdered, outraged, and violated innocent men, women, and children in Belgium. 'Murder, lust, and pillage,' the report said, 'prevailed over many parts of Belgium on a scale unparalleled in any war between civilised nations during the last three centuries.' The report gave titillating details of how German officers and men had publicly raped twenty Belgian girls in the market place at Liege, how eight German soldiers had bayoneted a two-year-old child, and how another had sliced off a peasant girl's breast in Malines. Bryce's signature added considerable weight to the report, and it was not until after the war that several unsatisfactory aspects of the Bryce committee's activities emerged. Finally, a Belgian commission of inquiry in 1922, when passions had cooled, failed markedly to corroborate a single major allegation in the Bryce report. By then, of course, the report had served its purpose. Its success in arousing hatred and condemnation of Germany makes it one of the most successful propaganda pieces of the war.

It is perhaps the case, then, we have learned nothing and forgotten nothing: according to Jowett and O'Donnell (1992) 'on October 10, 1990, a fifteen-year-old Kuwaiti girl named "Nayirah" had shocked the Congressional Human Rights Caucus when she tearfully asserted that she had watched as Iraqi soldiers took fifteen babies from their incubators in

Al-Adan hospital in Kuwait City' and 'left the babies on the cold floor to die'. Subsequently the *New York Times* revealed she was the daughter of the Kuwaiti ambassador, and that the public relations firm of Hill & Knowlton played a role in this: George Bush 'used the dead babies story more than ten times in the forty days following Nayirah's story'. (See also Bennett 1996.)

The story of the dead Kuwaiti babies continues to fulfil its designated task as atrocity propaganda. Rampton and Stauber (2003) remind us that 'the babies from incubators story did resurface briefly in December 2002, when HBO television premiered a "based on a true story" docu-drama entitled *Live from Baghdad* which recounted the adventures of Peter Arnett and other CNN reporters . . . [it] included actual footage of Nayirah delivering her false testimony and left viewers with the impression that the story was true'. Although the credits did acknowledge that the story was 'unsubstantiated', *Washington Post* television critic Tom Shales apparently reviewed this programme and wrote, 'The horror wreaked on Kuwait is brought back vividly during a sequence in which Wiener and his team travel to Kuwait to investigate allegations that Iraqi troops had ripped babies out of incubators as part of their plundering – remember?' These authors add, 'it may be unfair to single out Shales for his part in "remembering" an incident that never happened'.

Dehumanisation

What is perhaps curious is the voracious need of propaganda to demonise, and the ease with which it does so: any propaganda campaign can easily degenerate into mere vindictiveness, and many do, summoning up the imagery of the dehumanised enemy.

Nor is this dehumanised 'other' necessarily a certain group of individuals, every single member of the enemy population can be included. Gertrude Himmelfarb (1994) has complained that even some feminists do this, and modish feminism has eschewed the individual account: 'if women are victims generically, by the same token men are culprits generically'. Thus she claims that at the University of Maryland posters named sixty randomly chosen male students with the headline 'Notice: these men are potential rapists', and others had the names of all 15,000 men. (These were course projects in feminist art.)

To kill – and in history the function of propaganda has often ultimately been the creation of a mind-set that facilitates the act of killing – it is necessary to objectify. The 'other' is essentially an abstraction, a cipher either for evil or for inferiority. All reference to common humanity is bleached out, and when it does creep in, as for example between kidnappers and hostages, killing becomes more difficult, as George Orwell describes in *Homage to Cat-*

alonia, where a nationalist soldier he is about to shoot proceeds to urinate unawares, reminding Orwell of their common humanity and thereby saving his life. The 'other' is reduced to broad brush strokes, a few attributed dominant characteristics – whether the Marxist 'class enemy', the communist of the 1950s United States, or *Punch* magazine's nineteenth-century image of the Fenian as a savage whose features are barely human. Such polemics dwell on the symbols of otherness – facial types, dress. Eventually the mere symbol, such as communism's image of the silk-hatted capitalist, will suffice, the fuller picture is already understood so well that the symbol alone will signify it.

It is also important that propaganda stresses our superiority and the enemy's inferiority, that it teaches us that a vast chasm separates our merit from their redundancy. Naturally the Nazis paid particular attention to this. The German social welfare state was contrasted with British class injustice (Hitler proclaimed it was a war against Britain's ruling class), the British worshipped money and embraced the Jews ('Lord Cohn: the Judaization of the English upper class from D'Israeli to Hore-Belisha', Herzstein 1978); they were also deceitful, concentrating electronic beams in fishing boats, etc., and 'the splendours of plutocratic ritual are contrasted with the misery caused' (Herzstein 1978). This belief in our superiority is particularly useful as an incitement to the least privileged in society, taking their resentful focus away from those who stand above them to those who languish beneath them. They become grateful for their small privileges, and despise those who lack the good fortune to be members of the *Volk*. (The Orange Order and its political manifestations would be an example of this.) In order to dehumanise the enemy, it is necessary to put into circulation stereotypes which deny his autonomy as an individual character. In *Jew Süss* ('the best propaganda film of the Third Reich') a new Jewish stereotype is created, one different from the ghetto Jew of other Nazi propaganda, for Süss Oppenheim is a court Jew, and the ugly message is that some Jews have a veneer of civilisation, and they are the most dangerous (Herzstein 1978). A secondary merit of this stereotype is that it mobilises the latent envy of the have-nots for the polished, smart and successful. George Orwell's novel *Nineteen eighty-four* depicted a mythical dictator, Big Brother, and his fictitious enemy, Emmanuel Goldstein, who is a focus for populist rage, with acolytes roaring at Goldstein in quotidian hate sessions

The enemy will more usually be a real one, but the purpose of propaganda will be to motivate us by making us really hate. In Rwanda, Hutu propaganda such as Radio Interahamwe portrayed Tutsis as homicidal aliens who had to be liquidated, even though they had been in Rwanda since the fifteenth century. An atmosphere of extreme paranoia arose in which mass murder could masquerade as civic duty. As Block (1994) explains,

Hutu race ideology was derived from the 'hamitic theory' of the European colonisers, which posited the existence of superior northern African races – African Aryans, in fact. Hutus had their own version of this theory, and the foreignness of the Tutsi was a central tenet of Hutu propaganda. Radio Interahamwe was owned by their henchmen, it was hate-filled, increasingly virulent and singled out politicians who deserved to die. In ten weeks the militia killed half a million people, helped by Hutu civilians. Throughout the slaughter the radio continued to encourage Rwandans to fill the half-empty graves: 'When you kill the rats do not let the pregnant one escape. We made the mistake thirty years ago of letting them flee into exile, this time none will escape' (Block 1994). The parallels between Hutu propaganda and the Nazis – racist ideology, the enemy as a rat (a scene in *The Eternal Jew*), their threat to a superior civilisation, the need to eliminate them entirely – are almost too obvious to merit comment.

The language of contempt
In the process of dehumanising, it is particularly important to manufacture a new language, to separate us from the victim group and to render them contemptible. Such language may contain a distinct image of inferiority, such as Charles Murray's 'underclass', thus performing its ideological duty of devaluing them or, since words accumulate new meanings, terms not originally intended as vindictive, such as 'Sambo', acquire derogatory reference. Name calling, one of the methods of propaganda cited by the Institute for Propaganda Analysis in the 1930s (Alfred Lee 1986; Elizabeth Lee 1986), is a way of instantly positioning and stereotyping an adversary by highlighting the key features which mark them out as other than us and represents the essence of their debasement. The Croats referred to the Serbs as terrorists, but the Serbs themselves exhibited a particular fondness for name calling: all Croats were Utasha (German allies in World War II), while Bosnian Muslims became 'Turks', a particularly inflammatory term, given the long history of the Balkans under Turkish occupation (Zimmerman 1995). Bin Laden exhorts his followers against 'Zionists and crusaders'. If the enemy is not really an alien, we can still find the ways of making them appear to be so. Language is used to divide us from others in our own country, Foulkes (1983) for example, making comparisons between the concept of un-American and Brecht's reference to the prevalence of the term un-German in Nazi Germany.

The diaries of Victor Klemperer (1998) are in part a study of the colonisation of language by ideology intent on severing the bonds of common humanity with another segment of the community; the Jews become for example a hyphenated entity, Jewish-Bolshevik. Democracies at war have also found it necessary to manufacture a nomenclature of derogation, often with racial overtones: Huns, Nips, Wops, Argies and Yellow Peril were preceded in an earlier generation by the (rather kinder) fuzzy-wuzzy. Americans needed a rhetoric of enmity as well after Nine-eleven. For Geraldo Rivera of the Fox network, Al-Qaeda were always 'terror goons', US forces always 'heroes' (and the network audience was 50 per cent higher than the previous year). CNN was thus forced to 'burnish its patriotic credentials': it had 'ordered its correspondents to refer to the 11th September attacks each time footage is shown of civilian casualties in Afghanistan' (*New York Times*, 11 November 2001).

Otherness and the media

A good story needs a villain. Narrative structure in novel and subsequently film often arises from polarity, especially the primordial tension between good and evil, more particularly so since the evil personality evokes a raw, debased energy whose arousal and ultimate subjugation provide narrative momentum. Partly, too, this is because in literary terms it is easier to portray evil than good. Villains test the hero's competence and virtue, provide narrative drive and create opportunities for rich characterisation which the merely saintly cannot offer. (Even Dickens found it difficult to make virtue interesting: as Oscar Wilde said, one would have to have a heart of stone not to laugh at the death of Little Nell.) This structural imperative for a villain in the production of media texts creates a need to find appropriate targets and therefore the debased causes with which villainy is likely to associate. The Mafia cannot, of course, sustain this role single-handed: there is villain fatigue, and political correctness. New villains are needed, and it is this which makes Hollywood, not institutionally or endemically but on occasion, a propaganda machine.

An example of this is popular culture's engagement with a new villain, Big Tobacco (*Sunday Times*, 23 March 1997). Assaults on this provide opportunities for exposing the corruption of power and the avarice of business while avoiding accusations of being anti-business. In *Gasp!*, a novel by Frank Freudberg (1996), a dying smoker seeks vengeance against the faceless corporate monoliths who fed off his addiction; in *The Runaway Jury* (John Grisham 1996), anonymous corporate executives play with a major cancer lawsuit; in *The Practice*, a US television series, a young woman lawyer fights her old law professor in another court defence of cancer victims. The fact that these works stand primarily as entertainment, and that good entertainment often demands a villain, need not affect their status as propaganda. They stand squarely with the traditions of US populism as discussed by M. Kazin in his book *The Populist Persuasion* (1995). Oshinsky has argued (*New York Times*, 12 February 1995) that its rhetoric had always stressed the fight between good and evil, the manichean universe, between the virtuous majority and an unworthy elite: 'Populist spokesmen tended to portray their opponents as the enemies of ordinary people, and thus of democracy itself', an interesting and clever link (for example, Williams Jennings Bryan and Father Charles Coughlin, and subsequently Rush Limbaugh). Joe McCarthy declaimed a deep liberal establishment conspiracy to advance the communist cause; another example would be Charles Coughlin's claimed conspiracy of the Jewish plutocracy (Warren 1996).

The need for narrative structures also dominates the manufacture of our news (Bird and Dardenne 1988). The essence of news is story telling, and again, stories demand, often if not usually, a villain to give them narrative drive and ethical meaning. The *Daily Mail*, for example, plays to the prejudices of the English middle class like a Stradivarius: a daily procession of bogus asylum seekers, thugs, illicit social security claimants, EU excesses, social worker stalinists and politically correct lunacies parade, menacingly and outrageously, through its pages. The reader is invariably left in a state of repressed rage. The editor of the *Daily Mail* knows what he is doing. The media's need for stories with villains also coalesces with our need to blame someone when things go wrong. With the Atlanta bombing, the only 'evidence' against Richard Jewel was that he fitted a profile drawn up by a police psychologist. This demonstrates aptly how our need for villains and instant answers can contaminate the process of public judgement.

Dobkin (1992) discusses Nimmo and Coombs' view of television as pseudo-reality. (They claim the 'romantic quest structure' has been particularly important in television news, while McGee called the quest a 'universal structure' that gives meaning to political practices and rituals.) Dobkin also quotes CBS news reader Fred Graham: news stories on CBS tended to become two-minute morality plays with heroes, villains and a tidy moral to be summoned up at the end. Graham added that despite the fact that many important events did not present clear-cut heroes, villains, morals, the correspondents became experts at pointing them.

Jewel was no terrorist, and real terrorists are the ultimate 'other'. However, the language of denigration confuses, not clarifies, the issues. In the first place, governments can be terrorists yet are seldom described as such (that of apartheid South Africa, for example). Instead, oppressive governments are seen as 'maintaining order', 'conducting operations', etc. (Steuter 1990). Second, the international media's reaction to groups such as the Tamils is seldom uniform and may change over time, their ethical judgements calibrated by a language which graduates from terrorists to guerrillas to freedom fighters: 'the choice of these terms is the formulating of our social judgement rather than the description of a set of phenomena' (Steuter 1990). Thirdly, there is a rationale for terror which the language of denigration or pejorative hyphenation, while entirely justified as a visceral emotional and moral response to some bloody outrage, serves to obscure. The use for example of biological metaphors such as plague removes terrorism from the realm of social analysis, and the motives of terrorists are trivialised with words like 'game' or 'blackmail', or illicit linkages are made, e.g. 'communist-oriented ANC' (Steuter 1990). When the motivation of terrorist activity is made to seem this irrational, policy makers are led to say that force is the only option available.

Social integration

The creation of enemies is easy. The right inflammatory rhetoric, judicious selection of facts and malicious parodies of custom can successfully demonise vast swathes of the human race: 'there are many situations where the society in question lacks the cognitive instruments to see the message that is hidden behind the myth and will accept the causation that is being offered as proper explanation for its fate. The use of xenophobic narrative and scapegoating is an easy next step' (Schöpflin 1997). There is a particular call for the media to pioneer the responsible role. A climate of contempt is created for the enemy's culture, with even the more sophisticated members of the media competing in parody, for example the assertion in the *Daily Telegraph* (12 September 2001) and elsewhere in the British media that Islamic martyr-warriors believe they will be awarded seventy-two virgins as brides in heaven (with no authority from the Koran, which along with the other 'faiths of the book', Judaism and Christianity, explicitly forbids suicide). Those stigmatised as hostile 'begin to accept the demonic role assigned to them and behave in accordance with it' (Schöpflin 1997).

Jewel's case was a moral tale of our times that illuminates our need for heroes and villains: feted by the Olympics' business sponsors, he himself did not seek publicity but was soon its victim. Finally the *Atlanta Journal* announced, 'Hero guard may have planted a bomb', and offered a full profile of the loner as publicity-seeking drifter hero wannabe: he was the 'unabubba', investigated exhaustively by the FBI, followed on motor cycles. Yet fitting the profile was the only 'evidence' about him. (www.augustachronicle.com/headlines/102996/jewel.html)

Thus the activities of the news media compromise in large measure the search for villains, and the press thus creates whole categories of social enemies. Yet in Britain the *Sun* newspaper, once notorious for its social insensitivity, now takes a lead, with two pages devoted to the defence of ordinary Muslims, featuring profiles of five British Muslims (www.thesun. co.uk). Hollywood could be a powerful force, for if its media products today have a common ideological denominator it is the importance of social integration: we can inspire inclusion just as we can incite exclusion. Partly this is a matter of symbols – for President Bush to visit a mosque after Nine-eleven was, as visual rhetoric, one of the most significant things he could have done.

Hollywood's need for enemies

Good entertainment needs an enemy. Hollywood's prolonged romance with the Nazis (see Uklanski 1999) was due not so much to a predilection for history as to the ability of Nazism to project superb villains. The need for enemies is inherently political, since in choosing our enemies we define what we are and also what we are not; our values are illuminated and defined by their obverse, and this process has a political character, since it involves choice over ultimate ends and means, what we as a community stand for or against. We understand ourselves by our selection of enemies. Thus drama needs binary opposition to create those attributes that are key in dramatic suspense: fear (there can be no dramatically effective enemy of whom we are unafraid: we desire their demise because of their unfath-omable wickedness and coldheartedness), and identification – the 'our' (good) side stresses the best of our values and character.

Changing values do not result in a sophisticated and mature vision in which complexities of perspective and character are taken on board. They simply create new sorts of villain to replace the Red Indians, Nazis, Mafiosi and gangsters, complete with all the traditional attributes of villains, and Big Tobacco fits the bill admirably: rich, amoral, deceitful, powerful, it has no redemptive virtue. In *Feds* a mephistophelian pseudo-militia, CigSoc, attempts to besmirch the good name of an anti-tobacco prosecutor by secreting cocaine in his home, one character remarking, 'obscene profits and the fear of losing them are turning otherwise decent people into lying, deceitful manipulators' (*Sunday Times*, 23 March 1997). Political correct-ness and global harmony are, it is claimed, playing havoc with traditional sources of treachery. These workings can be seen, for example, in the farm film. It is the manichean good–evil universe that has been a staple of Holly-wood from its first beginnings. On the side of virtue are the family and its farm and the role of agricultural labour, a synonym for honest toil. The vil-lains are the banks, which foreclose on farms after having been promiscu-ous in their lending, and, beyond them, the big business which pressures them, 'masking their complicity with the allusions to the free market' (Webster 1988).

Hollywood has always needed villains. The little guy or girl against the rotten system, a decent man badly wronged who needs to be avenged are classic Hollywood down through its history. It is when the enemy is given some sort of political-social character, and often this is necessary both to give the conflict meaning and because social political ideology is a major source for difference, that considerations of propaganda arise.

Yet enemies are not necessarily conceived as either human or indeed subhuman in propaganda. They can be turned quite simply into an abstraction, the enemy is portrayed as a mere elemental force of nature like a storm or forest fire. There are World War II films in which the enemy hardly appears and the real theme is man's mastery of hostile nature and its taming by solidarity and team work. The war film *Fires were Started* never sought to answer the question 'By whom?' Thus the enemy came simply to represent all that man must battle against to be a man, connecting the wartime public with all the natural oppressions that their ancient ancestors had endured.

Enmity in action: Slobodan's propaganda war

There was nothing inevitable about the genocidal 'ethnic' tension of former Yugoslavia. People had intermarried and lived together for years, and countries, as with Czechoslovakia, can and do sunder peacefully. That, for ten years, they had been killing each other in an orgy of fratricidal butchery not seen in Europe since World War II owed everything to the determination of Slobodan Milosevic and his henchmen to sustain dominance through the toxic agency of propaganda and their understanding of its power to mobilise the emotions of fear, rage and hatred. Through propaganda they created a rhetoric of alien threat that is always the necessary preamble to mass murder, and they sought to synthesise ancient and modern fears, the old terror of the Turk neatly elided with modern fear of Islamic fundamentalism.

The crisis thus arose also out of the propaganda tradition of communism. Marxism-Leninism, the post-war ideology of the Yugoslav state, was never a 'mere' belief system alone but a proselytising creed whose evangelism was an integral part of its ideology. This supplied a ready-made methodology for attaining and sustaining power. Nationalism was just a way for Milosevic's henchmen to retain control by reviving ancient and long dormant tensions: yesterday they were communists, today fascists. Power, not ideology, was what mattered to them. For the French theoretician on propaganda, Jacques Ellul (1973), 'ideology and doctrine are mere accessories used by propaganda to mobilise individuals. The aim is the power . . .'. This was abetted by some structural similarities between communism and ethnocentric nationalism. Both, for example, diminish the individual, making the substitution of one ideology for the other relatively easy. This propaganda assault was contrived round four principal themes: the Muslim as social and cultural alien, the threat of an Islamic super-state, the international conspiracy against Serbia, and the atrocities of Serbia's enemies.

The first great theme of Serb propaganda was the foreignness and degeneracy of their Muslim neighbours. Orders to kill are seldom enough, they must acquire moral legitimacy through the bestowal of social sanction, and murder obtains its alibi through this rhetoric of otherness. This perception of the alien is not natural but socially constructed, it has some shallow basis in ancient differences, but mostly it is a fabrication. In Rwanda genocide was preceded by several years of anti-Tutsi radio polemics stressing Tutsis' foreignness even though they had been in the country for 800 years. The same was true of Nazi Germany. (Before then, the extinction the Jews faced was real enough – via intermarriage.) For Salecl (Zimmerman 1995) 'all nationalism, national identification with the nation is based on the fantasy of the enemy, an alien who has insinuated himself into our society and constantly threatens us with habits, discourse and rituals that are not our kind'.

In Bosnia this was achieved by sarcasm, by such devices as merging a Muslim newscaster's voice with film of chattering chimpanzees, or Serb newscasters mumbling phrases from Muslim burial rites with satirically bowed head; the stress on Muslim racial pollution, however, comes straight out of the imagistic lexicon of the Third Reich: 'it was genetically deformed material that embraced Islam. And now, of course, with each successive generation this gene simply gets more concentrated.' To Radavan Karadzic, Muslims were 'an urban population with no attachment to the soil' (Zimmerman 1995).

Another theme dear to the Serbs was the vision they had pedalled at various times of a 'Greater Albania', or of a muscular Islamic fundamentalist state digging deep into the heart of Europe and embracing Bosnia, Kosovo, Albania, Turkey and Iran. They spoke of a threatened Serbdom and the extinction of Serb identity. Serbs were the guardians of Christendom who had merely been defending themselves and European civilisation from Islamic fundamentalism. Serbs, then, were the defenders of the West, and the West was too craven, myopic and ungrateful to realise it. Schöpflin (1997) in his taxonomy of myths speaks of myths of redemption and suffering, 'where it is clear that the nation, by reason of its particularly sorrowful history, is undergoing or has undergone a process of expiating its sins and will be redeemed or, indeed, may itself redeem the world. East European myths posit a bleeding to near extinction so that Europe could flourish. These myths should be understood as myths of powerlessness and compensation for that powerlessness.'

Then there were the atrocities of Serbia's enemies. For the Serb leaders the believability of this was crucial to their programme of ethnic cleansing.

Serbs claimed to have found proof that Muslims were planning to circumcise all Serb boys and kill all males over the age of three and send women between the ages of fifteen and twenty-five into a harem to produce 'janissaries' (Zimmerman 1995). Of course this is ridiculous, but propaganda does not have to ask for belief to be effective, people (as we have seen) become co-conspirators in magnified fantasies of their own bigotries and fears. Similar accounts also appeared about the activities of KLA in Kosovo even as the Serbs mutilated that nation. Projecting your own crimes on to your enemy is a familiar propaganda technique (as in the Nazi film featuring British concentration camps of the Boer War: Ohm Kruger, in Herzstein 1978).

Zimmerman (1995) also discusses Nato's great anti-Serb conspiracy (for no propaganda is complete without a conspiracy). After the Dayton accords, Serb anti-NATO propaganda shifted into hyperbolic mode, and the psychological prologue for the Kosovo war was strenuously prepared. NATO 'with their military transporters and tanks . . . are running over children and mothers on your Serb roads, arresting our best and bravest warriors who fought in the war only to save their people and Serbdom. They are bombarding us, poisoning us with radioactive bombs, destroying our homes and bridges, taking us to court . . . they want to exterminate our seed.' According to Zimmerman the Serb media manufactured the ultimate fiction, that NATO had used low-intensity nuclear weapons in Bosnia, and people were contaminated by radiation. One historical parallel was thus irresistible: films of NATO peacekeepers merged with archive footage of German soldiers, and television maintained a sentimental diet of World War II partisan films. The international community had betrayed the Serbs. The International War Crimes Tribunal was cast as a partisan body with no further aim than to criminalise Serbs. These themes were articulated through techniques of rhetoric, myth making and information control.

Control – of information, of images – was the core of Serb propaganda methodology. Zimmerman discusses how Milosevic had long learned to muffle internal critical voices almost to the point of silence by such devices as manipulating the cost of newsprint. By banishing all Western media from Kosovo he denied the West that which would most galvanise it into military action, visual images of massacred civilians, of which we could see the merest peep. The images and information the West got from Belgrade were also controlled: journalists could be expelled, telephones cut, pictures censored. The effect of information control on Milosevic's own people was, however, incalculable, and, as journalists such as John Simpson reported, most of them simply could not understand why the West was attacking them or assumed it was some malevolent international conspiracy against Serbia.

Another technique was the invention of specialised vocabulary, for words were the Serbs' stock-in-trade. All Albanians became potentially 'terrorists' or 'Turks', Muslim and Croat were 'evildoers', *ustasha*, Islamic *ustasha*, *mujahadeen*, *jihad* warriors, Muslim extremists, Muslim hordes, *ustasha* butchers. All Muslims became 'fundamentalists', and contradictions did not matter, the Muslim was the terrible terrorist but he was also simultaneously the smiling, dull-witted *balije* (rude peasant) (Zimmerman 1995). Such words direct thinking, they are sensitising concepts, in that a word or phrase is seldom value-neutral but embodies a picture, an image or an ethical judgement. To get our opponents to use our choice of words is the greatest propaganda triumph, though in the case of the term 'ethnic cleansing' – so reminiscent of *Judenrein* – this rebounded on the Serbs and propaganda became counter-propaganda.

There were, of course, the myths. Montgomery has argued, 'if Yugoslavia is to teach us anything, surely it is about the malleability of historical memory, myth and identity' (Zimmerman 1995). A mythic, folkloric Serbia had been created, with Kosovo as a kind of holy land, its sacrosanctity in no way diminished by the fact that for well over 500 years it had ceased to be Serb. Schöpflin (1997) speaks of myths of territory, a land where purity was safeguarded, where folk virtues were best preserved before contact with aliens. These interlocked with other utopian self-sustaining myths, such as that of the Serbs as gallant warriors, the image of martial prowess defined by a nightly television advertisement. Schöpflin further argues that:

> The Serbian myth of Kosovo essentially begins with the redemptive element, in that the defeat of Kosovo Polje is explained by the choice of heavenly glory over earthly power. Self-evidently, this is an *ex post facto* rationalisation of the military defeat of the Serbian forces by the Ottoman armies in 1389 and the subsequent conquest of Serbia; today the Albanians are reconfigured as Turks, the ancient enemy.

Myth, he adds, makes communication difficult, since 'mythical language is for intra-, not inter-community communication'.

Murder is a deeply unnatural act. We have no inherited predisposition to kill. We do it because we have been persuaded to, because our deepest emotions have been colonised by somebody else. The murderers going about their work in Kosovo were not monsters but normal men. Yet their barbarism is incomprehensible unless it is placed in the context that explains it, years of saturation propaganda at once sentimental, self-pitying, vindictive and xenophobic.

> The real culprits in this long list of executions, assassination, drownings, burnings, massacres and atrocities furnished by our report, are not, we

repeat, the Balkan peoples. . . . The true culprits are those who mislead the public opinion and take advantage of the people's ignorance to raise disquieting rumours and sound the alarm bell, exciting their country into enmity. The real culprits are those who, by interest or inclination, declare constantly that war is inevitable, and by making it so, assert that they are powerless to prevent it. The real culprits are those who sacrifice the general interest to their own personal interest. . . . And who held up to their country a sterile policy of conflict and reprisals. (From the report of the International Commission to inquire into the Course and Conduct of the Balkan Wars of 1912 and 1913; Zimmerman 1995)

Part III

Case studies in propaganda

5

Privatising propaganda

The rise of single-issue evangelism

Single-issue groups are a focus of modern propaganda and they have been effective at constructing what appears to be the natural social order of things. Yet single-issue groups as a political force reach back down the generations, but from the middle of the twentieth century they have increasingly had more impact than other forms of political action, e.g. in the 'civil war of values' over abortion. They are testament to the ability of minorities to influence government agendas, and participation in them has become part of the leisure market, part of the competition for people's attention. People find them more empowering than party-political participation. The force of single-issue group persuasion determines to an extent who are the social winners and losers – what groups, for example, receive the lion's share of medical research budgets. Ultimately this success vindicates the status of the assertive emotional appeal, for single-issue groups are in the business of exploiting the emotions of anger and pity, and they use propaganda in its radical forms in their pursuit of a partisan-generated, mass-media-retailed public narrative.

The chapter goes on to discuss another expression of privatised propaganda – that of the modern corporation, particularly significant in an era when the social/civic public persona of the company infuses its brand identity.

Historical impact of single-issue groups

Properly considered, the effect of single-issue groups on our social and political culture may seem beyond measure. They have guided the hand of history, and the structure of our legislation reflects their differential effectiveness. Power lies most with those who propagandise best. Some would see single-issue groups as the essence of democracy itself, others as antidemocratic and the sponsor of a fragmented polity (they might remember Burke: 'it is seldom that the loudest complainers for the public good are those most anxious for its welfare'). The impact of such movements' propaganda is manifest in the outcome of our legislative battles today. Mink is not farmed in the United Kingdom, nor are cats reared for the purpose of vivisection, as a direct consequence of the propagandist agitation and militancy of animal rights groups.

If there are winners in these propaganda battles, there are also losers. Limited funds are distributed inequitably among the myriad social causes thirsty for government cash. The critics of single-issue groups have been caustic. They say that their propaganda distorts the agenda. Worse, they say that the wrong side often wins: the siege, for example, of Huntingdon Life Sciences by animal rights activists helped make it impossible for Cambridge University to build a new centre for primate experimentation (*Times Higher Education Supplement*, 28 November 2003). Yet such experiments are mandated by government in order to test new drugs, and, in as much as animal systems replicate those of humans, they offer the best hope of finding cures for such conditions as Alzheimer's, Parkinson's, Huntington's and other degenerative diseases of old age.

The public resonance of causes has little to do with logic. The farming of battery hens, for example, may objectively be seen as cruel, yet it figures only peripherally in the sights of the animal rights activists. The images of vivisected dogs possess power far in excess of those tragic hens, even though the numbers involved in the one case are trivial and in the other enormous, and the reason is simple: the dogs represent vulnerable affection, and the hens are food. The ban on genetically modified crops in Europe constitutes another good example of the power of single-issue group propaganda to influence the agenda; alternative articulations – the argument that such modifications make for higher yields for Third World farmers – are scarcely audible.

We often erroneously equate single-issue groups with the hip counterculture of the 1960s and its later metamorphosis into savvy modern cause marketing. Certainly since those days they have become more effective, and to a significant extent they have substituted for mainstream political activity. Yet a glance at the history of the past 200 years reveals not merely the antiquity of single-issue groups, but that their propaganda also sculpted the history of times before our own. The activism of the Anti-slavery Society and William Wilberforce sponsored a sophisticated propaganda, such as the writings of Olaudah Equiano (Plimmer and Plimmer 1981) or the notorious graphic image of exactly how slave body freight might be compressed into a slave ship. England in the nineteenth century abounded with such powerful cause movements, from the Royal Society for the Prevention of

Cruelty to Animals (RSPCA), founded in 1824, to the National Society for the Prevention of Cruelty to Children (NSPCC) founded as the London SPCC in 1884, to the Chartist movement with its demand for universal manhood suffrage and annual parliaments. Those were their halcyon days. The Suffragette movement in all its glory was of course a single-cause group, but not all nineteenth-century agitation cohort groups bequeathed a similarly benevolent legacy. The temperance movement, and such factions as its US women's affiliate, sponsored Prohibition in the United States and the consequent illicit community serviced by industrial-strength organised crime, whose legacy remains manifest in the hard drugs problem. The Fenian Society, and later Sinn Féin, were other nineteenth-century issue groups whose bequest we may regard with some ambivalence.

The legacy of these great causes litters the landscape of history, and yet we are in the main oblivious to their legislative achievements and the extent to which those achievements were a function of persuasive propaganda. The nineteenth and twentieth-century movements are so much naturalised that we forget that such features of our social landscape were not something innate but were planted there by the coherent agitation of organised groups. The Zionist movement, for example, gave rise to the state of Israel, yet Zionism was an organised single-issue group using propaganda as such groups do. For example, Tom Segev (2000) has described the serial propagation of an image of a tough new Zionist man, beginning well before World War I, with the aim of reversing traditional stereotypes of Jews as gentle and urban. Single-issue groups can be entirely the handiwork of charismatic individuals such as Huey Long in the 1930s with his 'Every man a king' campaign, or groups could accumulate popularity but have only ephemeral influence, as with Britain's Peace Ballot Union with its 2.4 million anti-war votes (Gardiner and Wenborn 1995).

Single issues today

Yet it is on the post-war order that our attention naturally focuses. The civil rights movement changed America for ever; the anti-Vietnam War movements left their legacy (perhaps even in the bellicose foreign policy of George W. Bush). The anti-apartheid movement (for example) had a significant impact on the international isolation of South Africa and its boycott by many businesses, but other liberal groups such as the Campaign for Nuclear Disarmament (CND), with its college-scarved, duffle-coated Aldermaston marchers, were clearly less successful.

We would err in regarding modern agitation groups as primarily left-wing, since the radicals' hyperbolic style was plagiarised by the right, and groups such as the US National Rifle Association found voice in this new order. The so-called 'new right' reinvented propaganda and updated its techniques for a modern era. One might suggest a linkage with earlier epochs of political evangelism in the United States, particularly the exertions of the rabidly reactionary 'radio priest' Father Charles Coughlin in the 1930s. An even older persuasion tradition goes back to the early exchange between politics and religion in the United States, where evangelising business and political communication techniques were borrowed from those of the pastor and pulpit, themselves refined by the need to compete in a market place of religions (Moore 1994).

Today the so-called 'civil war of values' in the United States is principally orchestrated by the single-issue groups, the environmentalists, pro- and anti-abortionists, the protagonists and antagonists of school prayer and many others. But a huge new cluster of activities has grown around the Anti-globalisation Alliance, a network of very loosely affiliated groups whose common denominator is a visceral antagonism to a world which seems increasingly bland, homogeneous and corporate (Klein 2001). In Britain, established groups like CND were joined by ephemeral ones like Road Alert (which co-ordinates anti-road protests), or the Advance Party (it represented ravers and festival goers). There has even been the Global Network for Anti-Golf Course Action, and Greenhouse, a group responsible for co-ordinating the 'ethical shoplifting of mahogany products' (Richardson 1995).

Issues embraced by the Anti-globalisation Alliance include the repudiation of Third World debt, the environment, the critics of genetically modified food, the opponents of US wars such as the 'Not in my name' campaign in the United Kingdom, the anti-nuclear groups and so forth. What distinguishes the propaganda of this coalition, which has targeted in particular the Group of Eight as well as some of the big international brands, has been its reliance on information technology to inform and involve a casualised membership and to organise it into activities of public protest which can, via means like text messaging, be ordered almost immediately. This has given the coalition and its various constituent parts a visibility, flexibility and unpredictability which its ancestors never enjoyed. The membership can be educated and organised in ways never previously possible and their power is understandably feared by their targets, governments and large companies.

Whereas governments were the universal object of propaganda agitation in the 1960s, today it is the corporations that to some extent have replaced them. 'Consumerism' and 'globalisation' are now part of a rhetoric of reproach, not exact terms but resonant rhetorical brands conscripted in an ideological war. (What is perhaps important is not so much the meaning of the terms as the dominant public idea of what they mean.) The radical dynamism of global free markets is seen as sandblasting the authenticity of cultures and demolishing traditional authority structures; the organisational form of this radical dynamism, the global corporation, is viewed as an unchallenged extraterritorial force of immense power.

Why single-issue groups?

Consumerism

Membership of activist groups may be a manifestation of a more general consumerist drive towards novelty. Gronow (1997), speaking of consumer behaviour in general, argues that consumer demands are no longer determined by an 'economy of needs' but by an 'economy of desire and dreams', or the yearning for something new and unexperienced. Richardson (1995) sees them as a variant of consumer culture. Single-issue group entrepreneurs compete in a market place for political participation. (Yet their publics are fickle: the turnover of organisations like Friends of the Earth is considerable, in some cases 60 per cent per year.) A consumer dynamic operates with an intelligent identification of political wants, positioning and segmentation.

Ideal self

The propaganda of such groups also operates in the theatre of fantasy wish fulfilment. Participation can give a sense of power over events, of framing agendas, that the ordinary citizen customarily lacks; they pander to our daydreams about saving the world. Membership is a way of affirming this ideal or symbolic self, a conscript in the battle for justice, the self we aspire to be or wish others to take us to be, a tangible advertisement of our social identity both to ourselves and to the wider world, in line with the claim that consumers use symbols of their desired identities in the hope of having those identities affirmed by others. The propaganda of single-issue groups will, or should, exploit all such needs

Another aspect of the connection between propaganda and single-issue groups is the importance of the 'will to meaning'. This was the principle by which the psychiatrist Victor Frankl (1963) sought to replace the Freudian 'pleasure principle', theorising that the frustration of the will to meaning precipitates emotion and neurosis. Involvement in single-issue groups is a way of giving life meaning to many people. Social commentators have spoken of the 'new individualism', a (perverse?) rejection of what is socially endorsed by the majority and that is the public expression of some idiosyncratic private identity. Such individualism involves the exchange of the macro-culture for the micro, and the symbols and rituals of subcultural acceptance can be political: from the propagandist confetti of stickers, badges and passive membership we seek inclusion by graduating to more embodied forms of involvement.

Strategies of issue groups

Tactics: the creative act
Social propaganda is viewed as the province of the anti-establishment challenger. This legitimates certain of its characteristics, such as its raw, unproduced tone. Attention-getting devices, the imaginative tactics of public visibility, are at a premium and a substitute for the more generous funding associated with, for example, social marketing. This perspective, however, is at best a half-truth, for some groups (such as Greenpeace) are rich, many are semi-domesticated by the political establishment, while others of course do buy commercial media, both to crusade for some current cause and (in particular) to recruit new members.

Nevertheless the grand PR gesture is almost costless, and it may be effective if it can somehow capture a public mood. For instance, in Washington DC (30 September 1996) anti-gun protesters lined up the shoes of 45,000 victims alongside a reflecting pool. (The figure matched the number of victims in the last year for which statistics had been available.) A piece of simple direct-action propaganda; by choosing an item of victim property they invoke the memory of the victim. And that is what is distinct about the propaganda methods of single-issue groups, the creativity of the public space, the imagination to stage gripping media actualities which will resonate with their target markets. A good example is the squadrons of naked models summoned by PETA (People for the Ethical Treatment of Animals). Among the more cynical devices (*Sunday Telegraph*, 10 November 1996) was the setting up by the French National Front of soup kitchens. Creativity is an essential property, since repetition of the same formulas leads inevitably to the exhaustion of the interest of the political consumer. One reason for the failure of communist propaganda was that it had become stylistically moribund. After the Zhadanov decrees, only one idiomatic representation of human character became permissible (Perris 1985).

Examples of propaganda entrepreneurship are legion. For example, in 1984 two social revolutionaries published a pamphlet attacking McDonald's, with chapter headings like 'McGarbage', 'McCancer', 'McMurder', 'McRipoff', 'McTorture'. They accused McDonald's of underpaying staff, destroying rain forests, torturing animals, corrupting children and exploiting the Third World. As *The Economist* commented (25 February 1995), the effect of the resulting lawsuit was to publicise charges which even the most radical of McDonald's customers in seventy countries would have dismissed. (This story is testimony to the potential power of the individual author in the propaganda wars.)

Tactics: video technology

The mid-1990s saw the first real migration of the issue advocates to elections, and evangelists of all forms of social cause, not merely parties, political candidates and governments, now colonised elections via commercial television advertising. Paul Newman voiced a brutal thirty-second television message about a recent shooting incident. Reading from a newspaper, he said, 'Matilda Crabtree, fourteen, jumped out of the closet and yelled "Boo" to scare her parents.' He paused briefly, then added, 'and was shot to death when her father mistook her for a burglar. Before you bring a gun in the house, think about it' (*Sunday Times*, 5 November 1995). The partisan video is just as important a source for propagandised television as is the paid advertisement. An example is a film of Greek abattoirs. In the video, sheep, goats and pigs are seen to have their throats cut without being stunned. The then British Agriculture Minister, William Waldegrave, saw the video and claimed to find the images 'truly appalling' (*Sunday Telegraph*, 8 February 1995). The killing of an animal – this time the kosher killing of a cow – was also a central signifier in Fritz Hippler's *The Eternal Jew* (1941; Herzstein 1978).

In numerous cases the media faithfully relayed these lucid self-produced images that the social propagandist had selected to articulate the cause best, and the cost is minimal. (This was the case in, for example, the Shell–Greenpeace Brent Spar debacle.) Even simple technology can have toxic propaganda effects. A cassette tape is also a potentially powerful conduit of propaganda and, heard by dozens of people at clandestine gatherings, can be used to whip up sedition in places like Saudi Arabia.

The propaganda techniques of those evangelising groups are limited only by the human imagination. But nearly all of them seek to exploit in some way the power of the vivid emotional appeal; and seldom do they offer rigorous or even evidence-based argument. (Statistics are merely another rhetorical brand.) For example, two particularly famous films were made against abortion, *Eclipse of Reason* and *The Silent Scream* (Branham 1991), and both used the old device of convert testimony which has appeared in many guises, for example the traditional housewife narrating her conversion from a rival brand. Convert testimony is impressive since it implies a case strong enough not only to dissolve but also to entirely replace the social bonds of participation in a former cause. The convert here was Norma McCorvey, the Jane Roe in the landmark 1973 US Supreme Court ruling, Roe v. Wade, which established a woman's constitutional right to terminate a pregnancy.

Targets

The propagandist has distinct targets; at least, intelligently directed propaganda is conceived with some specific group in mind, for no propaganda could succeed that was aimed at some amorphous, undifferentiated mass. Propaganda succeeds best when it eschews any idea of general persuasion and focuses on a defined population. Britain's schools are an example – targeted by among others the British Field Sports Society, the League against Cruel Sports, Animal Aid; the Research Defence Society and the Vegetarian Society. 'The classroom will be the battleground because knowledge is passed on more effectively by children than by their teachers' (*Daily Telegraph*, 11 September 1994).

Another target is the cadre of movement members themselves; much propaganda is made by, and for, the propagandist. The object may be merely to strengthen belief, to make an intense appeal to the converted, since the aim is minority reinforcement. Given that social propaganda operates in the politicised theatre of minority grievance, it can become offensive to dominant values. This is especially so since today 'Western cultures are rife with subcultures resulting in a plurality of belief and behaviour systems with each subculture seeking self-legitimation of their lifestyle and members of the subculture being indoctrinated to believe that their subculture alone speaks the language of truth about life and how it should be lived' (O'Shaughnessy 1995). It may not even matter who is alienated when the aim may be exclusively attention seeking, as it is in the case of terrorism, where the target is the partisan constituency rather than any broader court of public appeal. Only this could make intelligible the tactics sometimes used.

Often single-issue evangelists are only soliciting their own, a task made much easier by new technologies allied with precision marketing techniques like direct mail. They speak to their own in the strident language of non-compromise, and their own hear them well. Partisan propaganda may succeed only with the partisan and fail utterly in gaining new converts to the cause. If an entire perspective or mental paradigm of a situation is to be challenged successfully, indirect means of persuasion are necessary because a direct approach typically meets with resistance and counter-arguments. Single-issue propaganda may typify the direct approach and the results are sometimes counterproductive. Direct action propaganda, for example, would seem difficult to explain in general persuasion terms, since it can involve intimidatory strategies. Yet the population of interest for direct activists may be very small and the rest of us irrelevant. Thus, Operation Rescue in the United States sends flying pickets to target abortion clinics since it has identified doctors as the weak link (*Independent*, 9 December 1993).

Terror tactics
Organisations like Greenpeace and many other radical organisations attempt (as indeed does terrorism) publicity seeking in their use of direct-action propaganda, but their targets are usually pointed and considered,

and the action is carried out in a dramatically stylised way: there is, normally, no intention to injure – indeed, many such organisations entertain an overtly pacifist ideology. But there may be an intention to provoke the authorities into some act of casual brutality. Nor does the media success of, for example, Britain's Friends of the Earth necessarily lead to influence: Friends of the Earth suffered a forfeit of credibility with the decision-making elites.

Some, however, go further than this. The abortion wars are fought with special virulence. In one incident, protesters stole 4,000 aborted foetuses from a pathology laboratory and allegedly threatened to disclose the mothers' names (*Independent*, 9 December 1993). 'Wanted' posters gave doctors' names and addresses. Another example comes from Texas, where militia claimed that Texas was a sovereign nation and mounted a decade-long campaign of paper terrorism which aimed to choke the Texas courts and banking system with a flood of bogus property claims and bad cheques (*The Times*, 22 February 1997). This demonstrates the power of very small pressure groups to cause mayhem. The method chosen here is explicit repudiation of the authority of the state by abusing the organs of legitimacy. The blackmail tactics of Peter Tatchell's group Outrage (*Daily Telegraph*, 15 March 1995) would be a further case in point, since they systematically demand that establishment figures declare their homosexuality or be revealed.

Even organisations like Outrage are only part of a continuum. Organisations that began as conventional propagandists can host the cancer of a terrorist wing which is ostensibly repudiated by the mainstream, as with the murder in the United States of Dr David Gunn by anti-abortion activists (*Independent*, 9 December 1993) and of Dr John Britton (1994) and Dr Barnett Slepian (1998). Propaganda can thus assume the most delinquent forms of homicidal nihilism known to the human race. The aims of such violence are myriad: to secure attention, intimidate, remind, exhaust and, especially, provoke. Its success in achieving them is testament to the power of this type of propaganda. At its most extreme, therefore, propaganda is terrorism and terrorism is a form of propaganda activity.

Self-murder in the political sphere is one of the most impressive forms of propaganda. Martyrdom has historically helped to cement the relationship of nations to causes, and great religions to their adherents, but that species of martyrdom which is entirely self-authored, the hunger strike, has been notable for its impact at certain critical junctures of the twentieth century. Such activities awe others and ennoble the cause, adherents are provided with a role model; the enemy is unnerved by such levels of determination. The fast is the antecedent to martyrdom and contains the promise of martyrdom. It was much used by Gandhi in his propaganda campaigns against the British, and also by Irish nationalists at significant moments in their country's conflicts with Britain – Terence MacSwiney in 1920 during the troubles; Bobby Sands in 1981 followed by nine other starvation martyrs. Martyrdom creates cults (Kevin Barry, Horst Wessel, Steve Biko).

Impact of single-issue group propaganda

Pressure groups are the inventors and merchandisers of the contemporary legislative agenda. Many movements such as the environmentalists arose out of single-issue groups and not parties, but eventually landed on the party's menu by that route alone.

Just how effective can propaganda and direct action be even where public opinion is alienated? Laws can be strongly or weakly enforced, and legal rights are therefore effectively negotiable and governed not just by the theoretical support of public opinion but also by its intensity. Thus the campaigns targeting clinics and doctors seemed to be working, and the National Coalition of Abortion Providers began to claim that harassment of doctors was having a serious impact on the availability of operations, particularly in rural areas, the south and Midwest (*Independent*, 9 December 1993). Fewer medical students are being trained to perform abortions. Only 13 per cent of Americans believe abortion should be illegal, and public opinion is pro-choice, but it is not *passionate* about that right. In a democracy the agenda is often influenced less by the quantity of public opinion than by its concentration.

'The best lack all conviction, the worst are full of passionate intensity.' W.B. Yeats's phrase could rank as a description of propaganda, and it is through its agency that dynamic concentrations of partisan individuals are created, directed and sustained. A US example is the National Rifle Association, which is rightly feared. In one case a senator due for re-election attempted to stop the Bill that made the illegal bullets capable of piercing police armour. He defied the Senate leadership 'with irrelevant and dilatory amendments', yet the ban was enacted only after 'a bitter six year struggle against the gun lobby' (*New York Times*, 27 December 1976). Another instance of persecution by issue groups was an election in South Dakota. Senator James Abdnor, who was of Lebanese descent, had always voted not only against aid to Israel but against all foreign aid. Fund raising, much of it from outside the state, raised $90,000 to fight Abdnor. 'Inquisition, pogrom, antisemitism', accused one letter from a Congressman, appealing for funds to support Abdnor's rival. It denounced the radical right's 'requisition' of South Dakota, 'bigotry and hate' in the state, and attacked Senator Abdnor's refusal to authorise aid to Israel (Binyon 1986). In underpopulated South Dakota television advertising is crucial and so, therefore, is raising the funds to pay for it. Abdnor flew to Israel to assure them he was no antisemite. He still lost. Pro-Israel groups also helped to defeat Charles Percy, chairman of the Senate Foreign Relations Committee.

Yet the propaganda-driven approach can also be counterproductive. Those who actually possess the power of decision are antagonised by the propagandists' tactics when propaganda becomes merely a form of emotional self-service. For example, in the United Kingdom propaganda that is transmitted in advertising format has to meet certain standards of truthfulness. When Vegetarian Society advertisements claimed that studies had connected meat with increased risk of heart disease and cancer, the authorities argued that no such causal link could be shown. In the other advertisements, a picture of a joint of meat was accompanied with the words 'No wonder it's called the joint, these are just some of the harmful substances found in meat'. The Advertising Standards Authority condemned the society's use of 'inaccurate and emotional' language (www.asa.org.uk).

Corporate propaganda

Doghouse industries

Corporate propaganda, or what is customarily described as public relations, is usually seen as the province of a pariah industry or companies in crisis. This would include such 'apology' industries as Big Tobacco or firms with a reputation for pollution, or organisations which find themselves in extreme crisis, as did Mobil over the *Exxon Valdez* disaster in Alaska or Union Carbide at Bhopal in India. In these cases the crises are similar to political crises and demand the same kinds of propaganda expertise. Often indeed truth is the best policy, as when Tylenol suspended its product after dangerous public tampering or when Perrier withdrew its bottled water for a period after a health scare. Such approaches are frequently adopted by companies with a disreputable past: 'thus a TV campaign showed misty-eyed college graduates eager to start saving the world as employees of Dow Chemical. The aim was to change Dow's somewhat tarnished image following its association with producing napalm and Agent Orange during the Vietnam War' (O'Shaughnessy 1995). But some industries find themselves permanently in the doghouse, and that old staple the cigarette industry has been joined by the petroleum, pharmaceutical (Big Pharma), fatty and fast foods industries and, by now, apparently, much of Wall Street and the finance industry.

Propaganda is the medium through which such outcast industries fight back. The cigarette industry, for example, has not sought to justify its world proselytisation of nicotine addiction but rather to rationalise it on grounds of freedom of choice, for it is of course continually coerced by law into making propaganda against itself. New accuseds have joined them in the corporate dock. The pharmaceutical industry is collectively charged with ignoring the plight of Third World countries in relation to AIDS and the cost of drugs. Other companies, particularly those that manufacture symbolic and even idealised brands, notably Nike and Gap, stand accused of exploiting Third World labour. Such charges stick, they cohere with traditional and even inherited popular stereotypes about the ugliness of big business which are for instance celebrated in the popular cartoon series *The Simpsons*. The accusations against certain companies have in themselves become a tradition, such as the troubles the Swiss firm Nestlé has encountered in its exports of powdered baby milk to poor countries. This anti-corporate propaganda is now more influential than ever because, perversely, of the salience and ubiquity of the corporation's greatest friend, the power brand. For people feel betrayed when the brand which they prefer publicly (and thereby promote) fails to live up to its proclaimed idealism.

So companies need propaganda. A company like Microsoft, long accused of ruthlessly exploiting its monopoly, would do well to digest a manual on propaganda rather than ingest more vapid forms of corporate enema such as public relations. One company which is buying into a propaganda approach is McDonald's, whose new image is a basket of free-range eggs:

> Which comes first, the chicken or the egg? We think it's the chicken. The welfare of our chickens is always a priority at McDonald's. And that means when you're enjoying one of our breakfasts, you can be sure you're only eating free-range eggs. Talking of good eggs, we recently received the Good Egg award from the British Free-range Egg Producers' Association, which recognises our commitment to animal welfare. All our products also carry the Lion Mark, an independent assurance of food quality. Which goes to show that, like the chicken, the customer always comes first at McDonald's.

The charismatic corporation

Certain companies and corporate individuals, however, do not wait to get into political trouble before turning to propaganda, Rather, these charismatic organisations thrive by generating hyperbole. Richard Branson of Virgin or Anita Roddick of Body Shop personify their organisations, they shrink-wrap them in personality. Charisma can become the core identity of the company and constitute a kind of floating equity, as with the Virgin brand, which ceased to have a distinct focus on records and flight, and stands not for a particular activity but for a particular approach (or rather, it did). Even ordinary executives, men and women who have been suits all their lives and never founded a company, can aspire to charisma, as did Lee

Iocacca at Chrysler when he attempted to re-establish credibility of the company in a series of television advertisements which showcased him walking the plant, talking to workers. Charisma can of course be destructive, as for example where Enron's Ken Lay created a stellar personal image which won the trust of investors, or the plausible founders of dot-com start-ups (remember them – the youthful faces, the open shirts?), who charmed a world into credulous faith when all we had was show.

Explicit propaganda

Moreover, as the political vulnerability of business increases, especially in certain industries, the temptation is to seek out the narcotic of political propaganda deception. The following example is fictitious, but not uncommon: in the United States a 'Committee to Protect Our Kids' Future' created advertisements critical of government, but this 'committee' was merely the fig leaf of major environmental polluters (Johnson 2001). And Californians were deceived by misleading political advertising into signing a petition, but Big Tobacco orchestrated this (Ansolabhere and Iyengar 1995). Advertising is increasingly being brought to bear by partisan groups on such major legislation as trade agreements and health care. Entire industries now seek a propaganda-driven approach to fortify their status, as illustrated by former US Secretary of Health Richard Shweiker's campaign on behalf of the insurance industry, where $5 million were spent on a television blitz and seven million pre-printed cards were sent to Congress.

Brand propaganda

The company is no longer an agency of production independent of its own self-articulation. This is particularly so as product benefits now converge, so that, to create the differentiation critical to selling, companies must construct a distinct personality for themselves. It is with the phenomenon of branding that propaganda has its most obvious associations with the corporate world. Today the company is more than a mere manufacturer. It is, or can seem to be, philosopher-king, familiar face and the authoritative arbiter of values. Within the nexus of the brand it offers trust, friendship, community. When the company appears to repudiate this offer, as in the case of Gap and Nike, outrage is the consequence. A brand is an offer of affiliation, an invitation to a public expression of solidarity: companies have achieved the astonishing, persuading their customers to become their perambulatory billboards. For such customers it is an act of trust and the company must not betray them and thereby undermine this public identity they have espoused. Companies, the brand authors, are our identity definers, yet they comprehend neither the full significance of this nor why people repudiate them with such ill grace when they feel betrayed by some action of the firm or exposure of its activities.

Brands telegraph identity, they indicate values, social style and aspirational social community, they help us stand out or stand in. Product is a form of social articulation and confers social visibility; even what we drink is social and therefore identity-driven. The expressive meaning of goods (Nozick's symbolic utility) is critical today, and because of this businesses whether they will or no are actually in the propaganda game. Since products are identity definers they have an inherently political element. People discover community through the shared meaning and community of the brand, brands link us with others, a separator and a collator, and a fundamental expression of group membership. The brand becomes a friend, and as with a friend the familiarity becomes a way of constructing our lives. Part of the strangeness of 'abroad' is the absence of familiar brands.

Brands are propaganda because the role of brands is often to symbolise social ideas and emotions such as youth and energy. Branding is condensed meaning. Great brands resonate, they crackle with associations. In the implicit universe of the brand, meaning is created by its advertising and made resonant by its traditions and imagistic equity

Propaganda and advertising: selective value advocacy

Advertisements have no social mandate to be equitable or socially representative, they converge, in various ways, on the idea of constructing illusions, images, fantasies round the product, and such projections are never value-free. What the values of advertising's social communication leave out is actually as important as what they leave in. It is legitimate to discuss propaganda in the context of advertising because values that are – if they are – enlisted in the service of product advocacy are also communicated in their own right, and nor are they necessarily subordinated to the product appeal. (The advertisement may even appear to be advocating the values rather than the product.) For Pollay (1986) advertising is a 'distorted' mirror in that it 'reflects only certain values and lifestyles' and a 'distorting' mirror in that it provides 'reinforcement of some values [and thereby] strengthens them or expands their domains of salience'. For Schudson (1982) 'American advertising, like socialist realist art, simplifies and typifies. It does not claim to picture reality as it is but reality as it should be . . . it does not represent reality nor does it build a fully fictive world. It exists, instead, on its own plane of reality, a plane I will call capitalist realism.'

Consumers do not always buy primarily for high performance in the product's use-function but its potential for achieving some preferred life vision or the fantasy created by its advertising, becoming the co-perpetrators of their own illusory beguilement. Marlboro, for example, gives off an implicit message that cigarettes are healthy; in the lore of Madison Avenue, 'advertising doesn't always mirror how people are acting, but how they're dreaming'. In many mature and established markets technical and other product performance benefits may converge. Propaganda considerations arise because image becomes the only basis of differentiation, and the projection of image is intimately bound up with the communication of values. If 'advertising pours meaning into the brand', a part of that meaning has to be social, since products themselves are a form of social/political articulation.

Advertising has social effects independent of the sale of the product; 'the effectiveness of advertising should be defined not only in terms of the ability to manipulate consumer demand in the market place through gimmickry but also in terms of success in propagating an ideology of mass production/ consumption and a specific way of life' (Albritton 1978). Since value orientation is made intrinsic to product appeals, this raises the possibility of inherent social advocacy being sufficiently determinate to be called propaganda. Stern (1988), for example, has described using 'American cultural myths as core stories prefiguring surface ones'. She described how Budweiser used the Horatio Alger story of a hard-working young outsider's achievement of success. The carpenter (he has a Polish name) is accepted via post-work beer drinking with co-workers, symbolising his acceptance by his peers and thus his Americanness. The original advertisements promoting the launch of Revlon's 'Charlie' fragrance (a trousered woman stepping out boldly in military stride) are generally credited with the success of a fairly modest perfume, but they work by an explicit appeal to feminist values, still radical at the time. Advertising is the corporate enthronement of the normative, and this legitimation role is important in the war of values, for advertising domesticates: it neuters what would appear threatening in the radical media.

6

Party propaganda

This chapter on political negativity is confirmation of the Enmity thesis in propaganda. American political propaganda today, a blizzard of thirty and fifteen-second commercials, embodies a culture of defamation. The political advertisement is an actual political event with independent political consequences, even historic consequences, such as 'Daisy' or the infamous Willie Horton advertisement. As the chapter argues, this kind of toxic negative propaganda can also fail (high risk, high reward). These poisonous diatribes seemed for a time to have become normative, with an important ethical and democratic consequence in the non-participation of many Americans in the voter process. Yet coherent if not entirely convincing ethical defences have been made of this phenomenon.

Introduction: blandness and negativity

Cinema, the advertising industry, journalism all present conceptual problems, and their status as propaganda is always therefore open to challenge. Not so political campaigning and political advertising, for they wear their insincerity on their sleeve: this is a game played by universally understood rules, with a capacious element of charade. Party political advocacy, particularly in the United States, would appear to embody two in particular of the characteristics we commonly attribute to propaganda, that is, the creation of enemies ('negative advertising') and duplicity. If we achieve self-definition through the recognition of what we are against, a world made intelligible via binary oppositionals, the emotional endowment of political propaganda is necessarily substantial, since politics is so intimately concerned with the affirmation of values. Thus a political issue is not merely a product to be merchandised but a vibrant value symbol connecting with an individual's sense of who and what they are at the deepest level.

The propagandising of US political processes is partly attributable to developments in the mainstream media or what is familiarly described as 'dumbing down'. In Dennis Johnson's (1997) words, 'traditional sources of information on politics – public network television news, newspapers, and weekly news magazines – are losing viewers and readers, losing market share, and losing their once dominant influence . . . throughout America, local news formats are homogenised and formulaic: news, weather, and sports, with happy talk and audience entertainment as the operative cultures'. The quotidian event in any political campaign in the United States today is the thirty-second or fifteen-second 'spot'. According to Ansolabhere and Iyengar (1995), voters bypass information that entails more than minimal acquisition costs. Thus the audience is an inadvertent one, so political campaign propagandists have permission to proselytise the most detached of citizens. Herbert Klugman's thesis on 'low involvement learning' (Schudson 1982) has intuitive plausibility in this context.

Lifestyle propaganda

Yet party political propaganda may be neither negative, polemical nor duplicitous in content but rather may embody much the same soft stylistic references as does consumer product advertising. A better descriptor would therefore probably be as a propaganda/ marketing hybrid. The harshness we might associate with classic propaganda, or its ideological primness, is lacking in such texts. This is sometimes so in presidential campaigns, for example Ronald Reagan's famous 'Morning in America' montage, which was classic lifestyle advertising celebrating citizens, sport and leisure activities and social rituals such as weddings – pure imagery without content that you could interpret how you wish.

Often such propaganda draws from the same symbolic stock as consumer advertising. For example, in 1984 the Republican National Committee frequently showed a sequence of a girl riding through the countryside with her boyfriend. They are wholesome and attractive, apparently this is a health advertisement. But no, she begins talking to us about politics. She is intelligent and college-educated, no chic clone, and explains firmly and persuasively why she is a Republican. This kind of political propaganda merges forgettably into a cultural landscape of benevolent consumerist imagery. It is the polemical that the critics notice.

Negative advertising

The association between negative political advertising and the traditional forms of vindictive propaganda are obvious. Such 'advertisements' bear telling comparison with the tactics of Goebbels in, for example, his sordid campaign against the (Jewish) deputy Berlin police chief Isidore Weiss (Rutherford 1978). In fact the origins of both are contemporary with the beginnings of the mass media: the first filmed political advertisements were as coarsely negative as anything which exists today. For example, Blumenthal (1984) has described the first cinema political commercial when MGM targeted the socialist candidate for California governor, Upton Sinclair, in 1936.

> Reporter to old lady in a rocking chair: 'Who are you voting for, mother?' 'I'm voting for the Republican, Frank Morrison, because this little home may not be much, but it is all I have in the world. I love my home and I want to protect it.' Next, the reporter approaches a bedraggled bearded man in a mangy over-coat. 'I am voting for Seen-clair,' he replies in a stilted foreign accent. 'His system worked well in Russia, so why can't it work here?' And, in another film, an army of hoboes is depicted hopping off a freight train and whooping it up on arrival in the Golden State. 'Sinclair says he'll take the property of the working people and give it to us,' says one of the bums. Ten million dollars was garnered to fight Sinclair, and twenty thousand billboards proclaimed, 'If I am elected governor, half the unemployed in the country will hop the first freight to California. – Upton Sinclair.'

Metropolitan sophistication is unaware of the extent of negative propa-ganda in provincial US politics. Thus the Clinton campaign sponsored fifteen months of negative advertising during the 1996 presidential pri-mary but it went undetected because it occurred in non-metropolitan regions 'below the radar screen of the national press' (Johnson 1997). Charles Guggenheim was particularly vitriolic on the subject of negative political propaganda:

> in the last ten years Americans have been forced to endure an epidemic of neg-ative political advertising. Visual and aural manipulation abounds. Every tool of the advertising craft has been exercised to prove opponents lazy, dishonest, unpatriotic, dumb, cruel, unfeeling, unfaithful and even criminal. . . . Ask any seasoned media advertiser and he will tell you what he can do best in thirty seconds. Create doubt. Build fear. Exploit anxiety. Hit and run. The thirty and sixty-second commercials are ready-made for the innuendo and half truth. Because of their brevity, the audience forgives their failure to qualify, to explain, to defend. (O'Shaughnessy 1990)

Negative extremes

This vindictiveness has little to do with real attitudes towards the candi-date, who has merely been conscripted, voluntarily or not, into a civil war of values. The candidate constitutes a convenient symbol of enmity and does duty as such, for example by being positioned as 'weak on crime' whatever the truth of their views. Negative advertising foments public outrage and channels it towards the opposing candidate even though in any objective sense the issue raised is irrelevant to the election. Outrage needs an enemy. Thus in the See case Polly Klaas (Chapter 2) was not an issue but a symbol. (The candidates' views on retributive justice may in fact be identical.) Propaganda politics are thus a way of expressing your rage at what has become of our world, and implicit in their appeal is nostalgia for a superior and vanished social order, so that voting becomes an act of social identification.

Negative political advertising is yet a further example of the salience of fantasy in propaganda texts, for, again, it does not make the error of asking for belief but, rather, the target is exhorted to join in the sponsorship of a fiction. The enemy and their errors are made luminous, and this fable of blame is exaggerated to the point of comicality. A fantasy may be dishonest, but it is not a lie, because no one is really deceived by it; it is made possible only because of strong mutual dedication to shared values and norms

Limitations of negative propaganda

Yet the propaganda of negativity well illustrates some of the important limitations of propaganda as persuasion. We cannot preordain interpretation. Since individuals have autonomy, the impact of a message in propaganda will be intended but it can never be controlled. The reaction of its targets is seldom predictable: in the Alabama Supreme Court election (Chapter 2) Harold See still won. (A negative ad is as much a statement about the values of the attacker as the defender, and extremes may alienate.) Polemical propaganda strategies may backfire, destroying not their targets but their creators. In Canada the election which brought Jean Chretien to power also exterminated the party, the Conservatives, who were the initiators of the polemic.

Failure in negativity: the case of Canada

This case also illustrates the influence of press filtration, since propaganda must address its public through independent media, and this is an offer that free media can reject. The aim of the Canadian Tory advertising was to stigmatise the leadership qualities of Liberal Jean Chretien, a sequence of ugly photographs depicted him becoming increasing confused, with the comment 'I personally would be very embarrassed if [Chretien] were to become the Prime Minister of Canada' (Whyte 1994). One of these images (intentionally or not) revealed the crooked right side of Chretien's face (from nerve injury sustained in youth). Yet there seemed ample strategic justification for a negative approach, since private polls had shown that the largest segment of the least committed liberal voters were dubious about his leadership, and focus groups agreed: Chretien was incompetent, it would be embarrassing to have him represent them at international events, and nobody ever mentioned the pictures (Whyte 1994).

Yet the electoral consequences of this strategy were devastating (*Globe*, 16 October 1993). The media seem to have determined that they would be, affixing an interpretation on to the text that said the advertisement was a grotesque attack on physical disability; thus to be Tory was to hate people with disabilities. Television reports chose the worst parts of the images and the script; pundits denounced. For most voters, their only exposure to the advertisements was through the interpretative framework attached by television. They never did 'decide for themselves'. An experiment at Simon Fraser University found people reacted far more negatively to the broadcasts about the advertisements than to the advertisements themselves. The result of this election was the worst ballot-box defeat of any ruling party in the entire history of Western democracy itself. The Tories, previously the largest party in Canada, were left with just two seats. It had become 'politically incorrect to be a Tory' (Whyte 1994).

Britain in 1992

Another example of failure in negative propaganda is the British general election of 1992. In *Jennifer's Ear* two child actresses portrayed the allegedly true story of two little girls with glue-ear, one immediately treated privately, the other repeatedly delayed on the National Health Service. It was shown in the second week of the election campaign. Again the strategy and execution seemed to make sense. The Conservatives were probably at their least credible when they claimed that 'the NHS is safe in our hands', and it was natural for Labour to seek to exploit their area of perceived greatest vulnerability. A powerful 'attack' advertisement at the start of the campaign would put the Tories on the defensive where they had least to defend. Such an advertisement should not be rational but emotional, seeking to achieve the kind of resonance with viewers and media reduplication that the sinister 'Willie Horton' had achieved in the United States. That resonance would be gained by a human story, and not abstract argument. If the story was also true, grounded in fact, the power of its symbolism could sustain the entire Labour campaign.

The failure, as with the anti-Chretien advertisement in Canada, lay essentially in the fact that the advertisement further irritated already suspicious media that were determinedly fault-finding. They criticised *Jennifer* for accuracy, undermining the claim to truthfulness that was central to its power to persuade. Moreover the charge of 'exploitation' of a sick child was what actually reverberated with the public, not the attack on the National Health Service: the child's vulnerability worked against, not for, Labour's advocacy. Newspapers discovered the identity of the real child and pursued the family. Nor was it clear whether the failure to treat was due to lack of resources or incompetence (Butler and Kavanagh 1995). That week, *Jennifer* constituted 'nearly 20 per cent of stories on both main television news programmes': Jennifer Bennett and her glue-ear 'received more coverage than housing, transport, pensions, law and order, defence, foreign affairs or Europe – indeed, than several of those put together' (Harrison 1995). Harrison further argues that 'before the election the NHS had seemed Labour's strongest suit. However, the momentum the party had built up by the middle of the campaign was never regained after the Jennifer Bennett affair broke on 25 March.' The press became direct participants in the creation of propaganda and not mere conduits of it. The demonstrable impact of this kind of news manufacture may seem to negate any attempts by parties to promote themselves. Under this argument, party political propaganda may be viewed as the poor relative of press activism, its impact must be seen in the context of other significant drivers of political influence.

Press attack

The press thus functions not only as news provider but also as news interpreter. At times even a free press can conspire to present a powerful 'dominant view' against which all other opinion is perceived as deviant. When opinion becomes universal among major press protagonists like this, nimble propagandists can rarely redeem the situation. In 1992 the Labour Party under Neil Kinnock was leading at the polls. The press 'decided to crucify him'. From December 1991 to 9 April 1992 the relatively apolitical *Sun* readers registered an 8.5 per cent swing to the Tories (McKie 1995). The press sought to demonise the Labour Party and its leader (Seymour-Ure and Scott 1995). Propaganda-like distortions were the order of the day. For example, the *Sun* in the *Jennifer's Ear* case presented Jennifer's father as being opposed to Labour's use of the story when the reverse was true.

Manipulation

All advocacy is manipulative, and propaganda is a branch of advocacy. We have argued earlier (Chapter 1) that deceitfulness is actually part of the vernacular understanding of what propaganda is even if it is not an integument of its lexical definition. US party propaganda deceives, not always, or even usually, but often. It is difficult to speculate on the political meaning and consequences of the deceit, since it would be astonishing if voters were so naive as to be unaware of it. Once again, such advertisements are not rational acts of advocacy but an invitation to share a fable about some common social enemy, and they therefore, as we have argued previously, represent an offer of affiliation.

Candidate propaganda is also subtextual, sustaining toxic issues on the live agenda via its mastery of the language of coded imagery. An example of this would be Jesse Helms's advertisement against a rival (black) candidate, Harvey Gant. White hands crumpled a letter of rejection, with this text: 'You needed that job. And you were the most qualified. But they had to give it to a minority because of racial quotas. Is that really fair?' (Ansolabhere and Iyengar 1995). Propaganda is about value affirmation and not 'mere' policy, and in this case the advertisement is about tribal loyalty. A typical Helms advertisement would feature these words being written on the screen and spoken by an actor: 'I voted against the Martin Luther King holiday. Where do you stand, Jim?' Such commercially hired 'voices' are the *sotto voce* of the campaign, a kind of *alter ego* for the candidate, an anonymous agency speaking on his/her behalf and murmuring the things they cannot (dare not) say, as with the 1988 Bush Senior campaign.

Fakery

The level of manipulated imagery in party propaganda is notable, such as the controversial George W. Bush subliminal television advertisement which flashed 'DemocRATS' at the boundary of perception. Thus a University of Oklahoma study of over 2,000 political advertisements from the 1950s onward found that more than 15 per cent were manipulated in some way and the number of adverts using altered images, according to the National Science Foundation, rose from 13 per cent of those made 1950–62 to 70 per cent post-1980 (*USA Today*, 23 May 1996). One diminutive senator was made to appear bigger by being filmed in a chamber with small nineteenth-century seats (O'Shaughnessy 1990). Such manipulation has long been customary – the lowering of Bush senior's voice in a 1988 advertisement was not untypical, while his 1988 Boston harbour commercial successfully falsified Dukakis's excellent environmental record.

Party propaganda sometimes transcends the boundaries of distortion to the upper realms of fabulous invention and lying. This is a venerable tradition. A Lyndon Johnson photograph of the 1930s showed him with the President; a third politician had been airbrushed out of existence (Johnson 1997). Richard Nixon did the same kind of thing in the late 1940s, and earlier of course Stalin had notoriously manipulated images of himself and other Bolshevik leaders, including Lenin. In one case a senator was actually dying but sufficient shots of his re-election announcement were pasted together to conceal the imminence of his demise.

Today technological resources are being actively used to edit truth. A 1996 study found 28 per cent of the 188 commercials scrutinised contained questionable use of technology: 'news conferences that were never held, debates that never took place, use of audio or video to stereotype or ridicule opponents' (*USA Today*, 23 May 1996). Johnson (1997) comments:

> in *Forrest Gump* the hero is made via digital technology to blend into a 1962 White House ceremony and Kennedy's face is made to appear as though he is talking to Gump. This method is used in American politics, and one researcher who contrasted original and doctored versions of the same advertisement found viewers gave higher marks to the deceptive advertisements. Even Senator John Warner of Virginia found that his consultant had doctored a photograph in the Senate race.

Once more, the appeal in such cases is not to reason; again we see the target being invited to join a mutual hallucination of solidarity as co-partner in the production of hyperbolic meaning.

In defence of negative propaganda

In fact the ethical argument over negative party propaganda is a complex one and does not admit of any easy resolution. As Banker (1992) argues, we need to distinguish between argument and argument form: 'an individual "negative" political ad is an argument, at least implicitly. As an argument it may be reasonable or unreasonable. That does not mean that all "negative" ads, the argument form, should be discouraged.' What though seems clear is that negative advertising reinforces partisanship and corrodes the political centre. That may be the effect, and it is presumably sometimes the authorial intent as well.

But incendiary propaganda can incite counter-attack from opponents, who now have access to instant rebuttal facilities via the internet. Second, all partisan propaganda is subject to arbitration by an independent source its sponsors cannot control, the 'free' media with their now ubiquitous 'adwatches'. As has been argued, to commission political propaganda is to undertake a journey but not to control its destiny. For a party propaganda text exists in its own right as an autonomous political event with independent political consequence; it is not merely a paid messenger or conduit of persuasive information from encoder to decoder. The fact that harshly negative advertising is such a volatile weapon thus brings its own restraints.

Moreover context legitimates ritual and rhetoric, and a political context is ultimately about the leadership and future direction of the nation, and therefore may merit higher levels of *ad hominem* rhetorical aggression than are permissible in other communications situations, including commercial ones. Perceived character is an integral part of the political 'product' which we exchange for our votes, and in practice it is less easy therefore to create some neat dichotomy between 'character' and 'issue' and declare the one off-limits to public curiosity. These points are a valuable corrective to the tendency in much of the literature to dismiss negative propaganda as an unqualified loss for American public culture, but they are not an entirely satisfactory riposte to the critics of political negativity, for by the early 1990s fifty states with 62 per cent of the voting-age population suffered full negative campaigns (Ansolabhere and Iyengar 1995).

Public benefits of negativity/political propaganda

It would thus be dishonest to pretend that propagandised politics had nothing useful to deliver. It is ironic that the phenomenon can be defended in instrumentalist terms. Ansolabhere and Iyengar (1995) review the evidence that political advertising increases public knowledge of salient issues by increasing the amount of information in circulation. Banker (1992) argues that it 'can be viewed as supplying voters with alternative perspectives for understanding political reality', it enables us to 'reframe political facts, to allow the public to see it from a different perspective'. Negative propaganda can introduce legitimate public concerns into the election that might otherwise have been ignored, since no issue can be successfully 'manufactured' and sold without some underlying resonance in public opinion; to argue otherwise is perhaps to entertain the notion of a jejune electorate and a stimulus–response, or hypodermic, model of political communication (Kraus and Davis 1976).

Banker discusses a case in point, where polling revealed that an incumbent candidate (Senator Jeremiah Denton) was perceived as rich and aloof: projective polling suggested his rival focus on Denton's use of official monies to pay country club membership and on his anti-social security vote. In this context, the negative propaganda can be justified as an awareness exercise which led to a more informed, if more embittered, contest.

Impact of negativity

Around 70 per cent of the costs of an American congressional or senate campaign are generated by television advertising. These costs of propaganda are thus mortgaging the US political system to moneyed vested interests, about this there can be no ambiguity. No US politician, for example, dares to seriously criticise the actions of the Sharon government of Israel; in consequence the US possesses no independent freedom of action in the Middle East and is not accepted as a neutral party there. But the Israel lobby uses its power exactly like any other big US political lobby. The NRA is no different. The blame lies not with the lobbies that exploit their freedoms but with the systems that license them.

Ansolabhere and Iyengar, in their revealing book *Going Negative* (1995), provide substantial experimental and quantified evidence for the effectiveness of negative advertising. They discovered that exposure to a single campaign advertisement in experiments increased support for the sponsoring candidate by nearly 8 per cent, and that in the 1988, 1998 and 1992 elections the victors in one in three US Senate races, one in three governorship contests and one in nine US House races won by 7 per cent or less. These authors claim that 'more intensive advertising by the losers might have reversed these outcomes'. They claim independents are only responsive to negative commercials, an astonishing conclusion, and that negative advertising reinforces partisan loyalty: negative advertising freezes out the centre from political participation in elections, since negative races reduce turnout by over 7 per cent. On the evidence specifically for the effectiveness of negative advertising, they found positive–negative versions of the same advertisement in their experiments led to a 9.5 per cent versus 19 per cent lead. For low-interest voters the negative advertising created a 24 per cent increase in favour of their party and thus 'weak partisans are easily made into strong partisans'.

We have argued that a negative advertisement is also an autonomous political episode in its own right with independent political consequences. Thus some individual negative propaganda texts have become famous as historical events in themselves. (A television ad showing the legend 'Agnew for Vice-president' against a backdrop of increasingly hysterical laughter was one of the more successful of the genre.) Above all there is 'Daisy' (Tony Schwartz 1964). The fear aroused in Daisy is for the future of the entire human race: the tender image of the small girl with her symbolism of our future is contrasted with the robot male voice in nuclear countdown, and then Lyndon Johnson's voice lends an epic note of high authority: 'These are the stakes – to make a world in which all of God's children can

live, or to go into the dark. We must either love each other, or we must die.'
The explosion is a harbinger of armageddon, a signifier of the extinction of
the human race, the covert (and duplicitous) message being that Barry
Goldwater would actually lead the United States into nuclear holocaust.
Thus in 1964 the strategic positioning concept of President Lyndon John-
son was as peace candidate.

The most famous negative propaganda event was the Willie Horton
commercial, about a convicted killer who raped, having been given week-
end parole in Massachusetts. Horton, who was black, was 'run' as a kind
of anti-candidate by the Republicans. And in another commercial legions
of eerily silent prisoners were shown walking through a revolving door.
These images hit US liberalism at its most vulnerable point, an ideologically conditioned inability to sound vengeful on crime. Shortly after
'Horton' Bush soared past Dukakis in the opinion polls. Then, since
Democrats had always been more believable on 'quality of life' issues, film
of noxious Boston harbour was repeatedly shown. Thus the Bush Senior
campaign was run on symbolism – the flag, Horton, Boston harbour. In
that election there was real ambiguity about the future performance and
policies of the candidates, with one-third of voters undecided even late on.
Whenever there is ambiguity like this, decision makers fall back on symbols that signify a particular stance, to be interpreted for or against a particular set of values. Dukakis, a Democrat, did not understand this – or,
more properly, he did not understand propaganda. Whether or not 'Willie
Horton' and 'Daisy' affected the course of American history, they were
significant political events.

In the post-Nine-eleven climate, however, many commentators concluded that negative advertising was becoming less visible because it was
now more subtle. There was a new genre, the anti-negative negative, 9 per
cent of political commercials (*New York Times*, 24 October 2002). And then
there were the advertisements with female voices, more sorrowful than
angry: 'harsh negatives are not working. Harsh, vitriolic, dripping with
sarcasm'. Alternatively a dual private/public strategy was pursued: frown-
ing mailings and smiling television ads. Mr Gephardt's 'sunny' television
contrasted with mail shots on Medicare cuts featuring a slack-jawed Dr
Dean with a tabloid-style headline 'Caught' (*New York Times*, 12 January
2004). The internet (which is exempt from candidate endorsement rules)
could be similarly employed as the 'private' voice, its caustic imagery
excised from 'public' (mainstream) media. Contrast George W. Bush's initial
suburban-safe, airbrushed 2004 campaign television advertising with a
video on his campaign website:

> A woman, sitting at a keyboard, seeks information about Senator John Kerry
> on the internet. She unearths all sorts of scandalizing titbits. 'More special

interest money than any other senator. How much?' she says. The answer flashes on the screen: $640,000. 'Ooh, for what?' she says, typing out 'Paybacks?' and then, reading aloud from the screen, she says, 'Millions from executives at HMOs, telecoms, drug companies.' She adds, 'Ka-ching!' (*New York Times*, 22 February 2004)

Techniques, targets, technologies

Propaganda is increasingly the political task. Even in the 1930s Father Charles Coughlin could use his polemical radio broadcasts to bombard Congress with 200,000 telegrams the next day. In the words of one Congressman, 'I am not only a news maker, but a news man – perhaps the most widely read journalist in my district. I have a radio show, a television programme, and a news column with a circulation larger than that of most of the weekly newspapers in my district' (O'Shaughnessy 1990).

The internet has particularly strong propaganda applications, containing everything from fund raising to policy ideas from that 'sprawling ideological shopping mall', the Heritage Foundation. Thus 'campaign contributions can be solicited; policy papers posted for voter inspection; interactive chat lines established, so that the campaign can respond to questions from voters; volunteers recruited; candidate schedules publicised; and press releases and other announcements posted' (Johnson 1997). The internet is still in its infancy as a political tool, and its latent power remains as yet unrealised. The common properties of this new propaganda medium when exploited for political propaganda purposes are:

1 *Speed.* Mail shots can be sent overnight, but responses can be placed on the web within seconds. The fluidity of political situations is now extreme, since parties and politicians can post immediate replies. As US President Bill Clinton made a State of the Union address there was a mere two-minute delay between his statement and the Republican reply (Johnson 1997). The Republican web site, linked up to GOP-TV, listed 'a daily calendar of Clinton scandals and misdeeds'.
2 *Scope.* One million can be mailed, but many millions can be e-mailed.
3 *Precision targeting.* You reach exactly your ideological fraternity. Because the audience is select, the compromises of mainstream media are not needed, exactly the compromises mainstream marketing must make – audiences can be addressed in their own language, the language of emotion and unreason.
4 *Pressure.* Legislatures can be suffocated with e-mails.

5 *Reach*. Extreme economy is combined with extreme reach, and millions can be solicited at trivial cost. This contrasts with television and indeed direct mail: a commercial 'spammer', for example, needs only one sale per 100,000 messages to break even.
6 *Information*. Copious amounts are available at the touch of a button, and although this is not of general value to a mass electorate, it influences the press, for example, as journalists scour campaign web sites.
7 It is, or can be, *personal*. It is hardly realistic for a politician to persuade his acolytes to type dozens of letters to their friends, but e-mail provides that facility in seconds, while a good internet chain letter can reach millions and still command the endorsement of a friend. It blends the power of personal endorsement with the exponential reproduction of a text.
8 It is *multimedia*: moving image, sound and print.
9 *Interactivity*. This special property of the internet is a unique benefit, since propaganda is at its most powerful when co-production triggers self-persuasion.

Moreover it will initiate new actors on to the political scene, a minority party or candidate moving exclusively via the internet in the early stages, accumulating repute, funding and support before turning to mainstream media for imagistic capital. The key to the Howard Dean campaign was the new forms of direct involvement and participation that the internet permitted. The campaign was the inverse of a hierarchical approach, seeking volunteers and donations from website conversations: Blog for America permitted visitors to post any message they wanted and received 40,000 hits per day, and by November 2003 there were half a million e-mail addresses on the Dean database, while the campaign had raised $5 million in the last days of September alone (*New York Times*, 21 December 2003). The campaign in Tennessee was 'so virtual it does not even appear to have a telephone'. Nor, of course, are politically significant actors on the web largely or even mainly the political parties; thus moveon.org sponsored an anti-Bush advertising contest and found 1,500 commercials on its website: the two comparing Bush to Hitler received national publicity (*New York Times*, 11 January 2004). The internet does not, however, possess those peculiar properties of inadvertence common to other propaganda media such as television and posters, for these trespass unbidden on our consciousness, whereas the internet commands that we actively solicit information.

Negative propaganda has, however, become something of a stylistic rut in US politics; not everyone shared the instincts of the hard line. Electorates became wary of it, while duplicity can be exposed; as a strategy it represented and continues to represent high risk/high reward. It would be pleasant to envisage a future with more ethical, more benevolent alternative scripts in circulation. That is unlikely. There never was a Golden Age of political good manners and mature argumentative exchange in the United States, and negative propaganda will therefore always remain a strategic choice. The hope is that it will not become the only one.

7

Propaganda and the Symbolic State: a British experience

This chapter discusses the rise of the Symbolic State. It aspires to introduce a new formula into the political lexicon. It argues that Britain's 'New' Labour government embodies a propaganda phenomenon for which the word 'spin' is descriptively inadequate. New Labour actually represents something much more radical and important than that – an entire regime whose core competence has lain in the generation of imagery, that is, propaganda-driven. Its directors recognise that, in a sense, words speak louder than actions, and that the production of the correct imagery is politically more significant than the creation and execution of policy, the old concept of governing. Hence government's momentum and apparent dynamism derive from symbolic action. The idea of spin is part of this larger universe of meaning (defining spin as the affixing of a stabilising interpretation on to a fluid event). This also includes the use of data and its manipulation. Thus saying is easier than doing, with consequences either invisible or divisive. A skill hitherto numbered among a repertoire of governing skills has now become the principal one. While the chapter discusses the ethical and the social consequences of this evolution, it also suggests that such propaganda, or 'Symbolic Government', is the almost inevitable response of governing elites to an inquisitorial and relentless modern media.

The Symbolic State: a new idea in politics?

Why language is important

We define 'Symbolic Government' as government where the creation of symbolic images, symbolic actions and celebratory rhetoric have become a principal concern. Appearances do not just matter. They are the main part of its business. Symbolic Government is an entirely new kind of government. This is not to say that previous regimes did not engage in it frequently – but what was just an important tool of government has now graduated into becoming its central organising principle, absorbing therefore much of the energy of government.

The objective of this chapter is to elevate, or place in circulation, the notion of Symbolic Government as an alternative propaganda paradigm for viewing government today, with Britain as exemplar. The claim is that the management of the state's communication may even rival in importance the management of the state itself, at least as far as its rulers are concerned. Such propositions are perhaps frustrating, since they can neither be proved nor disproved, merely argued, without the satisfaction of final closure. Yet to engage in such an argument is no mere exercise in rhetoric, and our further justification lies ultimately in neither the truth nor the falsity of this proposition so much as in its value as an additional conceptual window on to the enigma of modern government and of propaganda in general. Its status is as another tool of interpretation.

A contemporary mythology

It is not merely a cliché that Britain has entered a new era of political manipulation, it is part of our contemporary mythology. The media were at first beguiled by their new manipulators, and the excesses of Blairite 'spin' can certainly be seen as the political riposte to years of sustained media persecution of politicians, as exemplified by the *Sun*'s (8 April 1992) eight-page extravaganza 'Nightmare on Kinnock Street' as its preamble to the 1992 general election. Thus Peter Mandelson was ennobled as the 'Prince of Darkness'; spin became celebrated in documentary, in classy soaps (*The West Wing, Spin City*) and dramas (Kosminsky and Jackson's *The Practice*). There are popular books, and there is a considerable media account. The idea that we are being professionally manipulated by government is apparently believed by nearly everybody.

How then can a review such as this one possibly be saying anything new? Our central argument is that, though the fight to present a favourable account of events to the media is well understood, the larger picture – the extent to which the entire apparatus of government has become propagandised, preoccupied with the pursuit of imagery management – is often lost. The word 'spin' is descriptively inadequate, since to speak of 'spin government' would restrict its activities to the provision of lucid sound bites. Much more is going on in Symbolic Government, and 'spin' rests beneath its conceptual umbrella as part of a larger universe of symbolic management.

The idea of Symbolic Government

The modern Symbolic State is therefore not the same as a state which from time to time uses rhetoric and symbolic enactments as one of a number of governing instruments. The persuasion–propaganda concept forms the essence of its political culture. Lacking an ostensible ideology or core beliefs, at least in the eyes of its critics, it may even seem that the purpose of power has become power itself. Symbolic governments campaign permanently, and what is critical to them is the appearance of momentum.

Symbolic Government is also government by narrative – the small narratives by which governments account for their daily work, and the meta-narratives, the big themes, that lend their many activities coherence and give them direction. The Symbolic State tells stories about itself. A good story beats logic or reason. Simmons (2000), for example, demonstrates how stories help managers persuade more effectively than rationally based argument. The propaganda structure of Symbolic Government may be seen as comprising a number of key components, viz. the constant assertion of progress in all things, the cult of statistical 'proof', symbolic actions and subjects of attack, hyperbolic language, obfuscation via quantificatory obscurity, the generation of 'tableaux' – i.e. the setting out of symbol-rich theatrical scenes such as visits to politically significant groupings, people or places; acute sensitivity to generated imagery and its deft management; on occasion, the manufacture of enemies/targets of derision; and of course spin, the affixing of a plausible interpretation on to a fluid situation.

Then there is, of course, the Leader. Symbolic Government is unthinkable without leaders who are actors as well as enactors. They perform. In the United States this is a derived consequence of the tripartite role of the President – monarch, chief executive, commander-in-chief. Such a role cannot be executed without some significant symbolic embroidery. Ronald Reagan defined the essence of this symbolic presidency, and his successors are his imitators. The Symbolic Government of Ronald Reagan was managed via a series of luminous, symbolic visual episodes that telegraphed the core values of the regime. Symbolic people were also incorporated into this theatre. Clintonism was in some ways a modern, sensualised reworking of the Reagan politics of imagery. Reagan's intimate, self-disclosive style – the 'feminine' rhetorician, to use again Hall Jamieson's terminology – was reflected in the quotidian Clinton performance, the empathetic 'I feel your pain' pose so parodied by satirists. The familiar Tony Blair idiom owes much to this Clinton exemplar of how a left-leaning leader may ingratiate himself with a middle-class culture, while during the Afghanistan and Iraq wars all of George W. Bush's actions were permeated with symbolism – his flying jackets, backdrops of square-jawed military listeners, his (brazen?) fighter-jet touchdown on the ramp of the aircraft carrier *Abraham Lincoln*, the surprise 2003 Thanksgiving appearance to the troops in Iraq. (But symbolism when exposed can backfire, as when boxes of ostensibly American export goods, used as a crafted backdrop to a speech by Bush, were exposed by the *New York Times* as having their 'Made in China' labels taped over.)

Rhetoric

The idea of Symbolic Government resolves into two interdependent components, rhetoric and symbolism, that is, the verbal and the visual. Both are in essence imagistic, the one creates images from language, the other from vivid pictures. Yet in Symbolic Government they coalesce, the one is unthinkable without the other.

The power of rhetoric

Rhetoric is the core of political persuasion. Contrary to rational choice theory, the words actually used are very important; alternatives are chosen via their descriptions, and these can vary in persuasive content. Descriptions connect a theme with our key emotional concerns, thus raising the possibility of a change in perspectives. Language does not simply declare a stance, it biases perceptions and gets us to think in certain ways, 'the names we give to things organise our thoughts'. Foulkes (1983) for example, or the wartime diarist Victor Klemperer (1998), described how one of the rhetorical achievements of the Third Reich was to get enemies to use its language – their words and phrases entered everyday discourse, became embedded in the culture, since words are not neutral tools but embody perspectives.

US history could even be calibrated via a sequence of epic rhetorical episodes, not least the presidency itself: 'Ask not what your country can do for you . . .', 'Peace with honour . . .', 'A kinder, gentler America'. It is significant that the inventor of Symbolic Government, Ronald Reagan, was a masterly practitioner of rhetoric, exploiting anecdote and metaphor. The essence was simplicity, such as for example his dismissal of Carter: 'There you go again.' His particular gift was to draw from an imagistic stock shared by all his viewers, that is, from vernacular language and the media rather than from classical texts and the Bible, since these were no longer common ground. Thus Colonel Gaddafi, for example, became 'the flake', an economic piece of populist derision. The power of the Reagan presidency was in large measure rhetorical in origin.

Britain's experiment in Symbolic Government has a number of distinctly rhetorical components: graduating from its easily remembered campaign phrases, couched as advertising slogans and often repeated, into a new political language, or at least a language in which politics was more important. Rhetoric was a significant part of the 1997 campaign by which Labour attained power (Jones 1999), one which was larded with urbane slogans such as 'Labour's coming home', 'stakeholder society', 'Education, education, education', 'Tough on crime, tough on the causes of crime', 'It's time for a change' (and who could disagree?) (Draper 1997). There were all the 'performative utterances' (Austin 1962) such as the rhetorical salvoes launched against harmless targets like 'Cut NHS bureaucracy', 'We won't spend £60 million on a new royal yacht while patients lie on trolleys in hospital corridors' (Draper 1997). In government, policy was presented in new ways. For example, the 1999 budget eschewed the old dry forms of presentation: it was 'fat and glossy' with headings such as 'Building a better society'.

The rhetorical vision

New Labour's critics argued that 'exciting' ideas provided a veneer of policy-wonk respectability but no substance – their value lay in the generated imagery. During the 1997 election the messages had been simple: uncosted promises on school class sizes, tax, jobs, the health service and crime, cast as Big Ideas, such as New Labour's promise (Jones 1997) to establish three-week intensive literacy summer schools (never carried out). Problems, in so far as they are solved, are solved rhetorically.

Thus was also a suspicion that policy arose out of rhetoric and not the other way round. While New Labour did not usher the concept of the 'rhetorical vision' into politics, it certainly embellished it. For Dowling (1989), who first used the term, a rhetorical vision is a coherent but dramatic explanation of reality, with a sanctioning agent to justify acceptance and promulgation. For the purposes of elucidating the phenomenon of Symbolic Government, however, we seek a different definition: rhetorical vision as an impressionistic idea, which is summoned and sustained not by a measured response to a felt need, or reflection on the results of empirical enquiry, but by the allure of the image of some idealised state. One such rhetorical vision is New Labour's mandate to send 50 per cent of the population to university. Its deficiency is exposed by simply posing the question: why 50 per cent? No mature investigation, statistical extrapolation, inquiry or manpower study had led to the production of this figure, nor had a way of properly funding these numbers been suggested. Fifty per cent was a rhetorically seductive sum, suggestive of democratic empowerment and participation, and mass credentialisation, of making what had been until very recently the perquisite of a small elite become the shared experience of much of the population. Opponents could be declared elitist by definition (since they opposed the extension of the education franchise) and therefore unworthy of serious attention. Thus the rhetoric led the policy, an inversion of the traditional form, where policy is decided and rhetoric articulates it.

Bureaucracy and rhetoric

The functionaries of the British state had to jettison their old bureaucratic language for a new hyperbole, but reading it – as in this example – we are perhaps no wiser than before:

> Mr Milburn will be creating a top-level NHS modernisation board to drive through the changes in the NHS. In a move designed to overturn traditional Whitehall bureaucracy and hierarchy, board membership will include the brightest and best modernisers in the health service. The changes signal a vote of confidence in front-line clinicians and managers who are consistently trail-blazing new ideas. These are the people at the rock face with the experience and enthusiasm to drive home the modernisation programme. (*The Times*, 23 February 2001)

In this case the illustration uses some favourite New Labour buzz words, for example the word 'modernise' is used three times: dynamic metaphors are constantly employed, such as 'drive through', 'overturn', 'trail-blaze', 'people at the rock face', 'drive home'. An *enemy* is created for all this energy to struggle against – hierarchy, traditional Whitehall bureaucracy, against whom are opposed the forces of virtue. This was not a special announcement, but a typical Ministry bulletin to the press. Yet it acquires the character of self-parody. In one brief period Tony Blair made fifty-three speeches and employed the word 'modernisation' eighty-seven times. For New Labour, the staid old civil service must be tipped out of the capacious armchairs wherein it had reposed for generations and learn the funky new dance steps. No longer would the anachronistic language do, the pompous, anodyne announcements: instead a new rhetoric that positively salivated with pseudo-revolutionary fervour, a pastiche dynamism, a high-octane racy patter, the orotund verbalisations of the slick-talking salesman.

Much of the aim of the new-found presentation skills was to mystify rather than clarify. Hidden tax increases might be disguised under the weight of obscure technicalia (according to their more partisan critics). People could not 'see' these new costs; for example, the abolition of pension funds' ability to reclaim dividend tax credits (Draper 1997) amounted, critics claimed, to a £6 billion-a-year annual tax on retirement savings, but the formula was 'too complex for the media'.

'Spin'

The rhetorical aspects of Symbolic Government are today often called 'spin', whose meaning therefore overlaps with the domain of rhetoric, and it is an old political skill. In the end, spin-doctoring is an argument, another word for advocacy. For Moloney (2001) spin is 'a euphemism for propaganda. It is another step towards what Deccan and Golding have called the rise of the public relations state.' In fact it has been said that the ancestry of spin lies with Cicero and Aristotle.

The concept of spin derives from the recognition that no event is closed to interpretation, otherwise history books would cease to be written, because historical 'facts' are perpetually reinterpreted. For Nietzsche, all thought arose out of perspective; there are thus no facts, only interpretations. Reconfiguring issues in a meaningful way must connect with the concerns of the target audience, to their values and sense, perhaps, of lack of control. Since all events possess open texture, that interpretation which is decisive, memorable, coherent and perhaps metaphorically articulated gains acceptance as the paradigm through which that event is viewed.

Symbolism

'An empty symbol' – how often have we heard those words? It must be said that symbolism is only ever empty to those with a super-rationalist/functionalist view of how complex social systems operate. Any perspective that places meaning centre-stage also invokes the power of symbolism. Thus, for example, the value of Roosevelt's New Deal was in large measure symbolic. The fireside chats, arts programmes, the TVA, the grand construction projects, etc., were massive symbols of hope. What mattered was the symbolic, not the actual, mobilisation of the unemployed.

The political value of symbolism

Symbolism may mean the serial creation of meaningful imagery, or it may refer to a unitary symbol. In the 1997 campaign Labour Party political broadcasts conscripted the symbolism of the bulldog, hitherto an icon of old High Tory England. Labour were years ahead of the Tories in terms of their understanding of the new symbolic grammar of politics. Symbols are condensed meaning, they resonate, and to middle England, an essential constituency for Blair, this impertinent adoption of the iconic paraphernalia of traditional Toryism telegraphed one essential message: 'We are on your side.'

While a symbol may, of course, refer to a visual image or tangible embodiment such as the bulldog – the general sense in which the term is publicly understood – it may also refer to a sequence of expressive actions whose achievement is to generate symbolic properties. It is to this latter that New Labour principally dedicated itself via a constant stream of initiatives, targets and interventions. These were the symbols of purposive action and vigorous problem solving.

Symbolic action

In government, Labour political themes were articulated via symbolic enactments and symbolism drove policy, sometimes to the extent of caricature. For example, there was a Women's Minister, but she drew no salary (Draper 1997).

'New' Labour was initially seen – to its political enemies at least – as an anti-ideology, a bandwagon, one that sought to take the politics out of politics. The aim was power, to be attained by fabricating an incoherent formula of political eclecticism, rooted in consumerism. Such Symbolic Government could be described as a confetti mix of authoritarianism, 'radicalism', liberalism, populism. In the first term authoritarian-sounding threats were made – punishment for juvenile delinquents, claims that teachers would be able to be sacked in four weeks if they were incompetent, and curfews for the under-tens. And the liberal conscience was assuaged with claims that there would be a selective ban on weapon sales (but not to Indonesia), adoption of the European social chapter, adoption of the minimum wage (but at a low rate) (Draper 1997). Critics accused the government of taking no decisions at all or of seeking instant policy answers to every crisis (such as Tony Blair's demand that policemen should be able to march miscreants to a cash machine and fine them instantly).

One accusation in particular that began to make itself increasingly felt, and hurtfully, was the idea that the government's only method of dealing with deep-seated social problems was to create multiple symbolic initiatives, for example the case of Jack Straw or David Blunkett as Home Secretary. Initiatives perform a role in the Symbolic State. They give the appearance of dynamism, a riposte to critics who decry official inactivity. The claims and assertions that often began to appear in newspapers hostile to the government are epitomised by this one from the *Daily Telegraph* of 16 April 2002: 'David Blunkett has launched crime initiatives at the rate of more than one a week since he became Home Secretary last summer'. The article went on to review the previous ten months, during which period it claimed that as many as six different initiatives had been announced in a single month, initiatives such as (June 2001) £15 million to drive crime out of shopping centres; (July) a task force to protect children on the internet; (September) an on-line campaign to cut car crime; (October) extending the use of Antisocial Behaviour Orders and signing up top firms to a hi-tech drive to cut crime; (December) national rethinking crime and punishment initiative; (February 2002) a security boost for 3,000 shops in deprived areas; (March) further extension of Antisocial Behaviour Orders, new guidelines for tackling drug dealers on housing estates, action on street crime through a robbery reduction initiative, 10 Downing Street crime summit, new advisory panel for victims; (April) video identity parades in robbery hot-spot areas.

Symbolic empiricism

Academics accused government of ingeniously massaging data, some political scientists concluding, 'Britain is fast becoming some kind of social statistical Utopia' (*Guardian*, 7 October 2002). For persuasion in a Scientific Age must also be rational-empirical to be credible, that is, data-driven, evidence-based (Chapter 4). Traditional rhetoric is more suspect, propositions cannot just be asserted, but must be 'proved', and it is on this process of symbolic manufacture that Britain's government, and by extension its subordinate authorities – schools, police, hospitals – focus today. Results and performance data are sought to show that quantifiable improvements are visible in every theatre of national life. When health care became the area of greatest political vulnerability for the government, the search for positive data became frenetic. On 11 April 2002 Alan Milburn, the Health Secretary, announced that only two patients were having to wait more than fifteen months for an operation, compared with 80,000 a year before. Had this result had been achieved by making larger numbers of people wait up to twelve months? All newspapers attacked what they claimed was the manipulation of hospital waiting lists. The use of such single performance measures like waiting lists or league tables is popular in the UK public sector because multiple measures are too complex for the needs of persuasive communication. Under this culture of audit, therefore, what is difficult to measure may not be measured at all. Not surprisingly, the energetic demands of Symbolic Government led to fraud by public bodies: 'in one case, patients were asked by telephone when they were going on holiday, then given dates for their operations in that period' (National Audit Office, Wednesday 19 December 2001). Similar examples of manipulation emerged from the police and other public bodies. Another consequence of symbolism's appetite for benevolent statistics was, arguably, to inflame the tendency of central government to micro-manage rather than devolve. Scant trust here for Edmund Burke's 'little platoons'.

Implementation of Symbolic Government

Control

The phenomenon of Symbolic Government resides not just in the intellectual acceptance of a particular and novel paradigm of government by a major political party. The party must live the idea, must implement it, and this is a function of the kind of discipline and managerial skill traditionally rather alien to the inchoate, amateur ethos of political parties. Yet it was at this disciplined management of communication that Labour excelled. This focus on the centrality of presentation, and thereby on the necessity of an unambiguous and coherent message, does not admit of moral doubt or political debate. An authoritarian internal party culture may even translate externally into an authoritarian government. Thus Jones (1997) describes the lengths to which Labour Party operatives went to discourage the media from showing the banners of protesting trade unionists at a Labour Party event. Negative information tends to weigh more powerfully than positive information, and this may even be a consequence of our evolution. In a primitive state, recognition of danger may be a more important survival skill than the recognition of pleasurable opportunity.

This importance of control via centralised command was one of the lessons that New Labour learned from its friends in the Clinton Democratic Party, with its famous campaign 'war room'. The pre-campaign campaign for the 1997 election would include 'a synchronised propaganda offensive which featured an elaborate photo opportunity, a big-hitting news conference, a new poster campaign and a specially commissioned party political broadcast' (Jones 1997). During the election itself Blair addressed the press on only three occasions (*Independent*, 3 May 1997). Observers spoke of 'the disciplined, almost scientific way in which he had fought this campaign' (Harris, *Sunday Times*, 4 May 1997). The utility of each expenditure of energy was carefully measured, Blair describing foreign television crews as 'no-votes TV' (*Sunday Times*, 4 May 1997). Blair's arrival as victor at Downing Street was greeted by cheering crowds, but 'even the crowds were choreographed . . . nothing was left to chance, said a Labour official. New Labour's organisation demands that it never is' (*Sunday Times*, 4 May 1997).

The cult and culture of rebuttal

The history of New Labour's Millbank headquarters has entered our political mythology. The image of 'Millbank' – omnipotent high-tech control – was in some ways as significant as its function. During that election the party's Millbank headquarters were open twenty-four hours a day, hosting such new propaganda delights as the twenty-four-hour rebuttal units, and 'prebuttals', another idea from the Clinton heritage. Campaigners were linked: pagers, the internet and faxes helped keep its candidates consistently 'on message' with information from the £300,000 Excalibur system, where documents, speeches, statistics and press cuttings, backgrounds and details could be accessed instantly (Jones 1997). By 2002 the government was planning a big expansion of this 'knowledge network' for retrieval and co-ordination (*Guardian*, 2 August 2002).

New Labour intended to rule as it had campaigned. This manipulation of the free media was achieved by a skill that New Labour honed to perfection, the remorseless nagging of the journalistic cadre by such as Gordon Brown's spin doctor Charlie Whelan (Jones 1997): during the pre-campaign 'by issuing a constant flood of rebuttal statements Labour were forcing journalists to question the credibility of the facts and figures which Ministers were giving to the House of Commons' (Jones 1997). Charm as well as pester-power was used, Blair actually flying to Australia to address the assembled paladins of Rupert Murdoch's global media empire (Jones 1997). This is a kind of persuasion which depends for its effectiveness on the free media and their successful conscription, i.e. a two-step sequence of communication between initiator and target, with the media as interlocutor. It works only in so far as the media are unwilling to interrogate the process (that is, lazy?) or recognise it as propaganda. The economic cost is low for the communicator, who is not paying for the advocacy product. In many democracies, including Britain, parties are comparatively poor and tend not to own newspapers, publish books or sponsor documentaries and film. Manipulation of the free media is distinguished from classic propaganda in which publication is enabled either by private wealth or by public control. In other propagandist cultures the state has owned the media (Soviet Russia), or parties have owned part of the media (Berlusconi in Italy) or have had some other interest (e.g. Louis B. Meyer of MGM when chairman of the California Republican Party in the 1930s: Mitchell 1993). But in the United Kingdom the parties own no media and must rely on the entrepreneurship of public imagery.

This campaigning idiom, and to some extent this structure, is significant because it was a strategy not only for electioneering but also for governing. The campaign ethos permeated government. The central strategic and communications unit co-ordinated messages across government departments, and organised 'spin'. Private briefings were awarded to sycophantic journalists. It was recognised first that in order to successfully pursue advocacy, it is necessary to employ advocates. The old order of government information officers had insisted on the tradition that government departments provided objective information. The new order purged them, and after the first year of Labour in power twenty-four of the forty-four heads and deputy heads of ministerial information departments had been replaced. This was seen by their union as an attempt to 'sanitise' the Whitehall machine of press officers reluctant to deliver Labour 'propaganda'.

Why Symbolic Government?

Cynical media

There are also tangible reasons why Symbolic Government finds a stronger contemporary definition in Britain than in any other country apart from the United States. In part this is Labour's reaction to its own past, the enmity of the press and nearly two decades of exclusion from government. In 1992 Labour's bid for power was trashed by the tabloids ('It was the *Sun* wot won it': Jones 1997). It is also a response to the previous, Tory, regime, whose public relations ineptitude became the stuff of legend. The famous BSE farm crisis was a showcase of these vices. Here the role of rhetoric and symbolism in structuring the crisis was never seriously thought through by the Tory government. It had appeared maladroit, ultimately because it saw BSE as a technical problem, to be ameliorated by a technical solution, and not as a dense and foreboding theatre of symbolism. A crisis designed to be structured around technical communications inadvertently became organised and perpetuated through a series of impulsive rhetorical acts and incompetent symbolic events. The Symbolic State was also a response to the 'new' media of the post-Watergate era, an irreverent, enquiring ethos whose point of commencement is a fixed suspicion of those in power. The Conservative government had appeared to be hounded out of office (partly by the weight of scandals, some which seemed of press manufacture and objectively trivial) by a persecutory media whose demonstrable omnipotence made the evolution of the Symbolic State the only possibility for those aspiring to capture and retain political power.

Moreover, Britain's rulers had come to grasp the apoliticality of the majority. They recognised that much political information is not actively sought out but consumed inadvertently, therefore putting a premium on the creation of a public imagery. People lack time to investigate assertions, or the means to do so. They are dependent on the press.

The Symbolic State may also be a consequence of the demise of partisan, class-based loyalties and the decline of deference, making persuasion the core activity of rulers. Television in particular removes authority's fig leaf of dignity; Mayrowitz (1986) has described how television constantly exposes the 'backstage' of Goffman's dramaturgic model, and that it is inherent in the nature of the medium to do this, so that generations inhabiting a television-arbitered milieu are, quite inevitably, increasingly sceptical of the claims of authority. They therefore need to be persuaded.

No objective reality?

All governments everywhere have always sought to persuade their people at some point. This is axiomatic, otherwise indeed they would cease to govern. Modern conditions may make Symbolic Government the optimal way of running a government (at least until their publics become less credulous). Symbolic Government becomes possible when objective political reality is elusive, or even non-existent. Walter Lippmann, whose political experience spanned much of the twentieth century, stressed that 'the only feeling that anyone can have about an event he does not experience is the feeling aroused by his mental image of that event' (Bennett 1996). We inhabit a media-saturated environment. Baudrillard (1988) elaborates this idea: 'political and social experiences are so media-driven that traditional notions of direct, face to face reality no longer apply'. He uses the term 'hyper-reality' as a reminder that it is this distinct, constructed symbolic world that increasingly provides the raw material for thought and feeling (Baudrillard 1988; Bennett 1996). And, writing in 1994, Schlesinger and Tumber (Moloney 2001) found evidence 'for the existence of an inescapable promotional dynamic that lies at the heart of contemporary political cultures'.

Changing opinions, even those of our ideological adversaries, is always a possibility and therefore a theory of government which places argument at its core is always bound to succeed, for a time. Our principles, ethical and political, are our rules, but rules pitched at a high degree of generality. Individual policy preferences are connected with this rule system, but not tightly; we can always change our opinion in the light of new argument. Levitin and Miller (1979) have demonstrated that there is only a loose relationship between ideology and issue preferences. In choosing, people access multiple beliefs and considerations which may vary in their underlying coherence (Sniderman *et al.* 1991). For most people, most of the time, principles are flexible, therefore always raising the possibility that advocacy may prevail.

Consequences of Symbolic Government

Authoritarianism

When image is so fundamental the degree of control necessary to perpetuate it becomes a central organising principle of the state, an intolerance not of incompetence but of the appearance of incompetence. The level of imagistic control mandated by Symbolic Government can at some point cease to be merely manipulative and become actively autocratic. Britain made that passage: the pursuit of imagery to the exclusion of other social and ethical goals (such as freedom of information or internal party debate) could lead in several regressive directions, even, in times of crisis, to a level of authoritarianism alien to modern Western democracies. For example, during the foot-and-mouth epidemic of 2001 newspaper reports made accusations about the coercive and even illegal exercise of state authority. Officials tried to stop newsmen filming from public roads, blocking cameramen and threatening crews for straying on to DEFRA 'territory' (the name of the Ministry was itself a rebranding of the old, failed Ministry of Agriculture) (*Daily Telegraph*, 3 August 2001). Newsmen were made to strip in public and equipment was ruined by spraying it with disinfectant. Journalists on public roads spoke of being put in the back of police vans. And for much of the crisis farmers seeking reimbursement for disinfecting their farms had to sign the Official Secrets Act. Another example is the treatment meted out to a citizen activist who had been badly burnt: 'senior figures at the Department of Transport sent the secret e-mail to uncover information on the Paddington rail crash survivor Pam Warren in what has been seen as an attempt to discredit her' (*Independent*, 6 June 2002).

Cynicism

Ultimately the obsession with advocacy-driven news management can lead to the wholesale abandonment of ethics by government. An example is afforded by the case of 11 September 2001, when, notoriously, a special adviser to the Minister of Transport, Jo Moore, sent an e-mail within an hour of the attack on the World Trade Center suggesting it would be 'a good day' to bury bad news. The irony is that the news they proposed to 'bury' – a consultation exercise on expenses for councillors – was actually so trivial. For Miss Moore, in the words of one observer, 'instead of managing the news, she was the news'. On another occasion, warming to this theme, the *Sunday Times* made the claim that 'Moore had asked a government press officer to vilify Bob Kiley, the London Transport commissioner advising Ken

Livingstone, the Mayor. The civil servant refused and was shunted off to the virtual Siberia of the foot-and-mouth inquiry' (14 October 2001).

Manipulation and deceit

The Symbolic State can easily become the professionally duplicitous state. The power of government over the press is that of information. The press can dig for it, but that is a cost, and energy is not limitless. It is an inherently adversarial relationship but it is not an equal one – government wishes to conceal, the press wishes to expose – but government ('by turns cringing and bullying': *Guardian*) has more resources, its entire apparatus of governing, to exploit the press's brevity of attention span and thirst for drama/narrative momentum (since a newspaper is, after all, a product to be sold in a market place).

Many commentators, such as the Conservative journalist Michael Gove (see also Jones 1999), chose as an illustration of this duplicity the practice of regurgitating old extra spending announcements as fresh news. 'When Alan Milburn announced . . . that ward sisters would be given £5,000 to improve their patients' environment it was welcomed . . . but six weeks later the Department of Health informed hospital trusts that the policy was to be funded via a cut in their capital allocation' (*The Times*, 4 July 2000). Among numerous instances was the introduction of 'nurse consultancies' – for which, however, no new money was forthcoming – or when the respected *Times Higher Education Supplement* (24 November 2000) claimed that the government had chosen to include the compulsory tuition fees levied on the parents of students (an amount which over three years would reach £1.2 billion) as part of public investment in higher education.

Selling war

Kosovo

Foreign policy, including wars, received the same make-over as domestic policy, and was animated by the same governing idea, that is, the fabrication of the positive, a constant progress towards a utopian end. Newspapers quickly noticed how imagistic considerations now governed the conduct of war as well as peace. Thus the *Sunday Times* (11 July 1999) alleged that in Kosovo Alastair Campbell and forty spin doctors were 'parachuted in' to create a parallel media operation at NATO headquarters, and the British and US governments tried to perform a turn-round on the NATO propaganda apparatus. In particular their fictions included the destruction of an entire Serb brigade, Serb mass desertions, civic unrest and 100,000 missing Albanians (*Sunday Times*, 11 July 1999). Spinners had their serious critics in the liberal press as well. In the *Guardian* (12 July 1999) the journalist Alex Thomson made similar allegations about spin-doctor duplicity, claiming that NATO had 'lied about inaccurate bombing of Pristina and tried to blame the Serbs. It did the same thing concerning one of the tractor convoys.'

Iraq

The wars in Afghanistan and Iraq were fought with US technology and US polemic. Weapons were rhetorical as well as physical: 'Axis of Evil', 'Coalition of the Willing', 'War on Terror' (we now declared war on a noun), and soon even opponents of these wars were beginning to use the official linguistic formulas. One specific British contribution, however, apparently lay in the area of disinformation, and there were frequent press complaints about the effluvia of distortion arising from it. On 22 March 2002 Downing Street briefed that a biological warfare laboratory had been found in Afghanistan, and that Baghdad was supplying Al-Qaeda with weapons of mass destruction. Pentagon denials came too late for lurid newspaper headlines (*Independent*, 31 March 1992). In another case in the same article, the Special Boat Service had intercepted a freighter off the Sussex coast on the suspicion that it was carrying anthrax or bomb materials. In spite of press headlines like 'Armada of terror' and continued claims that a plot had been foiled, only sugar was ever found. A coherent explanatory pattern would make visible the role of British propaganda fictions in the causation of the Iraq war, and the reasons why Britain assumed this role lies in the extent to which the entire ethos of British government has become suborned to the demands of propaganda. The government of George W. Bush was said to be similarly purveying 'cooked' information (Paul Krugman, *New York Times*, 25 October 2002) – not least the bogus claim that Saddam was getting 5,000 tonnes of uranium from Niger (*Guardian*, 30 May 2003).

Even in the political crisis following the end of the Iraq war – a crisis whose essence was the moral and administrative ramifications of the Symbolic State – it remained still impossible to tell whether or not Symbolic Government had met its nemesis.

Other consequences

Symbolic Government has consequences, immediate and long-term. Symbolic Government is in itself an education in Symbolic Government. The longer people are exposed the more they learn about it and the more cynical they may become. The contrast between promise and lived experience becomes vivid, as was indeed the case with the propaganda of the old Soviet Union.

These are not the only potential consequences. The energy – and time – of governments and Ministers are inevitably finite, and today much of them is spent on presentation. *Spin Cycle* by Howard Kurz (1998) explains something, for according to this account Clinton and his team were engaged in permanent firefighting, pursued by their domestic enemies (Whitewater, Gennifer Flowers, Monica Lewinsky). Domestic ephemera, the search for the right imagery and the pernicious hectoring of the media were the main preoccupations of the US government at its highest levels. It did not properly function as a government in the usual sense, the sense in which its citizens would have expected. Was the threat of Al-Qaeda fitfully regarded because of the consuming demands of the public relations battle? It is an idle thought, but not perhaps an irrelevant one.

The failure to solve – or to demonstrate credible progress towards ameliorating – the problems of crime, health care, education and transport, which have a very direct effect on the daily lives and fears of voters, leaves them with an undischarged anger and no alternative, given an inarticulate and demoralised opposition. Professional politicians, and many of their civil servants, inhabit a world where primacy is accorded to language, yet effective polity resides in application as well as conception, and it is in execution that such governments seem weakest – even the Downing Street policy 'Delivery Unit' becoming in the end another expression of Symbolic Government. Language ceases to be a tool to describe the possible, becoming instead a kind of formula via which words self-mutate into events and actions. Symbolic Government confuses intent with execution, and presumes that the ideal can be verbalised into the real. Operational expertise, the translation of an idea into effective practice, derives from a fund of experience and the lessons matured from that experience, yet these are often external to the lives of politicians and bureaucrats, who take refuge in symbols of action rather than the substance of action: 'Then he [Campbell] let it be known to journalists that he had banned calculators in primary schools. Except that he hadn't.'

The British government admitted that it had indulged excessively in spin; it promised that it would disengage and deal frankly with the public. Such an admission strategy is simply that – an Admission Strategy. After all, the ultimate spin is to denounce spin.

'Symbolic Government' is the name not of an operational tool but of an orientation – the core theory of the organisation, its heart and its road map, the residence of its key competences, its way of being. And Symbolic

Government is easier than governing. An idea – such as the Tories' Citizens' Charter initiative or Labour's Individual Learning Accounts – may be inspired and have content, but fail, as these did, through (almost inevitably) inept implementation. Real problems are ignored when government finds it easier to conceive new rhetorical devices than new policies; verbal dexterity is an easier thing to acquire than political imagination; imagistic sophistication sits smugly alongside managerial incompetence, the collective incompetence of Britain's foot-and-mouth crisis, for example, with its £8 billion price tag. Communication appeared to fill the space vacated by ideas and ideology, a world of professional campaigners and amateur statesmen. Nevertheless, in the light of this predilection, Blair's later courting of unpopularity through his support of George W. Bush's Iraq policy and, even more, of higher education fees seems inexplicable and a repudiation of Symbolic Government. There is no easy or simple explanation of how a man so addicted to public goodwill should so perversely endanger it, save the hubris of long habituation to power.

Part IV
Marketing war

8

Nine-eleven and war

By the time of the Afghanistan war the United States had run down its propaganda apparatus yet faced selling the war to a sceptical world. The Taliban dystopia and the cave dwellers of Al-Qaeda seemed quicker off the draw, merchandising to an appalled international community their theatre of nihilism with its unique terrorist video mini-series and its star, Osama bin Laden. His multiple role articulations, saturated with symbolism, sought to terrify, but also to recruit. Thus the United States needed to evangelise war, and created the Office of War Information to lead a global campaign. Something was achieved, but at the ephemeral level, with no sign of recognition of the magnitude of the propaganda task or of the manifest need for deeper forms of cultural engagement.

Selling terror

The visual rhetoric of Osama bin Laden

This chapter argues that the propaganda strategies of Osama bin Laden were not primarily verbal, but based on a surprisingly modern insight into an aspect of the contemporary condition, that is, the response of most of the world's youth to the generation of visual imagery. His notorious video-tapes privilege image over language; they rest on the recognition that the sign symbols that have had most impact are the visual, not the verbal, the moving image, not the printed word. The argument is that Bin Laden uses in particular four techniques to great effect:

1 *The attribution fallacy.* The United States is to blame for all the frustrations experienced by the Islamic people of the Middle East.
2 *Resonance theory.* Those grievances that Arabs hold most deeply, against

which they feel helpless, are made luminous by Bin Laden's broadcasts, which surface all resentments in a graphic way such that they smoulder in the minds of their viewers.

3 *Role playing.* Serial semi-ritualised enactments that elide in the role of warrior-priest.

4 Bin Laden's broadcasts focus on the most venerable of propaganda themes, that of atrocity–revenge, the appeal of which is universal in every culture.

The war against the Taliban/Al-Qaeda was a physical war underwritten by a propaganda war. The United States saw with increasing clarity that it faced a persuasion task that was epic in scale: an international coalition had to be formed and sustained; the government of Pakistan had to be persuaded, since its support was crucial – but not too crudely, lest it be sabotaged by extremists; the Middle East and by extension the Muslim world had to be neutralised, and convinced that this was not the beginning of a war against Islam; Afghans themselves needed to realise that the war was not against them but against the Taliban. Failure in any one of these key persuasion tasks would have negatively affected the conduct of the war. Failure in all of them, though perhaps inconceivable, would have been devastating. There was dawning recognition that what we faced was the most bizarre public relations campaign in human history: the terrorists began to speak, publicly and often. The marketing of terror, whether by the Tamil Tigers, ETA or the IRA, had not really been done before. For no terrorist organisation had ever 'talked' like this or sought an alibi for so spectacular an act of genocide. The terrorist act itself had in the past been its own articulation.

Attribution fallacy

Bin Laden's thesis was that the United States and its surrogates were murderers of the innocent and murderers of the faithful. The Palestinian cause was a comparatively late co-option into the Bin Laden *oeuvre*, but it performed sterling service: his is a curious perversion of the culture of blame, the fallacy of projection-attribution. The United States and the multiple evils he invested it with became an explanation for all the Arabs' collective failures and frustrations, and the simplicity of this thesis, its status as a universal explanation for perplexing phenomena, made it classic propaganda, for it asserted no troubling tax on the intellect. The videos surprised commentators with the technical sophistication of their rhetoric and assumption of their viewers' modern imagistic literacy. Beyond this, serial role enactments by Bin Laden provided the core structuring device for the terrorist miniseries.

In contrast the strategic objective of US communication was to neutralise international Muslim and especially Arab Muslim public opinion (which rarely translated into overt support for Bin Laden). It was an opinion that the events of the second Intafada, by that stage over a year old, had worked up into a frenzy of loathing, of Israel and, by extension, the United States. Al-Jazeera had relayed nightly images of the suffering of the Palestinians, and it seemed that the United States was bereft of Arab friends: 'it would be very hard for an American official to go on Middle East radio or Al-Jazeera to say anything that will not get the opposite response to that which is intended' (Professor Shibley Telhami, *New York Times*, 11 November 2001). Arab opinion was further alienated by the treatment of Iraq, and specifically by the deaths of medically neglected Iraqi children.

Bin Laden as a communications phenomenon is the product of two technological aspects of the late twentieth-century communications revolution, video and satellite, and one entrepreneurial, the establishment of a pan-Arab news medium, a clone of CNN, at the end of the twentieth century. Al-Jazeera was originally a defunct project of the BBC and lays claim to BBC values. After its initial failure, it was subsidised by the Emir of Qatar. Al-Jazeera has proved to be both a product for an eager market and a political revolution. No longer, with supranational media, could Arab governments control the supply of information; such media are market-driven, not government-prescribed, and the United States resented Al-Jazeera, denouncing the alleged bias of its coverage (*Daily Telegraph*, 11 October 2001).

Selling terror

Yet US propaganda was not originally proactive but responsive. Operating under the auspices of a Taliban regime that did not even believe in television, Al-Qaeda generated a series of propaganda video-tapes whose rhetoric of defiance punctuated the conflict at regular intervals. The existence as a conduit of Al-Jazeera made this possible. These tapes (they included training videos and many images pre-dating Nine-eleven) were a rhapsody of hatred of America, some congealing round scenes plagiarised straight from the textbook of classic atrocity propaganda – in particular of the death of the Palestinian boy Muhammed Al-Durra. One target was recruits, another the court of Islamic opinion, another the West.

Propaganda themes of Osama bin Laden

The appeals of Bin Laden propaganda typify the genre rather than take it in new directions. They illuminate a universal-type structure recurrent in its history; the themes of atrocity, revenge, utopia, otherness and enemies, the manichean order, and the uses of the attribution fallacy, fear appeals and manipulation summarise the Bin Laden text. Thus Bin Laden was not an innovator in the content of propaganda despite the originality in methods of delivery: on the contrary he emerges as a refresher of old stylistic clichés, the rhetorical debris of numerous revolutionary movements, agitation organisations and totalitarian regimes.

Fear appeals

There was, of course, Nine-eleven. If terrorism was an extreme form of propaganda, Nine-eleven was the most extreme expression of terrorism ever invented. Bakunin spoke of the 'propaganda of the act', a sentiment with which Bin Laden would certainly agree: 'these young men . . . said in deeds in New York and Washington, speeches that overshadowed all other speeches made everywhere else in the world. These speeches are understood by now by Arabs and non Arabs – even by Chinese' (*The Times*, 14 December 2001). Fear was a central theme in Bin Laden's anti-American strategy. Abu Gaith, his 'finger-jabbing' spokesman, promising atrocities against Britain and a 'storm of planes' against America (*Sunday Times*, 14 October 2001). However, fear appeals in propaganda can (and frequently do) have the reverse effect – not flight, but fight.

Atrocity propaganda

Atrocity propaganda is the most resilient of all propaganda appeals. The Nazis used alleged Polish atrocities against ethnic Germans to justify their invasion of Poland in September 1939. The irony of this atrocity propaganda – it is, after all, the main mobilising device and the emotional core of the Bin Laden case – is that it is presented as essentially ancillary to the extinction of 3,000 civilians, from all nations. The enormity of the crime was followed by the enormity of the lie. An organisation that had just murdered two giant buildings now sought to portray the United States as the international psychopath. If credible, its power is beyond doubt, motivating armies to action and civilian populations to suffer deprivation. Bin Laden narratives are a continuous recitative of atrocities, real and imaginary. The chances, for example, of being sexually violated by Israelis are theoretic, yet here he goes: 'Your sister goes to bed honourable and wakes up violated, raped by Jews.' Bin Laden supplies us with a cacophony of images of pity, rage and terror. This stream of pictures is elaborated by devices such as fast cuts, superimposition and diagonal lines:

> then comes Mohamed Al-Durra. Cue to machine-gun fire. Diagonal lines rend
> the screen to reveal a father's stricken face. 'Mohammed,' intones a deep,
> robotic voice, as the face of Mohamed Al-Durra, mouth open in terror, flashes
> before us. Cut to Israelis bombarding a building on which Osama has super-

imposed the pitiful image of the boy huddling against his father – an image flashed a dozen times during the twenty-minute duration. (Magnet 2001)

Revenge

Revenge has a powerful presence in cultural texts, one that is venerable, the great theme of Jacobean drama (*The Revenger's Tragedy*, *The Duchess of Malfi*), and universal, a permanent item of Hollywood merchandise and of the dramaturgy of most cultures. It is scarcely surprising that Bin Laden should seek to exploit the power of revenge as an emotional appeal.

Bin Laden's rhetoric was, fundamentally, a rhetoric of revenge, of justi-fied punishment for unjustified crime: the 11 September attacks were the return for decades of 'humiliation and disgrace'. He chose themes that would resonate with an international Islamic target audience, and Pales-tine was grafted on to his key concern, the violation of the land of the Prophet. 'I swear to God that America will not live in peace before peace reigns in Palestine, and before all the army of the infidel depart the land of Mohammed, peace be upon him' (*Daily Telegraph*, 9 October 2001). The call is to revenge:

> Bush senior and Colin Powell all appear on the screen. With cowboy timing a watching figure reaches into his robe to grab a gun. He crouches and fires at the screen, in time to a martial rhythm. Smoke obliterates the face of Colin Powell. Cut to Warren Christopher and President Clinton. Boom! Cut to a close-up of Clinton, wearing his habitual self satisfied smile. The gunman's shadow blocks out Clinton's face. Kerpow! (Magnet 2001)

The ultimate call to revenge in almost any culture, the supreme talisman of vengefulness, is a murdered child, and the livid pain of the bereaved par-ents. 'Cut to the boy's lifeless body . . . '

Tony Schwartz's (1973) resonance theory of communication sheds light on why such appeals may work. Schwartz argues that a persuasive text is a co-production, the author merely surfacing emotions and sentiments already present, and using the viewer as work force. Resonance, this smoul-dering in the mind, was what Bin Laden was trying to achieve. To give legit-imacy, coherence and direction to his youthful Islamist targets, he focused on Palestinian woes, on Iraqi children, larded with quotations from the Koran and expressed in felicitous Arabic, and these resonated: 'among Bin Laden's attractions are his simplicity, eloquence and apparent sincerity, and the assumption that he has renounced his wealth for a life of piety' (*Sunday Times*, 14 October 2001).

Purity and contamination

Notions of purity are common in propaganda, and ideas of ideological, racial and imperial purity have been among its themes for the past two centuries. Communism, for example, sought to burnish ideology by a serial creation of enemies who threatened that purity – bourgeois revisionists, Stalin's kulaks. The Nazi pamphlet 'Keep your blood pure' (Herzstein 1978) epitomises this need for the absolutist insistence of some kind of unreasoning perfection.

The video rhetoric of Bin Laden was larded with notions of purity and contamination. In this one regard alone it resembles the rhetoric of Hitler, who created similar metaphors of plagues and so forth. The idea of purity is intimately connected with the concept of utopia, or the perfect society, and this indeed, with increasing zeal, was what the hosts of Al-Qaeda, the Taliban, were trying to bring on earth – the rule, in fact, of the pure.

Fantasy
We err if we treat the Bin Laden videos as conventional arguments or messages. Rather, their imagistic hyperbole is an invitation to world Islamic and specifically Arab opinion to consume a heady narcotic of dominion and the absolute, and in this they merely perpetuate the emotional core of propaganda activity in the twentieth century, from Mussolini's New Rome to Mao's Cultural Revolution or, less illiberally, De Valera's Land of Saints and Scholars.

The other
Recruitment videos denounced Americans and Jews as 'monkeys and pigs', demanding the murder of all 'infidels' (*Sunday Telegraph*, 21 October 2001), and this is made possible by the manufacture of a dehumanised 'other': those killed on 11 September were simply 'the enemy'. The magnitude of their egocentricity – the pain and death of Mohamed Al-Durra are 'real', those of the children in the airliners a statistic – is beyond the self-understanding of the authors of these images.

Manichean universe
There was the establishment of the necessary context of the manichean universe, a world divided between the 'camp of the faithful and the camp of the infidel'. This imagery of a manichean world with its binary oppositions is a common appeal in many polemical forms of persuasion, typically associated, for example, with cults where there is the confrontation of the elect and the condemned, those people outside the cult: Calvinism was a mainstream religious example. That enemy is not only the United States, against which all good Muslims must rise up, but also corrupt Arab regimes, the Koran-cursed hypocrites who 'back the butcher against the victim'.

Power, impact

US commentators began to fear the Bin Laden videos. Bin Laden began to seem a professional in the arts of propaganda. Commenting on his power to deliver almost instant rebuttal of George W. Bush, Frank Rich of the *New York Times* thought that 'through mature presentation, brazen timing and a cunning message, he upstaged the President of the United States on the day he sent American troops into battle'. According to Rich, he may be a cave dweller but, we keep being reminded, he is no caveman (*Guardian*, 15 October 2001). Many feared he was 'winning the propaganda war in the Muslim world' (Anton La Guardia, *Daily Telegraph*, 9 October 2001). The power of the videos in fact resided in convincing Westerners of their power, not in persuading Muslims. Journalists wrote that Bin Laden was 'now the most popular figure throughout the Muslim world' and similar meretricious nonsense. Journalists began to speak of poor exposition of the US case. The US government sought to suppress the Bin Laden videos (*Guardian*, 15 October 2001) so that five major networks all agreed to limit their coverage of Bin Laden's media forays (*Guardian*, 12 October 2001).

What was the real impact on the intended target, Arab public opinion? It is in fact difficult to gauge the real extent of Arab anger. Feroze Zakaria, editor of *Newsweek International* (*Daily Telegraph*, 1 December 2001), even claimed that 'after the first few days, these protests were tiny, often made up of just 1,000 people'. He concluded that 'most Muslims are struggling to combine their faith with modernity and have not given in to fantasists of a medieval Utopia'.

Bin Laden propaganda techniques

Visual rhetoric

These tapes constituted a language of imagery which was instantly recognisable as universal code and therefore transcended the linguistic barriers of the spoken word. According to Julia Magnet (2001), 'Bin Laden has hi-jacked sophisticated techniques for his video: it's as if Guy Ritchie, Stallone and Spielberg have banded together to make Jihad, the movie.' The brief views television audiences were accorded of the tapes made for a prevailing image of naivety. Not so, according to Julia Magnet. Bin Laden's media team have mastered the techniques of the MTV generation. 'Now, in a parody of the American flag, a puzzle of horizontal stripes emerge from each side of the screen, finally connecting to reveal two fighters facing down Warren Christopher. Bang, bang! Whoosh – the images disappear and the screen spins round to reveal . . . Osama bin Laden.' Julia Magnet points out the technique of repetition – images of Israeli brutality appear 'over and over'.

Manipulation

Bin Laden's expositions were hardly concerned with any objective notions of truth, referring for example to America killing Muslims and desecrating holy places for 'eighty years' (*Daily Telegraph*, 9 October 2001). They are, more-over, highly manipulated, since the same incidents are filmed from different angles, thus giving the impression of a moving sequence of atrocities.

The many roles of Osama bin Laden

Julia Magnet (2001) discusses the austerity of his physical performance which enhances an image of power more than elaboration would have done, power, in abeyance, subordinate to the iron will: 'his body language is gentle and controlled: only his right hand moves, and then never further off than six inches from his body. Rarely does he shake his fist, a gesture famil-iar in all propaganda. When he does, it is with weary anger: his cause is so self-evident that he does not need an indignant mime show.'

Cultural theorists have spoken of the dramatic performances of Clint Eastwood as 'the artful withholding of speech rather than the artless inabil-ity to speak' (Kellner 1995), and the same description could be applied here. Much of the impact of Bin Laden's theatre is contained in the characteris-tic Bin Laden facial mask. This otherworldly pose, this pseudo-mysticism, was integral to Bin Laden's dramaturgical synthesis of actor and holy man. Julia Magnet again: 'it is the eyes that grab you: otherworldly, luminous eyes that remind me of Charles Manson. They never meet the camera. It is as if he doesn't see this world – only the spiritual dimension.'.

For the novelist John Le Carré (2002) he is the consummate narcissist: 'his barely containable male vanity, his appetite for self, and his closet pas-sion for the limelight. And just possibly this will be his downfall, seducing him into a final dramatic act of self-destruction, produced, directed, scripted and acted to death by Osama bin Laden himself.' For Le Carré, Bin Laden is a man of 'homo-erotic narcissism'. And an actor: 'posing with the Kalashnikov, attending a wedding or consulting a sacred text, he radiates with every self-regarding gesture an actor's awareness of the lens. He has height, beauty, grace, intelligence and magnetism, all great attributes unless you're the world's hottest fugitive and on the run.'

Bin Laden had a wardrobe of serial roles, semi-ritualised enactments, articulated by stage props. He was, of course pre-eminently Bin Laden the soldier, the guerrilla freedom fighter, 'dressed in green fatigues with the white Muslim headscarf and a rifle propped against a rock behind him – the image of a believer and fighter' (*Daily Telegraph*, 9 October 2001). Then he was the Saracen sheikh, mounted in flowing robes on a white arab steed, the desert prince who would destroy all who threatened his honour and that of his kind. Or he was the scholar, staring at the camera against a rich backdrop of religious texts. Then, another frequent act, he is the holy man, the visionary, wrapped in some private knowing, his spirit soaring to the promise of paradise. Or there is a synthetic role, the holy warrior-priest, 'citing Islamic scripture, his rifle leaning against a rock beside him, every inch the austere holy warrior'. This combination would seem alien to Western eyes today, where soldier and priest appear antithetical functions, but if we reach back far enough in Western history we see unitary instances of it, as for example in the Templar knights, literally fighting priests.

Bin Laden could be regarded as possessing some affinity with the characteristics of the 'feminine rhetorician' conceived by Kathleen Hall Jamieson, who argues that this is the most persuasive style in a television-arbitered communications milieu, contrasted with the older histrionic-declamatory 'masculine' style as practised by for instance Benito Mussolini. Though lacking in her normative characteristics of intimacy and self-disclosure, Bin Laden is certainly the antithesis of declamatory.

Limitations of the tapes

Bin Laden's videos represent the tactical mobilisation of religion and tradition. Many in the West were culturally deaf to their imagery and, of course, ignorant of the power of Bin Laden's spoken Arabic. The complete tapes were viewed only by the Arab audiences of Al-Jazeera . What we saw in the West were effectively edited fragments, condensed images of an enemy posing to taunt us, and then little after the US government had asked for their cessation. Thus the narrative strengths of the videos had been denied us, or any sense of their sophistication.

In summary, there were two targets of persuasion, the international court of Islamic and specifically Arab opinion, and the United States and its allies. For Islamic opinion, the aim was to create an enemy, a dehumanised 'other', and to do so through mobilising the agency of atrocity propaganda and the concomitant emotions of anger and frustration, within the creation of a broader manichean framework of a world polarised between good and evil, the sacred and the contaminated. The United States, the other target, was the subject of fear appeals, there would be more demonstrations of the terrorists' power. The tapes also, it must be remembered, were a form of taunt to embellish the insult to US pride of Nine-eleven. What America saw served to enrage, not intimidate, and led to acceptance of military losses, the fear of which had previously immobilised US power.

The limitations of persuasion? Selling war

On 6 October *The Economist* spoke of 'another sort of war [that] is already under way . . . it is the propaganda war. That word has come to have a derogatory meaning, of the dissemination of untruths. In this case, America's task is (in truth) to disseminate truths, about its motives, about its intentions, about its current and past actions in Israel and Iraq, about its view of Islam.' One month after Nine-eleven and anxieties were beginning to surface about the effectiveness of the US case presentation: 'the propaganda war is in danger of being lost and America knows it. Its planes may control Afghan skies, but on-air supremacy was relinquished' (*Sunday Times*, 14 October 2001).

The United States had an actual communications problem that was external, and a potential communications problem that was internal. The public mood of horror, this sense of a shared universal victimhood, evolved quickly into patriotism, but America's governors could at any point have mismanaged that great swelling of loyalty and lost US confidence. That – after a shaky start – they did not do so is tribute to their propagandist skills, but their failure to similarly impress the larger world is testament to the limitations of those skills. Thus, communication as understood by US leaders in this crisis reflected the world from which they were drawn, that of the political campaign, and the consumerist context they had grown up in. Veterans who ran war rooms of presidential campaigns played a key role, and the lessons learnt in these areas – on anticipation, opinion research, energy of riposte and the production of eloquent visual imagery – defined the character of the US response from then on. The former political consultant John Rendon was brought in as a kind of propaganda subcontractor (Franklin Foer, *New Republic*, 20 May 2002). Within its conceptual limitations this approach worked, delivering a message of the day and targeting such Taliban allegations as downed US Chinooks and US atrocities at Mazar-i-Sharif.

This was a communications approach to win battles and not wars: no strategy, only tactics. The challenge is permanent attitude change in the Moslem world, the recognition that alienation of such magnitude cannot be assuaged by propaganda and marketing as usually conceived. So this becomes a timely case study about the limitations of conventional propaganda, since political initiative now becomes a necessary condition for its effectiveness: policy and propaganda are not conceptually discrete but interwoven. Ideas and initiatives may be communicated well or badly, but without them all we have is empty words. And a more mature idea of propaganda, which elevates it above the sloganeering ethos of campaign political marketing, is to seek cultural engagement, a missionary idiom which aspires to proselytise through classroom and library rather than sound bite and video postcard.

Internal: tactics of the home front – of symbols and myths

The visceral response of US government and people alike to Nine-eleven was to be the tactical mobilisation of culture and tradition, the bedrock of patriot propaganda in any era, the myths and the symbols that evoked the nation's self identity and gave it meaning. When nations are at war such totems are re-endowed with legitimacy and become once again the public currency.

The FBI employed one of its oldest tactics, the traditional Most Wanted list, this time of Al-Qaeda suspects. Bin Laden and his right-hand man headed the bill (*Daily Telegraph*, 11 October 2001). This, and George W. Bush's demand for Bin Laden to be caught 'dead or alive', in the language of the old west, connected the struggle with the honour and simple certitudes of the old frontier. It was a rhetoric as welcome as it was necessary, despite early errors – christening the war Operation Infinite Justice, the reference of George W. Bush to a 'crusade', picked up by Bin Laden in his references to the 'alliance of Jews and Crusaders'. The internal dialogue with the US public was managed in ways that exploited the traditional symbols of the American nation, for example 'this battle is being fought with weapons like $1 bills stuffed into envelopes by American children and mailed to the White House to help Afghan children' (*New York Times*, 14 October 2001). Then there were the resonant public symbols: Bush in flak jacket, Bush addressing the troops, the photographs of the firemen raising the stars and stripes in duplication of Iwo Jima, and the translation of their image into bronze, and into history. There were the humiliation rituals of Camp X-ray.

Private propaganda

Even individual Americans could and often did conduct a private propaganda war, with the core signature, the Stars and Stripes, flying from countless cars or homes and, frequent if not ubiquitous, the super-patriotic T-shirts. Another form of private propaganda lay in the area of caricature, cartoon and assorted iconography: 'it was the first move in an unconscious and subterranean propaganda war: the process of making the architect of the world's worst terrorist atrocity into a comic cult' (*Daily Telegraph*, 22 November 2001). The internet teemed with attempts to belittle Bin Laden via humour, such as the widely circulated Harry Belafonte parody ('Come, Mr Taliban, hand over Bin Laden, air force come and they flatten your home'). There were on-line games and commercial paraphernalia (herobuilders.com). In World War II humour, whether in films like *The Great Dictator* or cartoons like Donald Duck in *Der Fuehrer's Face*, was a defence mechanism, neutralising the threatening individual by placing him within the menagerie of popular media caricatures. The artefacts and images were not all amusing. Plaster statues of New York fireman began to appear, some with an angel at their side.

Symbolism

There was a war to fight, but there were also the dead to be buried. The rituals and symbols of bereavement were a necessary way of adjusting to the scale of the loss, notably the decision of the *New York Times* to publish an obituary for every single one of the Nine-eleven victims (unintended propaganda, but as powerful as it was inevitably prolonged). Such images also constituted a motivation to continue the struggle. In all this mystical and brooding theatre of symbolism, one man stood out as its supreme practitioner. It was not only Mayor Giuliani's ability to find the right language to articulate what lay too deep for tears, it was his comprehension of why ritual and symbol would be of such supreme importance at such a time, why they were not merely desirable but necessary. And so his rigorous attending of the firemen's funerals, his visits to Ground Zero, his constant visibility self-cast as a figure of dynamism and hope, were enough, but he gave more. Ultimately that extra was sensitivity to symbolism of a high order, but also imagination in symbolic conception and elaboration. What better way, for example, to deal with the terrible fact that for many relatives there would be no body to bury than to offer them an urn filled with the dust of Ground Zero?

Censorship

Propaganda is the denial, as well as the provision, of information. It is the antithesis of the objective search for and exposition of truth, as pursued ideally by a scientist, for instance. Propagandists present *a* truth, rather than *the* truth. The facts they espouse are probably not wrong, they are merely the most benevolent retrieved from a *smörgasbörd* of facts. Other data will be ignored, or even actively suppressed – that is, propaganda may be a coercive activity as well as a manipulative one. The imbalance of power between us and our leaders is exploited to the full. This is called censorship. The government argued that 'the shaking of his hands, the use of a particular verse of the Koran, anything in what he says or does could be a sign to someone somewhere that it is time to start a new phase of the attacks on America' (*Guardian*, 12 October 2001). Another aspect of this control was the strict limiting of journalistic access to the military, with none at all for special forces, with the media pushed to produce bland reports and presidential staff parsimonious in their contacts with journalists (*ibid.*). The trick was to tantalise with trivia.

External: tactics to persuade the world

By September 2001 the once great US global propaganda enterprise had shrivelled almost to extinction. The end of the Cold War had created a fresh mood and a new indifference. Radio Free Europe had lost over half its budget (*New York Times*, 11 November 2001). The US Information Agency had been shrunk and melded with the State Department (whose own public diplomacy fund was cut by 40 per cent in the Clinton years). The CIA no longer had 225, but twenty-five, propaganda personnel. In consequence there was no organised system that could swing into action once war was imminent (*ibid.*).

A problem facing any *ad hoc* group created to manage communications was global reaction to the human costs of the war. Civilian casualties would rank highest on the agenda of the United States' international critics, and US command of technology is a double-edged weapon: (1) it can save civilian lives but (2) there exists an imagistic gulf between the aerial armada of US weaponry and all those turbans and rifles straight out of *Lives of a Bengal Lancer* (Paramount, 1935). America, the injured party, had much to fear from the global retailing of the imagery of destruction, since, whatever the strength of the cause, the picture of the richest fighting the poorest nation on earth was inherently difficult to negotiate, and contained always the possibility of losing control of the conflict's meaning and a metamorphosis from righteous revenge to 'David *v*. Goliath', especially with the Taliban's daily enunciated claim that the United States was bombing civilians. It was particularly important to convey the idea that civilian casualties would be minimal – that everything would be done to avoid them. The strengths of smart technology were talked up, though perhaps not as crudely as in the Gulf War with its antiseptic rhetoric of collateral damage. The impression given was that a smart bomb would knock first on the victim's door and introduce itself. This was the promise of a war that would, uniquely, be free of innocent victims, with the offer of a science of killing that would destroy every enemy – even dropping over Afghanistan spy satellite photographs of Mullah Omar's number plate.

The task of this *ersatz* machine of instant manufacture, paralleling the Office of War Information in World War II, was essentially then the conduct of a public argument both with Al-Qaeda and with the United States' less murderous critics via the management of riposte, information and generated imagery. The response, though vigorous, was at the tactical level: 'soon they had set up a round-the-clock war news bureau in Pakistan and a network of war offices linking Washington, London and Islamabad that helped to develop a 'message for the day' (*New York Times*, 11 November 2001). A top advertising executive, Charlotte Beers, whose brands had included

Head 'n' Shoulders and Uncle Ben's, was bought in to the State Department 'to try to make American values as much a brand name as McDonald's hamburgers or Ivory soap', and appointed Under-secretary of State to 'sell the war' (*ibid.*). She:

1 Put Arabic-speaking ambassador Christopher Ross on Al-Jazeera. With offices and an audience of 35 million in the Arab world, it was a powerful force.
2 Placed Colin Powell on Egyptian television.
3 Put an interview with Vice-president Cheney in Britain's populist *Sun* newspaper.
4 Sent a 'catalogue of lies' to Pakistan's newspapers refuting Taliban claims, for example that the United States deliberately bombed civilians.
5 Began addressing groups of exclusively foreign journalists, especially from Muslim countries (*ibid.*).

As in a presidential election campaign, message co-ordination was paramount. The new White House 'war room' acted as message entrepreneur, for example 'that Al-Qaeda has hi-jacked a peaceful religion' (*ibid.*). The US government sought to manage expectations, including getting Americans to accept that many more Americans could die in the struggle (*Daily Telegraph*, 22 November 2001).

And then there was of course the enemy to fight. War is communication, and the techniques used by the United States did of course include the old psy-ops ones – leaflet drops, aerial radio stations. Since military activity is inherently propagandist, some missions were undertaken only for marketing purposes. According to one account, during the Afghan conflict 'every aspect of briefings can be part of the psychological warfare. At one briefing, officers showed night-vision video of an army Ranger raid in Afghanistan, in part to show that Taliban and Mr Bin Laden's terrorist organisation, al-Qaeda, that the US military could land and carry out operations on the ground.'

US long-term global strategy: cultural propaganda?

America's leaders ran the propaganda war like an election campaign, and its conduct illuminates the strengths and limitations of that ethos. It brings into particularly sharp relief the redundancy of political marketing-propaganda approaches when they are tasked with the deeper mission of permanent opinion change. A point-scoring public argument with the Taliban, with charge followed by counter-charge, may have been necessary but could never have been more than a holding operation.

Superficial?

Long-term more, much more, is needed. Even if America recognises this question there must be considerable doubt as to whether it possesses the answer. The international and Arab resentments were dealt with at the level of a PR campaign, but how could this, for example, go any way to combat the impact of the Pakistan madrassas with their 500,000 students? Changing attitudes, and even the values underpinning them, is a long-term proposition. Success or otherwise here would not be achieved by the overt polemicism, or explicit symbol systems that the public more customarily associate with the idea of propaganda. A 'hypodermic' stimulus–response model may be seldom applicable to any communication, since meaning is always negotiated in the semiotic process, but here in particular, where the antagonism is universal even if it is latent and passive, the only strategy worth talking about is a long-term and culturally oriented one.

Hollywood goes to war?

So now some Americans began to think of a deeper and more permanent form of propaganda to influence Middle Eastern opinion. There was talk about, and moves towards, enlisting Hollywood, with its semi-monopoly of global imagery. Why could it not illuminate the best in America rather than continually generate imagery of materialism, sex, violence and degeneracy (*New York Times*, 11 November 2001)? For one commentator, 'it is time for corporations to have a brand manager in charge of America'. Direct approaches were made by the US government to Hollywood. Officials talked 'with writers of big action movies as well as directors of music videos, experts in image manipulation' (*New York Times*, 14 October, 2001). Carl Rove, a senior adviser to George W. Bush, was to visit Hollywood. There were calls on Hollywood to develop movies that conveyed the goodness of Americans, for US corporations to market the values of family and community along with their products on shelves around the world (*ibid.*).

Hollywood may indeed be relevant in the drive for permanent attitude change. For it has always presented a fantasy America– originally one of American possibility, the wish-fulfilment of the émigré founders of Hollywood itself, then later a vision of a vibrantly decadent American dystopia. Neither was, or is, true. But a consistent theme of Hollywood down the years has been integration propaganda (in Ellul's terminology). One way forward would be to direct the same energy of inclusiveness towards Moslems as has been offered to other groups, and in truth this has begun to happen. The snarling, gun-toting Arab terrorists of such productions as *Navy SEALS* (1990) have begun to be replaced by more sophisticated portraits.

Cultural propaganda

The revival of foreign-language broadcasts was another idea, 'recreate the kind of propaganda campaigns that were waged against the Axis powers in World War II and against communism in the Cold War'. One commentator argued, 'it's time to bring back the idea of an Edward R. Murrow in Arabic, modernised of course, using satellites and short-wave' (*New York Times*, 11 November 2001). The projection of a more positive image of the United States gained urgency: news organisations 'should feature reports by Arabs through travel in America that can offer impressions that go beyond the stereotypes of narcissism and self-indulgence' (*ibid.*). There had to be a renewed commitment to ethics in international politics: 'we can't build civil society and democracy in these countries, but we have to stand for it. It has to be part of our flag. We have to be the standard bearer.'

Some ephemeral attempt was made to engage in these new forms of cultural propaganda. The best work of the CIA during the Cold War – its sponsorship of radio stations, or *The God that Failed*, or the great intellectual magazine *Encounter* – were recalled, even with affection (*New Republic*, 20 May 2002). The planned, though never executed, Pentagon Office of Strategic Information was aiming to fund US works in Arabic and more pro-Western English textbooks and Islamic theology courses, as well as computers and alternative curricula to counteract the madrassas. The proposed Arabic-language satellite channel was delayed.

Could it have worked?

Can much be realistically achieved via communication when two such different world views are in collision? Effective communication ties in with values, yet values themselves change only slowly over time. America is the author of the modern, and for traditional societies it is a threat in as much as it is the embodiment of the modern. Beyond this, there is a massive divergence of political and cultural perspectives between the Middle Eastern Moslem and the metropolitan United States. In Bosnia, Kosovo, Kashmir, in Gujarat, at Ayodh, in Chechyna and on the West Bank the Moslem sees everywhere impotence and the defeat of the Islamic cause and seeks a coherent explanation, and a culprit, for this defeat – and all of it against a historical background of a once dominant culture progressively disinherited since its political extinction in Western Europe in 1492. The United States becomes that explanation because a single, unitary, all-embracing explanation is urgently sought.

Yet for much of the Arab world the simple mantras of fixed hostility to the United States are probably a gross oversimplification of their private attitudes. 'Ambivalence' would probably nuance the character of their disquiet more effectively. The cultural totems of Americana are everywhere on display throughout the Middle East, and attitudes to the United States compound acceptance with rejection. This raises at least the possibility that while effective propaganda can never win the Arabs over to America's perspective, it could at least neutralise most of them. To do this, though, would probably be impossible in isolation, but it could work in conjunction with a renewed series of US foreign-policy initiatives, ones founded more completely in multilateralism than in unilateralism.

9

Weapons of mass deception: propaganda, the media and the Iraq war

Within an overall discussion of the formal propaganda efforts of all participants in the Iraq war, this chapter applies a conceptual approach to communications aspects of the conflict, specifically the overlapping roles of
myth, fantasy, rhetoric, deceit, the creation of enemies, and official manipulation. The Iraq war became a theatre of propaganda, and new developments such as the conceit of the 'embedded' journalist (when you wear the
uniform you buy the values) and such technical advances as satellite-
linked phones/cameras created a new kind of war, one synthesised out of
hundreds of video fragments. The conflict was structured by the twin foundation myths of the Weapons of Mass Destruction and the links between
Saddam Hussein and Osama bin Laden. This was a hybrid justification for
war, and in the early stages propaganda sought (against an increasingly
sceptical world) to embroider these justifications. Rhetoric and symbolism
also played a key role in structuring and sustaining the debacle. The creation of Saddam's enmity was critical. Thus significant ideas on propaganda that have been clarified by the war include: the continuing part
played by the rhetoric of enmity, the role of fantasy and willed belief in
propaganda, the significance and completeness of the coherent organis-
ing/ integrating perspective, the on-going role of myth (not least how
much can be fabricated in a conspiracy of false beliefs), the concept of emotional proof, the problem of imagistic control, and propaganda as the
search for retrospective justification. The propaganda war pursued by
the United States and Britain had its limitations, since in war press reaction
can never be controlled, only influenced, and much of what is 'war propaganda' is actually an after-the-fact interpretation/definition of events, or
sustained apologia.

Manipulation: the official propaganda war (1) The world

The British and US governments recognised that the propaganda war would be as critical as the physical war. International public opinion had to be at least neutralised if it could not be persuaded: 'faced with a sceptical audience at home, the government has invested almost as much thought in winning the propaganda war as planning its military operation' (*Daily Telegraph*, 20 March 2003). As a result the propaganda operation was enormous and, in the eyes of some, insidious. The task was much more difficult than in the case of Afghanistan. There the Taliban regime had allowed itself to become the launch pad for the worst attack on the United States since Pearl Harbor. The case for attacking the Taliban and destroying their regime, although not universally accepted, especially in Islamic countries, was relatively easy to defend and did not tax the art of the advocate. America could quite legitimately pose as aggrieved victim and carry forward the moral force of that role.

In Iraq the propagandists faced the supreme challenge to their profession, they had to make America's case effectively and credibly before a world that was at best sceptical, and at worst deeply hostile. The US case was vulnerable on so many fronts. US interests did not face a realistic threat from the Saddam regime; without the backing of the UN Security Council the war was in effect illegal; the United States was acting the bully in an illicit display of superior power; there was no just cause; the United States was indifferent to the loss of civilian life, was ultimately merely motivated by the need to secure its oil supplies, was only looking for an excuse to display its supreme military might in the aftermath of Nine-eleven, was a deviant member of the international community in exhibiting a consistent pattern of unilateral behaviour, was as a result arrogant and selfish and did not understand the ramifications of its actions, it falsely and with no good evidence portrayed Saddam Hussein as a 'godfather of international terror in order to justify its need for an enemy to attack. This, broadly, was the majority view of the United States in some countries, universally perhaps in the Middle East, but it was also the majority view in France and some other European countries, and it was the view of a substantial minority even in the British Isles. Where therefore could propaganda begin? What could it reasonably hope to achieve in the face of such hostility? In the view of one commentator 'one of America's most historic and bipartisan traditions is to do an execrable job explaining itself to the world. The average *Fortune* 500 company is far more sophisticated at getting its message across abroad than the US government has been' (Nicholas D. Kristof, *New York Times*, 8 April 2003).

bipartisan news

A new kind of media war

A vigorous, partisan right-wing media (Fox News) which had scarcely existed in the last Gulf War shaped the public meanings of this war. There were other salient changes. The visualities of war had attained new levels of immediacy and vividness. The public record had never before captured the sense of actually being in a war with such a degree of accuracy before. The new satellite video-telephones, evident first in Afghanistan, came into their own in this conflict, relaying their staccato imagery around the globe. The camera was everywhere, satellite-linked: technological advance had made it possible to connect up highly portable cameras to satellites and instantly relay the images. The pyrotechnics of the first Gulf War with their astonishing rocket-head recordings of attack seemed almost quaint by comparison.

The technology was not merely a passport to vivid news, it was the news. Observed one astonished reporter:

> Fox News broadcast extraordinary live sequences from moving vehicles of American armoured columns racing through the desert, their tracks throwing up clouds of dust. . . . Attacks commanded in real time by commanders hundreds of miles away are broadcast in real time to audiences of millions. . . . Satellite communications have become portable, allowing journalists to broadcast from anywhere as the troops advance through the Iraqi desert. (*Daily Telegraph*, 22 March 2003)

In the *Sunday Times* (23 March 2003) Sarah Baxter described the images as an army public relations dream, 'they showed live pictures of the American Seventh Cavalry barrelling towards Baghdad past the hulks of Iraqi tanks from former wars . . . It was the first time in the history of warfare that a wife could watch her husband invading a country thousands of miles away.'

 The major evolution was a US propaganda concept, that of the 'embedded' journalist. This was, of course, a high-risk strategy. It could have easily backfired. The senior command of the US military remembered well the adversarial role assumed by journalists in the Vietnam War. This one was to be very different. The concept of the embedded journalist presented, of course, many potential problems – the journalists might, for example, witness vicious behaviour by the troops and, what proved to be a real problem, the world's public were inundated with scraps of detailed parochial information from 500 (estimates vary) embedded journalists, including Arab ones, which served merely to heighten the general confusion and obscure any overall pattern. Nevertheless, the embedded journalist was probably a successful propaganda sleight-of-hand. Since the embedded reporter by definition shares the hardship of the troops and lives through their emotions alongside them, the bias will inevitably be towards the military. Many British television journalists wore elements of combat gear and one, the ITV journalist Bill Neely, was dressed entirely as a British soldier. It is a small step from wearing the corporation's uniform to adopting its values. According to Martin Bell:

> one peril of embedding journalists is that they will accept the campaign's vocabulary and agenda. The idea of embedding journalists is new. Such journalists, although not required to wear uniform, are in many respects auxiliaries of the units to which they are attached. They work under censorship, including self-censorship, as to broadcast sensitive information might expose them and coalition forces to Iraqi fire. (*Daily Telegraph*, 24 March 2003)

Bell pointed out how in the first Gulf War censorship was tighter and images were broadcast three or four days late. Moreover, again a propaganda triumph for the Americans, embedded journalists were obliged to pool their material for readers of other newspapers and other viewers, they could not travel independently, and interviews had to be on the record. Rampton and Stauber (2003) remind us that the Pentagon also 'offered combatants as journalists, with its own film crew, called Combat Camera. The dramatic rescue of Jessica Lynch was a Combat Camera exclusive.'

So this was a new kind of media war. Some commentators did in fact argue that the embedded reporters had been an error. Argued one:

> we drink thirstily from the Baghdad trickle and then turn round to be drowned by the coalition flood. The key problem is the embeds. They are all over southern Iraq like a cheap suit and they're all babbling excitedly, reacting, understandably, to every shot that is fired and every rumour that flashes around the battlefield. 'They're reporting every fight as if it's a major incident, every pinprick as if it's a mortal wound,' said a media manager at Centcom. The result is a deluge of reportage that simply cannot be assessed; it might be crucial, it might be trivial, who knows? . . . The reality is that it's harming the coalition by generating confusion, uncertainty and even depression. . . . The embeds are certainly tightly controlled, but the effect of their reports has been a massive loss of control for the military. The sheer volume of their reportage has swamped the media and repeatedly wrongfooted the generals. (Brian Appleyard, *Sunday Times*, 30 March 2003)

Qatar theatre

George Allison was commissioned to build a $200,000 stage set for the headquarters in Qatar. Allison was a leading Hollywood art director who had worked with the illusionist David Blain (*The Times*, 11 March 2003). According to *The Times*:

> gone are the easel and chart, solitary television and VCR machine with which General Norman Schwartzkopf showed fuzzy images of smart bomb raids during the 1991 Gulf War. On a set that will become instantly recognisable,

generals will present updates from two podiums at the front of the stage adorned with 50 inch plasma . . . screens and two 70 inch television projection screens ready to show maps, graphics and videos of action. Behind them will be a soft-focus elongated map of the world, as if to suggest that the world is united behind them.

The Times commented on the propaganda value of a stage set at the symbolic level: 'besides looking good on television the presentation conveys another message – that American technology is second to none and far outclasses anything possessed by the Iraqis, who will be watching the briefings on the Arab broadcaster Al-Jazeera . . . The technology gulf will be part of a psychological campaign abetted by the media . . .' And, commented Rory McCarthy in the *Guardian* (26 March 2003), 'a large US Central Command seal above the central podium delivers an unequivocal message of authority: an eagle sits on a Stars and Stripes shield with its wings outstretched to envelop a map of the Middle East and Arab world'.

Briefings

The briefings themselves were an important part of the propaganda campaign, with the black one-star general Vincent Brooks as a principal spokesman. Some observers were highly cynical: 'the messages are rigidly controlled. The media handlers in Qatar are in constant contact with Campbell, White House strategists and Victoria Clark, the press chief at the Pentagon. Every morning they agree what information will be put out in London' (Tim Shipman, *Spectator*, 29 March 2003). This same journalist complained of the deference of many correspondents: 'the Americans have hardly helped for calls of openness by asking supine questions that would have shamed even the 1950s BBC. It is not unusual to hear something along the lines of "Would the general like to tell us something about how vile the enemy are today?"' He suggested that the coalition was putting pressure on recalcitrant journalists. Commented Rory McCarthy:

> The front row of the briefing hall at the Central Command headquarters in the deserts of Qatar is largely reserved for the American television networks but frequently the toughest questioning has come from those further back . . . the milder style favoured by some of the US correspondents is reflected in a question posed by a presenter with the American network CBS, who asked at General Frank's first briefing on Saturday, 'The campaign so far has gone with breathtaking speed. Has it surprised you, or is it going more less as you expected?' (*Guardian*, 26 March 2003)

For one American journalist, Michael Wolfe:

Qatar

this whole thing (not just the news conference, but in some sense, the entire war) is a phoney set-up, a fabrication in which just about everything is in service to some unseen purpose and agendas. . . . What is most surprising about this to me is not so much that there are a lot of people who would mistake a news conference for an actual, transparent, official giving of information, but that the Pentagon would be media-savvy enough to understand this. (*Guardian*, 14 April 2003)

Rush Limbaugh gave out Wolfe's e-mail address: 'almost immediately, 3,000 e-mails, full of righteous fury, started to come'.

Manipulation: the official propaganda war (2)
Wooing the Arab world

The briefings were not politically deaf to the interests of the Arab world. They were translated simultaneously into Arabic, and Al-Jazeera was assigned a front row at the briefings. Arab-speaking diplomats were imported from the State Department to 'spin Arabs in their own language', and General Brooks was coached in Arab pronunciation. More generally 'Mr Bush hounds Cabinet members to give interviews to Al-Jazeera television, a new White House office flatters foreign reporters by spinning them, and the US began Radio Sawa to seduce Iraqis and other Arabs with sirens like Jennifer Lopez. The brilliant system of embedding journalists in US military units includes Arab journalists' (*New York Times*, 8 April 2003). Much was done under the auspices of the Office of Global Communications at the White House, which had been established during the Afghanistan war.

The coalition propaganda effort could look forced: 'the US effort to manufacture a huge global coalition involved an embarrassing effort to recruit micro-dots in the Pacific, and the White House proudly put out a list of supporting countries that included the Solomon Islands. When reporters asked the Solomon Islands Prime Minister about the support, he said he was "completely unaware" of that' (*New York Times*, 8 April 2003). Britain's Ministry of Defence boosted the effort by sending 160 media specialists to the Gulf, their message co-ordinated by Alastair Campbell (*Sunday Times*, 23 March 2003). By the beginning of the war the United States had already set up Radio Sawa, a populist radio station targeted at the Middle Eastern audience which aroused deep suspicion in the minds of Arab commentators: 'it seeks to brainwash and instil American ideas in the minds of the rising generation'. Congress had given $35 million to fund the station for 2002. The aim here was propaganda as entertainment, with the ideology and even US bias completely invisible. Radio Sawa is popular, 'the favourite station of more than 50 per cent of listeners in its target audience' (*The Times*, 15 November 2002).

The Iraqi people as target

We must first observe that the targets of coalition propaganda were diverse and required different persuasion strategies to achieve different objectives. One very important target was the Iraqis themselves, the Iraqi people in general, and the Iraqi military in particular. Ideally the United States wished the people to rise up and destroy their leaders, but this proved to be a chimera. It also wanted them to welcome the US troops euphorically and to tolerate a US army of occupation. The methods the United States used were the traditional ones of psy-ops – leaflets and radio broadcasts – for this particular target market. By late February more than 8 million messages had been dropped over Iraq (*New York Times*, 24 February 2003). The leaflets were aimed at troops but leaflets were also disseminated among ordinary Iraqis assuring them that the war was not a war of conquest and that Iraq would be run by and for the Iraqi people. Sixty thousand of these Blair-British texts were printed daily. 'There was an echo of New Labour propaganda in the leaflet when Mr Blair promised that a new representative Iraqi government would develop public services and spend Iraq's wealth not on palaces and weapons of mass destruction, but on schools and hospitals' (*Daily Telegraph*, 5 April 2003).

Radio was a particularly powerful instrument with such civilians. At this level the United States was using cultural propaganda, broadcasting in Arabic 'with programmes that mimic the programme styles of local radio stations and are more sophisticated than the clumsy preaching of previous wartime propaganda efforts. . . . Senior military officials say, for example, that the US radio shows broadcast from the EC-130 Commando Solo planes followed the format of a popular Iraqi station, Voice of the Youth, managed by President Hussein's elder son, Uday. The US programmes open with greetings in Arabic, followed by Euro-pop and 1980s US rock music intended to appeal to younger Iraqi troops, perceived by officials as the ones most likely to lay down their arms. The broadcasts include traditional Iraqi folk music, so as not to alienate other listeners, and a news programme in Arabic prepared by army psychological operations experts at Fort Bragg in North Carolina. Then comes the official message. 'Any war is not against the Iraqi people, it is to disarm Mr Hussein and end his government' (*New York Times*, 14 February 2003). Some argued that a major lesson learned in Afghanistan was the importance of explaining our presence there.

The Iraqi military

If the broadcasts to civilians carried a general message of friendship, the aural and literary message to Iraqi soldiers was more specific. One aim was, of course, to get them to desert so that no fighting would be necessary. Or to surrender. If propaganda really can achieve the goal of an evaporating enemy then it must rank as one of the most potent resources of the modern battlefield, raising also the possibility of a war whose casualties were light even among those who dared oppose the super-power. Clearly elements of the US leadership imagined that they could really stroll through Iraq and the entire opposition would melt away. Part of the aim of these communications, which also used television, was to stress that anyone who defended the Hussein regime would be brutally attacked and any war criminal would be put on trial. This process included, remarkably, direct attempts to communicate with commanders of Iraqi combat formations by military high-frequency radio, as well as attempts to reach the Iraqi military via their mobile phones (*Sunday Telegraph*, 29 March 2003). According to the *New York Times* (24 February 2003) 'American cyber-warfare experts recently waged an e-mail assault, directed at Iraq's political, military and economic leadership, urging them to break with Saddam Hussein's government. A wave of calls has gone to the private cellphone numbers of specially selected officials inside Iraq, according to leaders at the Pentagon and in the regional Central Command.' Missile operators were warned.

The military effectiveness of propaganda

US officers apparently had great faith in these methods. In the words of General Michael Moseley (*New York Times*, 24 February 2003) 'it pays to drop the leaflets. It sends a direct message to the operator on the gun. It sends a direct message to the chain of command.' Other military leaders claimed that propaganda had been integrated into military planning in ways never seen before – although they did not, of course, call it propaganda. In the words of General Paul Lebras, 'What we're seeing now is the weaving of economic warfare, psy-ops and other information warfare through every facet of the plan from preparation through execution.' The *New York Times* pointed out this truth (24 February 2003), that 'there are many ways to disable an enemy's operations'. Anti-aircraft radar, for example, can be destroyed from the air or captured on the ground but 'the enemy soldiers running the radar can be convinced to shut down the system and just go home'. The US military had within it a joint information operations centre based in Texas, and personnel from this joined the Central Command info-warfare team.

There was a final clever trick. When the war finished, the hunt began. After all, there was no formal surrender as on Luneberg Heath in 1945. The former Baghdad regime simply disappeared. It was at this point that the coalition created what must rank as one of the more vivid tactical moves in the whole history of propaganda, that is to say, to publish images of the fifty senior leaders of the regime as a pack of playing cards, divided according to their significance as spades, hearts, clubs and ace of diamonds (and already a collectors' item).

Rhetorical aspects of the war

Colonel Collins

'Shock and Awe' – these words alone remind us (and they were the brand name for the opening of the campaign) that the Iraq war was an exercise in rhetoric as well as myth making. All sides used rhetoric, the aim being to guide and bias perception. There is perhaps a distinction between rhetoric and eloquence, eloquence being its more elevated form.

Colonel Tim Collins of the Royal Irish Regiment achieved fame not in battle, the eminence of this military man rests on rhetorical skills alone: he apparently 'moved his men to tears' (*Daily Mirror*, 20 March 2003). In fact Colonel Collins's speech was a masterpiece of studied ambivalence, and it could be interpreted as meaning almost anything. The *Mirror*'s headline was 'Show respect', and quoted:

> If you are ferocious in battle remember to be magnanimous in victory. If someone surrenders ensure that one day they will go home to their family. We go to liberate, not to conquer. You will have to go a long way to find a more decent, generous people than the Iraqis. Show respect for them. Their children will be poor but in years to come they will know that the light of liberation was brought by you. Our business now is north.

For the *Sun* (20 March 2003), however, interpretation was rather different, under the heading 'Brit colonel's storming battle-cry' 'show them no pity . . . they have stains on their souls'. And here the colonel apparently became vengeful:

> The enemy should be in no doubt that we are his nemesis and we are bringing about his rightful destruction. There are many regional commanders who have stains on their souls and they are stoking the fires of hell for Saddam. He and his forces will be destroyed by this coalition for what they have done. As they die they will know their deeds have bought them to this place. Show them no pity.

Other parts of the speech can be regarded as studied masterpieces of political correctness and multicultural sensitivity: 'Iraq is steeped in history.

It is the site of the Garden of Eden, of the great Flood and the birthplace of Abraham. Tread lightly there. You will see things that no man could pay to see. . . . You will be embarrassed by their hospitality, even though they have nothing.' The colonel stressed that his men and the enemy shared a common humanity: 'if there are casualties of war, remember, when they woke up and got dressed in the morning they did not plan to die this day. Allow them dignity in death. Bury them properly and mark their graves.' There is an important rationale behind this kind of eloquence, for the men who fight, in the familial circumstances of a regiment whose comrades they have come to regard as brothers, the temptation to be ruthless to an enemy and kill gratuitously is present. In this sense, eloquence is a way of internalising discipline. Colonel Collins again:

> It is a big step to take another human life. It is not to be done lightly. I know of men who have taken life needlessly in other conflicts. I can assure you they will live with the mark of Cain upon them. If someone surrenders to you, remember they have that right in international law. The ones who wish to fight, well, we aim to please. If you harm the regiment or its history by over-enthusiasm in killing or cowardice, know it is your family who will suffer. You will be shunned unless your conduct is of the highest, for your deeds will follow you down through history. We will bring shame on neither our uniform or our nation.

Colonel Collins was far from being the only rhetorician of the Gulf war, his speech was not the only piece of striking rhetoric. Another voice of eloquence was that of eighty-five-year-old Senator Robert Byrd: 'I weep for my country. No more is the image of America one of the strong yet benevolent peace keeper. Around the globe our friends mistrust us, our word is disputed, our intentions are questioned, we flaunt our superpower status with arrogance' (speech delivered on the floor of the US Senate, 19 March 2003, www.commondreams.org). There was something of the Roman about Senator Byrd.

Coalition rhetoric

In contrast, the soundbites of the coalition were banal, even counterproductive. According to the *New York Times* (8 April 2003), 'US briefings, from Mr Bush on down, were always on plan, and our coalitions are always the largest in history.' The hyperbole of the coalition was a feature which irritated many commentators, but nevertheless it is an important facet of propaganda, starting with the 'Axis of Evil'. All Iraqi paramilitaries were to be 'death squads'. The war was a serial branding exercise. From 'Shock and Awe' to 'Coalition of the Willing', 'regime change', 'weapons of mass destruction' the entire exercise was punctuated with pithy and duplicitous phrases which were inserted into the public consciousness, bred and multiplied in it, so that the public space swarmed with them. In the end the events could not be read in any other way but through the language our theatrical directors had created for us. For effective rhetoric constitutes a way of seeing which crowds out other possible ways of seeing. This was the great insight of our spin doctors. And if circumstances change so could the rhetoric, hence the mutation into 'weapons of mass destruction-related programmes'.

Then, of course, there was the military jargon, itself an important part of the rhetorical war: targets were 'serviced', bombing became 'kinetic warfare', commanders could discourse on 'effects-based warfare'. Such pseudo-technical jargon, about as far away from the concept of eloquence as one can possibly get, is still as important as the burning metaphors of formal rhetoric. For what it does is effectively turn war into a technical process rather than a human catastrophe, and the jargon is usually successful at deafening us to the cries of suffering humanity. Eloquence, therefore, the glory of the English language as captured in Colonel Collins's heroic prose, is only one facet of the rhetoric of effective persuasion. Deracinated language and the language of the technical manual or bureaucratic process, or the witless argot of everyday speech, can do equal service as rhetorical performer.

Deracinated language can naturalise and neutralise the exceptional and the perverse in the colours of the everyday. Radio Sawa was rather good at doing this. Thus *The Times* (15 November 2002) contrasted reports on Radio Sawa and Radio Damascus. Radio Sawa described the death of a Palestinian thus: 'Palestinian is killed by Israeli gunfire in Nablus.' Radio Damascus: 'Despite the curfew imposed by the Israeli occupation army on Nablus for more than 100 days, tension prevailed today over the area of Nablus where a Palestinian youth, aged 15 years, was martyred and five others were wounded in various confrontations between Palestinian civilians and the occupation army'. An Iraqi diplomatic offensive was described thus by Radio Sawa: 'sources said Iraq was probably asking that Gulf States not allow the US to use their military installations as launching points for the attacks on Iraq.' Radio Damascus: 'diplomatic and political efforts continue against the US's insistence on aggression against Iraq. Iraqi Foreign Minister, Naji Sabri, said the US stood as a dangerous threat to the future of the region.' Language also performs the happy duty of obscurantism, as in 'Rumspeak':

> There are no known knowns; there are things we know we know. We also know there are known unknowns; that is to say, we know there are some things we do not know. But there are also unknown unknowns – the ones we don't know we don't know. And if one looks throughout the history of our country and other free countries, it is the latter category that tend to be the difficult ones. (*The Economist*, 6 December 2003)

Deceit and duplicity

Fabrication

Both in the run-up to the war and during the war itself there were increasingly voluble accusations that the British and US governments were fabricating evidence that favoured conflict with Saddam Hussein. There were
the charges that Bush himself was loose with the facts. The *Wall Street Journal* claimed in October 2002 that 'senior officials constantly make reference
to intelligence that could be neither proved or disproved. Both a senior
former CIA official and *USA Today* accuse the government of using biased
information' (quoted by Paul Krugman, *New York Times*, 25 October 2002).
This sleight-of-hand became visible when it was revealed that 10 Downing
Street had borrowed large parts of an old PhD thesis without acknowledge-
ment to help create a public dossier on Saddam Hussein. This work 'related
to events around the time of the Gulf War in 1991, but was presented by
the British government as up-to-date. The dossier also plagiarised from
Jane's Intelligence Review' (*Daily Telegraph*, 8 February 2003). Colin Powell
praised this dossier in his presentation to the UN Security Council on 5 February 2003. Such was the extent of the plagiarism that not even gram-
matical errors were corrected.

The document was not simply plagiarised, it was also altered (*Sunday
Times*, 9 February 2003). For example, the phrase 'helping opposition
groups' was changed to 'supporting terrorist organisations' and 'monitor-
ing foreign embassies' became 'spying on foreign embassies'. On 27 April
2003 the *Independent on Sunday* carried the headline 'Revealed: how the
road to war was paved with lies'. It claimed that there was no evidence of
chemical, biological, nuclear or banned missile activity by Baghdad:

> the case for invading Iraq to remove its weapons of mass destruction was
> based on selective use of intelligence, exaggeration of sources named. A CIA
> report on the likelihood that Saddam would use weapons of mass destruction
> was partially declassified. The parts released were those which made it appear
> that the danger was high; only after pressure from Senator Bob Graham, the
> head of the Senate Intelligence Committee, was the whole report declassified,
> including a conclusion that the chance of Iraq using chemical weapons were
> very low for the foreseeable future. On biological weapons, the Secretary of
> State, Colin Powell, told the UN Security Council in February that the former
> regime had up to eighteen mobile laboratories. He attributed the information
> to defectors from Iraq, without saying that their claims – including one about
> a secret biological laboratory beneath the Saddam Hussein Hospital in central
> Baghdad – had repeatedly been disproved by UN weapons inspectors.

The article also pointed out that a report released in autumn 2002 by Tony
Blair claimed that Iraq could deploy chemical and biological weapons

within forty-five minutes, but that Defence Secretary Geoff Hoon said that such weapons might have escaped detection because they had been dismantled and buried. The article concluded, 'Some American officials have all but conceded that the weapons of mass destruction campaign was simply a means to an end – a "global show of American power and democracy," as ABC News in the US put it. "We were not lying," it was told by one official, "but it was just a matter of emphasis."' Perhaps this is the definition of propaganda. In the end, the war's truths and its illusions – such as the packaged miniature epic 'Saving Private Jessica' – were hopelessly intermingled.

The creation of enemies

If public opinion was to support a war with Iraq, it was essential for the Anglo-American alliance to utterly demonise Saddam and his regime. Really Saddam made the perfect enemy, he was a stage villain ordained by central casting, complete with heavy moustache and fedora. The most important part of the construction of Saddam's Enmity was of course the notion that he was a direct threat to the safety of the West through both his alleged weapons of mass destruction and his alleged close link with Osama bin Laden. If this magnitude of threat was to be credible, Saddam had also to be made into a truly evil man capable of anything. We had to learn to hate Saddam, and this was not difficult. So in the prologue to the war the British Foreign Office drew up a twenty-three-page report (*Daily Telegraph*, 3 December 2002) which dwelt laboriously on the various medieval processes of torture employed by Saddam's executioners – the gouged eyes, hands pierced with electric drills, suspension from the ceiling, acid baths, sexual abuse, electric shocks, etc; son Uday maintained a private torture chamber; one militia man functions as a professional rapist; prisoners are kept in rows of steel boxes as found in mortuaries until they confess or die. And there is the amputation of the tongue as penalty for insulting the President (as mentioned by George W. Bush). The briefing where journalists were presented with this report by the Foreign Office also included a video show depicting the beating and execution of prisoners and the famous scenes after the gas attack on Kurdish villages (*Daily Telegraph*, 3 December 2002). This theme of a murderously evil regime was continued into the war itself.

Throughout the war expectations of the immediate discovery of weapons of mass destruction were constantly stimulated. The press built up the image of 'Chemical Ali' and his female Mini-me, christened of course 'Chemical Sally'; expectations of a chemical attack were genuine. The evidence in support of this contention, the discovery of protective clothing for Iraqi troops, was tenuous, yet reports claimed that 'US and British forces have found mounting evidence of a potential chemical or biological attack' or that the 'CIA's intelligence reports reveal that dozens of artillery shells tipped with poisonous Sarin, VX nerve agent or mustard gas have already been deployed. They have gone to troops in the Medina Division of the Republican Guard currently dug in South Baghdad' (*Sun*, 29 March 2003).

There were many other allegations of Iraqi brutality which were the extrinsic manifestation of an evil regime. Saddam's militia deliberately situated themselves next to civilian homes, defence installations stood in the suburbs; Iraqi troops advanced under a white flag, then fired; Iraqi troops deliberately fired on fleeing civilians. While there was some truth in these allegations, it was critically important for the coalition to create atrocity propaganda as a justification for war and as the ultimate manifestation, in atrocious acts, of Saddam's evil. And if atrocities could not be found they could always be fabricated. When Tony Blair appeared with George W. Bush at a news conference at Camp David he claimed that two British soldiers had been executed after their capture by the Iraqis. The evidence was that their bodies were lying next to their upturned Land Rover rather than inside it. Blair condemned 'the release of those pictures of executed British soldiers' by Al-Jazeera as an 'act of cruelty beyond comprehension'. The family of one of the dead protested, saying that the army had told them the soldier had died in combat (*Daily Telegraph*, 29 March 2003).

Myths of the war

Two foundation myths

We have argued that the confectionery of myth is the fundamental attribute of the activity of the propagandist. The Iraq war was constructed on two foundation myths. The first was that Saddam Hussein was concealing an arsenal of weapons of mass destruction, chemical, nuclear and biological. The danger was that he would use them, perhaps on the other Arab states, perhaps on Israel, perhaps, as he had before, on the hapless Kurds. The second foundation myth, that of the linkage between Saddam Hussein and Osama bin Laden, was intimately connected with the first. For if Saddam possessed weapons of mass destruction and had created a relationship with Bin Laden, it followed that Bin Laden had access to weapons of mass destruction: a suicide bomber, and a dirty bomb? The idea was dreadful. But was it true? It seemed to many all along that both ideas really were myths, myths in the vernacular sense of being untrue. Yet to admit to the untruth of these myths publicly would have destroyed the very moral foundation of the Anglo-American invasion, and so, after the conclusion of war, the Prime Minister was continuing to assert his increasingly laboured faith in the inevitability of their discovery.

The concept of emotional proof

Did the coalition leaders really believe in their own myths? This is not an easy question to answer, and at one level they surely did. The question is perhaps better put in a different way: not 'Did they fully believe in the myths?' but 'Did they believe in them sufficiently to be motivated to carry out an invasion of a nation of 25 million people with all the uncertainties and insecurities involved?' Perhaps the answer to this question may lie also in the concept of emotional proof, which is not the same as rational proof. *Emotional proof is where we feel intuitively that there is a causal connection which is highly significant to the creation of some event and yet which cannot easily be pinned down, but where we also believe this thing to be true because we have a deep emotional need for it to be true.* It is possible that this explains the peculiar determination of George W. Bush to exorcise the demon of Saddam Hussein. And in one sense he was right. The dominant, even the exclusive motive of Osama bin Laden was the presence of US troops on the soil of the land of the two holy cities, Mecca and Medina, and the contamination ascribed to it. Those soldiers were there to contain Saddam Hussein. Therefore Saddam Hussein was indeed an indirect cause of Nine-eleven. So remove Osama's *raison d'être* by removing Saddam. Indeed, Donald Rumsfeld announced the future withdrawal of US troops from Saudi immediately the Iraq war was finished. This is emotional proof rather than logical proof; the invasion of Kuwait put in motion the sequence of events which led to Nine-eleven. Saddam Hussein was not responsible for Nine-eleven in deductive logic, and yet, in emotional proof, he was.

Other Gulf War myths

There were two foundation myths to the Iraq war, therefore, but numerous other myths emerged to support the super-myths. One was that this war would fulfil the promise implicit in the first Gulf War, that war could be clean, that strikes could be surgical, that one could fight an antiseptic war without dead civilians. While the accuracy of modern electronically guided weapons is truly remarkable, the idea of deathless war must rank as one of those delightful myths by which democracies so often beguile themselves, a winsome conceit to deaden the pain of reality. Other support myths included the idea that the Iraqi people would rise up and destroy their rulers themselves, something in fact they were too afraid to do, and that they would warmly welcome their liberators – at best a half-truth, because of the ambivalence most Iraqis felt towards the United States. The war was also conducted with large helpings of disinformation, such as the rumours that Saddam had been killed (*Sunday Telegraph*, 23 March 2000: it claimed the CIA believed there was a fifty–fifty chance that Saddam was dead).

Foundation myths (1) Saddam–Bin Laden alliance

The alleged link with Bin Laden was also significant to the coalition, although they were sufficiently shameless to manufacture other causes of war when the lead justifications were disproved. The evil that Saddam had done could always be conveniently polished as an alternative justification, one which was in fact increasingly advocated, so that towards the end the war was becoming merely one of liberation of an Arab people from a great evil rather than the protection of ourselves from that same evil. Before the war much effort had gone in to proving that link with Bin Laden, Dick Cheney claiming that Iraq had trained Al-Qaeda fighters: 'That's why confronting the threat imposed by Iraq is not a distraction from the war on terror, it is absolutely crucial to winning the war on terror. The war on terror will not be won until Iraq is completely and verifiably deprived of weapons of mass destruction' (*Daily Telegraph*, 3 December 2002). The *Sunday Telegraph* (27 April) was announcing as its banner headline 'World exclusive: the proof that Saddam worked with Bin Laden'. The paper claimed it had discovered intelligence documents in Baghdad proving a direct link, and that one Western intelligence official described this as 'sensational'. Another headline claimed 'Bush always suspected Saddam was behind Nine-eleven'. The trouble with this is that any link can be proved between any regime in the world and there always exists transmission of information at some level. The real question is 'What is the significance of this?' On what point of the scale would Saddam be implicated? The UK tabloid press was also insistent, claiming proof of links with Al-Qaeda terrorists (*Sun*, 6 April 2003), and dutifully reiterating the point made by Colin Powell in his UN speech.

Maureen Dowd claimed in the *New York Times* (9 March 2003) that George Bush had cited Nine-eleven eight times in a news conference, and she quoted William Ryder: 'As a bogus rallying cry, Remember Nine Eleven ranks with Remember the Maine of 1898 for war with Spain or the Gulf of Tonkin resolution of 1964.' Ms Dowd added, 'a culture more besotted with inane reality TV than scary reality is easily misled'. Dowd pointed out that in a *Times*-CBS News survey, 42 per cent believed Saddam was personally responsible for the attack on the World Trade Center and the Pentagon, and in an ABC News poll 55 per cent believe he gave direct support to

Bin Laden: 'the case for war has been incoherent due to the overlapping reasons conservatives want to get rid of Saddam'.

Foundation myths (2) Weapons of mass destruction

The other foundation myth, that of weapons of mass destruction, received formal endorsement in a dossier presented to the British Cabinet Office's Joint Intelligence Committee published on 24 September 2002. Tony Blair argued that there was 'as clear evidence as you can get that he is continuing with his weapons programme and the threat is real, serious and continues' (*Guardian*, 24 September 2002). Blair added that Hussein 'will launch an external attack on his neighbours'. In February 2003 a Sky TV poll revealed that many Britons had now become convinced of the truth of this, with 79 per cent convinced Saddam possessed weapons of mass destruction and only 21 per cent doubtful (*Sun*, 6 February 2003). The myth of the weapons of mass destruction was in fact the principal justification for war. In the words of Paul Wolfowitz, 'President Bush's determination to use force if necessary is because of the threat posed by Iraq's weapons of mass destruction' (*Daily Telegraph*, 3 December 2002). British public opinion came quickly to believe that it had been manipulated into fighting the Iraq war (ICM poll results, 24 August 2003). Blair's claim that Iraq could launch weapons of mass destruction in forty-five minutes looked increasingly risible. Had No. 10 spin doctors really 'sexed up' the now infamous dossier? Had their bullying driven principal biological weapons expert Dr David Kelly to commit suicide? (It was also posthumous bullying – 'Walter Mitty' and so forth). For Blair's government, lost in a political Golgotha more desolate than any British administration had faced for many years, there seemed no obvious point of exit.

Partisan perspectives (1) The media war

Print

The print media had a vigorous and partisan war. So also did television. Increasingly the mass media seemed to forget their role as self-appointed fearless inquisitor after truth and became instead merely appendices of some vast semi-visible propaganda machine. In Britain the tabloids were violently divided. The editor of the *Daily Mirror*, Piers Morgan, embarked upon what can only be described as a propaganda crusade, one of the most aggressive and hyperbolic in the whole history of journalism. The *Sun* was somewhat less passionate, its bias precisely the opposite view, closely followed by the *Daily Mail* after some slight initial hesitation on account of the size of its female readership. Soon the *Mail* was lauding the war and jeering at the anti-war camp ('extremist links of the anti-war rally leaders who called children on to the streets'). The *Sun* embroidered the patriotic theme in its own inimitable way, featuring on 4 and 20 March sundry images of almost naked women with small strips of combat gear as the slight, final protectors of their modesty. Another *Sun* poster, 'The *Sun* backs our girls' (18 March), was fully clothed and featured a service-woman foregrounding a union flag.

Banner headlines were the order of the day, the *Mirror* manufacturing some classic ones, for example 'Coalition of the bribed, bullied and blind' (22 March 2003). These were effective because they were set against poster-size photographs such as the caption 'Beast of the skies' over a picture of a massive B-52. Another memorable heading was 'UNlawful UNethical UNstoppable' (18 March). And the *Mirror* was determined to take the enemy seriously, with a treatise on how Saddam could fight back, listing the ferocious biological chemical and terrorist weapons he could have at his disposal. Such perspectives are immediately problematic when war is joined, the accusation that the paper is behaving in an unpatriotic way. The *Mirror* determined to continue its anti-war campaign during the process of the war itself, a strategy which lost it readers. It confronted the accusation of disloyalty by an effective stratagem: on one page, a massive picture (18 March 2003) of Tony Blair with the banner heading 'He's let us down' while opposite was an image of a British soldier and the retort 'He never will.' The *Mail* was reduced to mocking opponents of the war, such as 'Cocky Robin and the roller-coaster ride to resignation'.

The broadsheets were less ideologically consistent. On their comments pages every one of them permitted opponents of the dominant view to articulate their perspective, and this was true of *The Times*, the *Telegraph* and the *Guardian*. Nor could the pro-war media restrain the anti-war sentiments of some of their cartoonists, *The Times*, for example, publishing what must rank as the most tasteless cartoon in history (showing Tony Blair zipping up and George Bush pulling up his trousers). The *Spectator* published a cover (1 February 2003) with the legend 'Poodle power', featuring a massive decorated Texan boot and a minuscule Tony Blair in World War II pilot uniform standing proudly upon it.

Television

The television media seemed equally partisan, or were perceived as such, with the BBC attacked by the government for the alleged bias of its reporters. This was a charge it found difficult to sustain, unlike the liberal criticism of Fox News: 'Flag-waving patriotism is unrelenting, from the

reporters embedded with the American heroes and liberators on the front
line in Iraq to the Rumsfeld-lauding talk-show host' (*Guardian*, 14 April
2003). Some idea of the chauvinist ethos of US television at this time is
given by Rampton and Stauber (2003):

> Networks quickly scrambled to give names to their war coverage, with corre-
> sponding graphic logos that swooshed and gleamed in 3-D colours accompa-
> nied by mood-inducing soundtracks. CBS chose 'America at War'. CNN went
> with 'Strike on Iraq'. CNBC used 'The Price of War' while NBC and MSNBC
> both went with 'Target: Iraq' – a choice that changed quickly as MSNBC
> joined Fox in using the Pentagon's own codename for the war, 'Operation Iraqi
> Freedom'. The logos featured fluttering American flags or motifs involving red,
> white and blue. On Fox, martial drumbeats accompanied regularly scheduled
> updates. Promos for MSNBC featured a photo-montage of soldiers accompa-
> nied by a piano rendition of 'The Star-spangled Banner'.

Liberals even began to suggest creating a liberal radio network as a riposte
to the Rush Limbaugh show or those hosted by Oliver North and Gordon
Liddy. 'Limbaugh entertains a 15 million audience with his pet obsessions
such as, in this particular context, the French' (*Guardian*, 19 February
2003). Observers spoke of a charisma deficit on the liberal left. In truth, the
nature of all media had changed since the first Gulf War little more than a
decade before, the rise of talk radio and the ascent of Fox News had permanently altered the centre of gravity in these media. A cavalier, choleric right
wing with its vivid personalities such as Bill O'Reilly and Anne Coulter had
made the days of liberal CBS anchors anachronistic, almost a part of history. Rampton and Stauber (2003) describe a Fox anchor berating a professor who had written an anti-war letter as an 'obnoxious, pontificating jerk
. . . A self-absorbed, condescending imbecile . . . An Ivy League intellectual
lilliputian'. And NBC's Mike Savage was dismissive of 'turd-world nations'.
The right had colour and the left had monochrome, and with the arrival of
the Iraq conflict the right-wing pundits were ready to evangelise the war
with their own boisterous nostrums.

Partisan perspectives (2) Private propaganda

A feature of the Iraq war was the level of private propaganda that it began
to generate, embodied not only in the assertive posters of the 'Not in my
name' campaign in the United Kingdom, which famously helped persuade
a million marchers on to the streets of London, but also in the private
initiatives of pressure groups and even of private citizens themselves. In the
United States, organisations opposed to the war articulated their opposition
in a classic American way. They advertised. Groups such as Bush Weakens

America printed dense copy in the press. Tom Paine dot-com created one of the best images: Bin Laden in the pointing pose of World War I Uncle Sam/Lord Kitchener recruiting posters with the phrase 'I want YOU to invade Iraq.' *Mad Magazine* manufactured 'Gulf War, Episode Two: Clone of the Attack', a photo-montaged pseudo-cinema poster festooned with images of warplanes, soldiers, explosions, and showcasing the various *dramatis personae* of the conflict.

The internet allowed individual initiative to surface in the propaganda war. For example, a retired sergeant of the Marine Corps, Ed Evans, wrote a kind of hyperbolic poem denouncing liberal treachery. Such texts, produced by individuals in their own homes, can attain extraordinary circulation, and possibly impact. If recipients are sufficiently moved to transmit them to every name in their address book, then by exponential process much of a country's population can be reached. Sergeant Evans, using the refrain:

I will not be manipulated,
I will not pretend to understand,
I will not forget,

went on to say, 'I will not forget the liberal media who have used freedom of the press to kick our country when it was vulnerable and hurting.' He argued that, speaking of the enemy, 'there is no compromise possible with such people, no meeting of minds, no point of understanding with such terror. Just a choice: defeat it or be defeated by it. And defeat it we must!'

I will force myself to:

Hear the weeping,
Feel their helplessness,
Imagine the terror,
Sense the panic,
Smell the burning flesh,
Experience the loss,
Remember the hatred.
I sat in a movie theatre, watching *Private Ryan*, and asked myself, where did they find the courage?
Now I know.
We have no choice. Living without liberty is not living.

Sergeant Evans urged his readers to 'keep this going until every living American has read and memorised it so we don't make the same mistake again'. Individuals could also engage in spectacular acts of vandalism which in the context of the Iraq war were appropriated as propaganda, such as the graffiti on the British war memorial at Etaples, 'Dig up your rubbish, it is contaminating our soil' and 'Saddam will win and will make your blood flow' (*Daily Telegraph*, 4 April 2003).

Celebrity propaganda

Celebrities had the public prominence to be noticed when they made anti-war points, famously of course Michael Moore at the Oscars. Madonna's video *American Life* 'features models in haute-couture combat gear lobbing grenades at the audience, leaving viewers uncertain whether their idol is against war or just currently enamoured of the army surplus look'. Apparently she avoided clarity on this matter, 'releasing a statement to the effect that she is neither pro- nor anti-Saddam but simply wants to stir debate'. During the Iraq crisis groups such as Musicians United to Win without War put their name to newspaper advertisements. Blur and Massive Attack joined in with such campaigns but did not create fresh anti-war anthems to replace those of yesteryear (Neil McCormick, *Daily Telegraph*, 13 March 2003).

Fantasy and propaganda: the European, Arab and Iraqi media

Media self-deceit

The media had been oversold, promised an easy walk-over; some British and European journalists rapidly became suspicious. Judged retrospectively, their comments seem rather absurd: 'whether they like it or not . . . there has been a psychological and military miscalculation of enormous proportions and it has spread a damaging and depressed uncertainty among the British and American electorates'. This article went on to claim:

> within a few days it was clear that the Iraqis were actually winning the propaganda war. They are winning because, in stark contrast to the coalition, they keep it simple. They broadcast the message: we're still here and we will win. Furthermore they let reporters in Baghdad say more or less what they like, censoring them invisibly to the viewer by restricting their movements. (Brian Appleyard, *Sunday Times*, 30 March 2003)

According to the leaked memo of one BBC defence correspondent:

> I was gobsmacked to hear . . . in a set of headlines today that the coalition were suffering significant casualties. This is simply not true, nor is it true to say . . . that coalition forces are fighting guerrillas. It may be a guerrilla warfare but they are not guerrillas. And who dreamt up the line that the coalition was achieving small victories at a very high price? The truth is exactly the

opposite. The gains are huge and the cost still relatively low. This is real warfare, however one-sided, and losses are to be expected. (*Sunday Telegraph,* 30 March 2003)

The media became extraordinarily pessimistic, especially in Britain: 'hopes, however over-optimistic, of a quick, clean victory were being drowned by the bloody blasts of high explosive and the whine of shrapnel' (*Sunday Times,* 30 March 2003).

The Arab press

Much of the Arab media supported Saddam Hussein as a kind of Arab saviour for his bellicose anti-Americanism, his status as the only Arab leader who had confronted the United States, as well as his boisterous support for the Palestinians. The quality of this endorsement should, however, be scrutinised, for many Arabs were not in fact blind to the violent excesses of the regime. They voiced support for Saddam as a symbolic anti-Israeli and anti-American gesture rather than from some deep adherence to his cause. Those Arabs who did go and volunteer to fight for Saddam met with real hostility from the Iraqi people.

During this war the Arab media appeared to be living a lie:

> Arab media are giving the impression that Iraq has already won the war. The mood is triumphant, and little attention has been given to the progress of the coalition forces towards Baghdad. 'Iraq has inflicted major losses on the coalition forces and the Americans and British are suffering a defeat they will never forget,' said a commentator on Syrian television. In Cairo, an editorial in the daily *al-Ahram* said Iraq had succeeded in turning the conflict into a long and bitter war and predicted that British and American public opinion would turn against it . . . the Qatar daily *al-Rai* praised the Iraqis for restoring Arab honour. (*Daily Telegraph,* 29 March 2003)

Such wilful self-deceit seems in retrospect pathetic, but given their geopolitical perspective it was hardly surprising. This suggests again the role of fantasy and self-deception in propaganda. Nor did the Arab news media alone articulate noisy support for Iraq. Again there was the pop music: 'the new video of Shaaban Abdel-Rahim, who sings folksy street music for the masses, flashes back to scenes from the last Gulf War and blasts the West for perceived double standards'. He topped Egyptian charts earlier with a song featuring the phrase 'I hate Israel,' after which US groups pressured McDonald's to drop 'his catchy jingle for their new falafel' (*Daily Telegraph,* 13 March 2003). Even near the end, some Arab papers continued to pretend that the alliance was nowhere near Baghdad, giving prominence to the verbal peregrinations of the Iraqi Information Minister, Mohammed

Said Sahhaf. The images of iconoclasm, the smashing of Saddam's statues, appear to have caused genuine astonishment in the Middle East, for such events 'overthrew the biggest lie in the recent history of the Arab world' (*The Times*, 10 April 2003).

Iraqi propaganda

Improbable though it may seem at this stage, the propaganda of the Iraqi regime had some admirers in the West, including those who began to say that Iraq was actually winning the propaganda war. Thus Hala Jaber claimed that Iraqi propaganda was working with the Iraqi people:

> they have cast the war as a *jihad* in defence of the motherland. Saddam has worked hard to rally the nation behind a sense of patriotism. Many say that he has succeeded. . . . [I]n the face of foreign invasion, internal political differ-ences are put aside. Arab tribes, Baath party members and religious sects had united under one banner, faith and culture – that of patriotism. (*Sunday Times*, 30 March 2003)

In practice the Iraqi propaganda machine, as described by the BBC corre-spondent Rageh Omaar, could hardly have been more cackhanded:

> by putting such severe restrictions on where we are allowed to set our broad-casting equipment, the regime ensured that many reports that they had dili-gently helped us to gather are simply never sent out. . . . [A]fter what are often useful briefings from the most senior Iraqi officials, we are unable to send our reports. . . . [T]he allegations that we are being seduced by a slick Iraqi propa-ganda machine are way off the mark. (*Sunday Telegraph*, 30 March 2003)

One of the biggest errors of the Iraqi regime was so to antagonise Al-Jazeera that it decided to exit Iraq (*Daily Telegraph*, 4 April 2003). The regime ordered one Al-Jazeera journalist out of Iraq and banned another from working. In doing this Iraq effectively neutralised its most effective propaganda conduit. Al-Jazeera had a world audience during the war of 40 million, the only television team in Basra, and a ruthless willingness to show images of civilian death which created powerful atrocity propaganda against the coalition.

In the end, of course, Iraqi propaganda became counterproductive as the coalition advanced. In the final days 'comical Ali', Information Minister Mohamed Said Sahhaf, began to command centre-stage. News about the war began to focus on the character of the Information Minister himself, whose hyperbolic optimism and tenuous grip on reality combined with an own-label brand of blood-curdling rhetoric to turn him into a Monty Pythonesque character accorded the honour of his own website, 'We love the Iraqi information Minister dot com' (*Sunday Telegraph*, 13 April 2003).

He became a cult figure, T-shirts appeared festooned with 'his most out-rageous lies' and the website was temporarily down owing to the blossom-ing of interest. Quotes of the day included such gems as 'I now inform you that you are too far from reality.' Aprons carried his marvels of spin, such as 'God will roast their stomachs in hell' or 'My feelings – as usual – we will slaughter them all.' According to the website 'he stands superior to truth'. The fascination was because he seemed surreal, a cartoon figure who simply contradicted such realities as the fact that Baghdad airport had been captured. Another gem: 'I'm here now to tell you, we do not have any Scud missiles and I do not know why they were fired into Kuwait' (*Sunday Tele-graph*, 13 April 2003). Finally he went on 10 April. He was the last intact member of the regime and had already seen US troops before he disap-peared after saying, 'No, no, no, maybe there are two or three tanks, but they will go.' Like Goebbels, he remained to the end; with the surrealism of his own performance the regime was in its final days pure propaganda without any kind of army, state or leadership, the propaganda ticking on for some days after the political entity whose vision it expressed had completely disappeared.

The limitations of propaganda: control

In a democracy the press can only ever be influenced and not controlled. Government information can only ever be an invitation to accept an inter-pretation. And this offer can be refused. America's problem in the second Gulf War was that so many foreign commentators simply rejected the per-spective of the US government. Some of these critics saw the war as part of the broader political problem of so-called American exceptionalism. For example, Henry Porter in the *Observer* (23 March 2003) produced a list of the United States' errors of omission and commission – the Land-mine Treaty, the International Criminal Court, the Kyoto agreement, the Anti-ballistic Missile Treaty, the 1972 Biological Weapons Convention's planned inspection powers, tariffs on steel imports, subsidies to its own farmers: 'It has become clear that America has been crudely manipulating many agendas in its own interests . . . there is a gathering conviction that America is, to use the word of the moment, in state of persistent non-compliance on too many protocols, agreements, treaties and conventions to number'.

Coherent integrating perspective. For other hostile observers, their antago-nism was part of a broader rejection of US culture, a stance by no means confined to Middle Eastern critics. Listen to what the novelist Margaret Drabble had to say:

I was tipped into an uncontainable rage by a report on Channel 4 news about 'friendly fire', which included footage of what must have been one of the most horrific bombardments ever filmed. But what struck home hardest was the subsequent image, of the row of American warplanes, with grinning cartoon faces painted on their noses. Cartoon faces, with big sharp teeth. It is grotesque. It is hideous. This great and powerful nation bombs foreign citizens and the people in those cities from Disneyland cartoon planes out of comic strips . . . . others have written elegantly about the euphemistic and affectionate names that the Americans give to their weapons of mass destruction: Big Boy, Little Boy, Daisy Cutter, and so forth . . . but there was something about those playfully grinning warplane faces that went beyond deception and distortion into the land of madness. A nation that can allow those faces to be painted as an image on its national aeroplanes has regressed into unimaginable irresponsibility. A nation that can paint those faces on death machines must be insane. There, I have said it. I have tried to control my anti-Americanism, remembering the many Americans that I know and respect, but I can't keep it down any longer. I detest Disneyfication, I detest Coca-cola, I detest burgers, I detest sentimental and violent Hollywood movies that lie about history. I detest American imperialism, American infantilism, and American triumphalism about victories it didn't even win. (*Daily Telegraph*, 8 May 2003)

This critique articulates the emotional core of anti-Americanism today, a sentiment that is by no means confined to the left. This diatribe would resonate even with some *Telegraph* readers, and it is ironic that the *Telegraph* of all papers should have printed the most eloquent attack on the war of all those that I have read. Eloquent because the article uses the image of warplanes painted with faces as the central organising metaphor for her polemic. The painted-face warplane is for her symbolic both of the military aggression, technological dominance and alleged cultural deformity of the US nation. Against such hostility, what can propaganda do except to recognise that propaganda elicits counter-propaganda, and in this context Drabble herself has been self-conscripted into the ranks of Gulf War propagandists.

The quality of her literary rage is almost intoxicating, but it is also astonishingly selective both of the evidence and of the reasoning behind US actions. It demonstrates the effectiveness in propaganda of the coherent integrating perspective; 'American imperialism' seems to plausibly meld together phenomena connected with America into a universal explanatory framework. What stands outside that framework – such as US interventions in Bosnia, Somalia and Kosovo, where no conceivable US interest was served by intervention, is conveniently ignored or awkwardly incorporated.

The management of anarchy

The problem with war propaganda is that the propagandist cannot control the media, merely try to persuade those who control the media, nor can we control the actions of the forces of our own side. Both elements may and probably will betray us. As in Vietnam, the media can develop a universal negative consensus: similarly, despite the best efforts of rhetoric and the management of imagery, our own forces can do the most craven and stupid things because their ability is ultimately defined by the lowest common denominator of intelligence of their own soldiers. Where this worked well, as at the Imam Ali mosque, where US troops fell in to the shout of 'Everybody smile' from the platoon commander 'as he told his baffled men to kneel down and point their weapons to the ground in a surreal act of submission' (*Daily Telegraph*, 4 April 2003), it can become useful propaganda for a cause.

At its worst it can make the pro-government case articulated by the most sophisticated propaganda machine ever created seem cruel and murderous. Listen to Lance-corporal Gerard of the Household Cavalry:

> there was a boy of about 12 years old. He was no more than 20 metres away when the Yank opened up. There were all these civilians around. He had absolutely no regard for human life. I believe he was a cowboy. There were four or five that I noticed earlier and this one had broken off and was on his own when he attacked. He'd just gone out on a jolly. I'm curious about what's going to happen to him. He's killed one of my friends and he's killed him on the second round. (*The Times*, 31 March 2003)

These two accounts show how far the American propaganda effort was dependent on the moral and military tactical decisions of individual soldiers and airmen. In the first instance, the lieutenant had acted with cultural insight and real initiative, instinctively recognising both the power of symbolism in that context and what particular symbolisation rituals he should order his men to enact. In the second, the pilot appears to have been blinded by the lust of battle; yet there is supreme political sensitivity in actions taken on the modern battlefield. There was an even more extreme example of this at Fallujah, thirty miles west of Baghdad, during a demonstration about the occupation of the local school. Fifteen people, including two boys, were killed: 'though the US troops say they fired in self-defence – and may well have done so – television footage of bleeding Iraqis, clearly unarmed, lying on the road, has shocked Western viewers' (*Sunday Telegraph*, 4 May 2003).

Events can also favour the propagandist; the symbolism, time and again, of the iconoclasm, the multiple populist beheadings of Saddamite statuary, and, ghoulishly, the discoveries of the mass graveyards of the murdered.

The crashing statues, the cracked cement heads, will be the image this war bequeaths to history, resonant symbols of propaganda value beyond price.

Media independence

The trouble with all these efforts at message production is that in the end propaganda is not a science but an immensely crude art. We cannot foreordain outcomes, we can only make intelligent guesses. Here, for example, is a cartoon in *The Times* of London (10 April 2003). It is captioned 'Budget day' and contains two images, one with the word 'Profit' underneath, the other with the words 'And loss'. The first is of a (cartoon) photograph in black-and-white of Saddam Hussein in a beret. The second (cartoon) photograph is of the famous armless boy, reduced almost to a torso, his skin a mass of bloody matted flesh. Such an image can effectively undermine the work of a legion of spin doctors. In propaganda, in a democracy, the free media may obey personal prejudices or economic interests and as such may indeed be effective propagandists for a government, but radicals who deny the media their independence are exaggerating. A newspaper is indeed a product, and as such it sells not just by sustaining expectations but also by selling novelty. So the press is inherently both conservative and radical, since the diet of unalloyed conservatism would bore even the most sedate of its readers. The press has to surprise us; in the Iraq war, even pro-war newspapers were sufficiently flexible to carry some anti-war messages such as the boy in the cartoon.

In this war, it is probably accurate to say, one particular event alienated the public most, or at least the kind of public that writes letters to newspapers and leads opinion. This was the apparent sacking of Iraq's National Museum of Archaeology by looters, many of them organised. Nothing in the war quite so antagonised intellectual opinion as this, the image of a nation ostensibly robbed of its cultural heritage, and by extension the entire world, given the significance of ancient Mesopotamia in the evolution of civilisation (though many artefacts subsequently resurfaced from safe storage). The inability of the US command to recognise this, and to engage in the simple expedient of sending in guards, was to many incredible. In this instance such indolence could almost cohere with the 'cultural Disneyland' libel propagated by America's antagonists. A conundrum of wartime propaganda is that much of the key imagistic material is completely out of the control of propagandists themselves, making their role to retrieve the situation after the fact, or simply hope that the world will forget. It usually does. These events also raised profound questions about the education of soldiers. An educational process which tutors them to be mere technicians is bound to end in such consequences when mere technicians go to war in a febrile social and cultural context.

The narrative production of the Iraq war was officially terminated with George W. Bush's fighter jet landing on the USS *Abraham Lincoln*. It was a theatrical tableau: the setting sun, the great 'Mission accomplished' banner, 'Commander-in-chief' painted beneath the cockpit, and (according to Democrats) a $1 million cost (Rampton and Stauber 2003). In the end came recognition, with the admission by Colin Powell, that weapons of mass destruction did not exist. It was a reaffirmation of Mark Twain's aphorism, that a lie can travel half-way round the world while truth is still tying its shoelaces.

Afterword

The impact of propaganda

The claims made for the impact of propaganda are of course extensive. To 'prove' them in a clinical sense is much more difficult. Certainly enemies have been more inclined to attribute their opponents' success to manipulative ability than to courage. Thus a British view of Napoleon: 'it is a mystifying truth that he has done more mischief by means of the *Moniteur* of Paris than he has ever effected by the united efforts of the cannon and the sword' (Taylor 1990).

It is certainly possible to choose particular moments in history where seizure of the propaganda initiative does appear to have been decisive, such as the significance of German newsreels in re-establishing the Hitler myth in the wake of the July plot (Taylor 1990). The campaign orchestrated by the London advertising industry in 1914 at the behest of Lord Kitchener was the most successful in history up till that time. Kitchener (Pollock 1994) recognised that Britain's miniature professional army would be no match for the Germans and had to be supplemented by a vast influx of new soldiers, but he also opposed conscription. Therefore a campaign began to recruit 3 million volunteers, and he succeeded in meeting this target. What other term could describe such a campaign but 'propaganda'? To say that 'communication' created a volunteer army the size of the current Irish Republic tells nothing about the intrinsic nature of that communication.

One can also argue that the influence of particular propagandists on the evolution of historical events is demonstrable, as one might for instance with Verdi and the Italian Risorgimento, with many of his operas an impassioned cry against tyranny, *Rigoletto, Don Carlos, Aida, I Lombardi, The Battle for Legnano*. He was a 'master of the rebellion genre' (Perris 1985). And emergent social phenomena can be attributable to powerful propaganda entrepreneurship: environmentalist, feminist and other contemporary agendas for example were not initiated by political parties but via the disorganised public evangelism of organised private groupings (see Richardson 1995). In all these cases it is impossible to isolate the influence of propaganda from that of other explanatory factors: the Risorgimento would have happened without Verdi, Hitler would have re-established his authority had the newsreels remained silent, reappraisal of the ethical status of abortion might, possibly, have occurred among the medical community without the evangelism of the Right to Life movement. At this level, then, belief in the power of propaganda is mere faith, made credible, of course, by persuasive examples and arguments.

Yet we come, again, to the problem of objective proof, and it is an insoluble one. How indeed does one ever 'prove' the effectiveness of propaganda in framing and forming the twentieth century, even if we believe that it did? The great revolutionaries of the twentieth century certainly had faith in its efficacy: as Hitler commented on the disintegration of German army morale in 1918 (propaganda documents were found on many prisoners), 'One could now see the effects of this gradual seduction. Our soldiers learned to think the way the enemy wanted them to think.' Hitler recognised the apolitically of most people, and that 'opinion and actions are determined much more by impressions produced on their senses than by reflection' (Blain 1988).

Belief is one thing, scientific evidence is another. Naturally in the communist and fascist revolutions of the twentieth century there was little incentive for anybody on either side to measure the effectiveness of the propaganda. One who did, an SPD organiser called Serge Chakotin (1971), in a controlled experiment applied 'new', i.e. copied from the Nazis, propaganda methods to four Hesse towns. The Nazis lost in every one of them, but won in the fifth town in the experiment, where the SPD had been using only traditional or 'rational' methods of persuasion. This of course raises a terrible thought: could the Nazis have been beaten with their own methods? If the SPD had really understood propaganda and the manipulation of emotion, might the Third Reich never have happened?

There are, however, still those who would downgrade the power and persuasiveness of rhetoric and propaganda (May 1982). Many historians dismiss notions such as the rhetoric of self-presentation as peripheral. A rational critique can, however, easily neglect the central role of communication in leadership, as practised say by Bernard Law Montgomery, who had actually taught 'Presentation' at staff college. In his excellent book *Eminent Churchillians* (1994) Andrew Roberts castigates the military incompetence of Admiral Lord Louis Mountbatten, Supreme Allied Commander South East Asia during World War II. Mountbatten, however, was a very skilful propagandist indeed, in a theatre (Burma) where morale was not a peripheral matter but the core issue. (He became the first military man to employ a a professional public relations expert, Alan Campbell Johnson.)

Other critics aim to debunk the notion of language power and theorise that any power in society, including that of language use, derives from the particular social formations on which it is based and which it legitimates. Such economic and social determinism is really a denial of the power of propaganda, its (often Marxist) proponents, for example, may merely see Hitler and Churchill as ciphers for economic forces. For them, the thesis of this entire book is in fact a nullity. This was not of course the view of Hitler himself, who after the Munich *Putsch* declared, 'All that matters is propaganda.' Other authorities more plausibly claim that the impact of propaganda lies not in moulding our thoughts but in setting our agendas (Kim *et al.* 1990). Kim *et al.* argue that the media are 'not successful much of the time in telling people what to think, but . . . stunningly successful in telling its readers what to think about'. They cite their study of the movie *Amerika*: those who did not see the programme pondered a different set of US–Soviet relations issues from those who did. The agenda-setting hypothesis has remained a major mass-communication theory. These researchers conclude from their investigation: 'the effects of exposure to the programme itself . . . seem to be minimal in the determination of the agenda for the post-programme discussion'. The implications for the study of propaganda are interesting, since the stress is on the power of the media to ordain issue priorities rather than dictate a particular line on those issues.

A singular example of effective propaganda comes from Northern Ireland (Demick *et al.* 1996), and unlike most public service campaigns this one had the attraction of an objective measure, the number of informer calls to a confidential telephone number. In the first advertisement, a young man is featured who knows a terrorist, and feeling guilty about his silence he rings the hot line after witnessing a shooting. There followed a 51 per cent increase in calls to the confidential telephone number. This advertisement, which ran for two years, is really a story of guilt and redemption through virtuous action: part of the aim was to destroy terrorist social networks by winning acceptance of the idea of putting public before private relationships. Its yield scarcely compares with some of the other spots which (between 1988 and 1992) produced astonishing call rises of 500 per cent or even over 700 per cent. With the cessation of violence came new images of present hope contrasted with past fear, of the young, and of community interaction, a metamorphosis as concrete blocks changed into flowerpots, guns into starting pistols. With phrases which might have come from a soft-drink advertisement, what may seem like the banality of ordinariness took on a new meaning ('Wouldn't it be great if it was like this all the time?'). For the first time the terms 'Catholic' and 'Protestant' were used.

Even better evidence arises from California, which has spent $836 million on anti-smoking advertising and education since Proposition 99 took effect in 1988, but the Center for Disease Control estimates that it has already saved $3 billion in direct health care costs and another $5.4 billion in indirect costs. *The Economist* (9 December 2000) claimed that 'many Californian women were put off smoking by a brutal television ad that hit the airwaves in 1997, in which a woman named Debbie tried to explain that she could not suppress her desire for another cigarette. She addressed the viewers through a hole in her throat, cut there after a laryngectomy that had been made necessary by her smoking.' According to this account, adult smoking rates in California have declined by more than 32 per cent since 1988. Young people have reacted even more energetically: in one year, from 1998 to 1999, the number of young smokers fell more than 35 per cent, cutting the rate of tobacco used by twelve-to-seventeen-year-olds to 6.9 per cent.

However, it is easy to find counter-examples, where propaganda insensitively administered has failed or even been counterproductive. Thus the Reagan administration intensified anti-Soviet hyperbole, believing in the outmoded 'magic bullet' theory of wartime propaganda 'which assumed that foreign audiences could be easily manipulated if the propagandist had good aim and the right ammunition' (Nichols 1984). In 1984 the administration spent $750 million on such propaganda. It de-emphasised the more influential cultural and information-oriented programmes and simply asserted that US propaganda was effective without supporting evidence or on the basis of fabricated evidence (such as Poles travelling west) and imaginative listening figures. A message must be received, not just created, and the audience is not passive but proactive. In Nichols's words, 'the effects of international propaganda are largely the product of audience needs and motivations rather than the intent and methods of the propagandist'. In the Soviet Union about 9.7 per cent of adults listened to Radio Liberty once a month or more in 1983, but about twice as many heard the more moderate Voice of America. (The BBC reached as many as Radio Liberty even though it broadcast less than 10 per cent as much.) Nichols concludes that blitzes merely exacerbated Soviet xenophobia and suggests that those who seek foreign propaganda are already alienated.

Soviet commentators were, however, impressed by the power of what they saw as Western 'cultural' propaganda. Thus Soviet critic S. Karganovic (1974):

> Western propaganda, however, is attempting to undermine the socialist consciousness of the people by means of 'sociological subversion'. This is a far more sophisticated weapon than the old fashioned broadcasts of Radio Free Europe. Sociological subversion uses movies, records, cigarettes, cars and

other indicators of the relatively high standard of Western consumer society to divert the attention of the people from their productive tasks.

The post-Nine-eleven new era of US 'public diplomacy' showed every promise of repeating some of the Cold War errors. Under-secretary of State Charlotte Beers's 'shared values' advertising campaign, authored by McCann Erickson, was withdrawn by the State Department after less than a month:

> Dubbed a Muslim as apple pie campaign by the *New York Times*, the shared values videos featured photogenic Muslim Americans playing with their children and going about their jobs. One TV commercial showed . . . Ismail, a Lebanese born schoolteacher who now lived in Toledo, Ohio. Her head covered with an Islamic scarf, Ismail was shown with her smiling children in her all-American kitchen, at a school softball game and extolling American values as she taught her class. 'I didn't see any prejudice anywhere in my neighbourhood after September 11th,' she said. (Rampton and Stauber 2003)

Impact on history

There has also been unquestionably a rising interest in retrospective verdicts on the twentieth century since the millenium passed. People are searching for meaningful ways of interpreting the chaos of twentieth-century events, and to call it 'the propaganda century' is as legitimate as any soubriquet. Propaganda must be understood not as a peripheral aspect of history but as a fulcrum. Previously political leadership had fallen to great military or aristocratic figures and hereditary castes: now it was the turn of populists/propagandists such as the ex-journalist Benito Mussolini. Propaganda was a necessary condition of dictatorship in the twentieth century.

It is not easy precisely to calibrate the role of propaganda and its significance in relation to other variables in historical judgement. For example, how relevant is it as an explanation for the collapse of Germany army morale in the closing stages of World War I? But, without doubt, that role – in war, revolution, capitalist–communist struggle, the rise of consumer society – has been significant. Wars and revolutions are unimaginable without the galvanising agency of propaganda. They are not created by popular sentiment alone, that sentiment has to be channelled, given reasons and an enemy, a leader figure, hope.

Propaganda also played a role in fomenting and sustaining both the National Socialist and Bolshevik revolutions (for example, communist cinema trains in the Russian countryside), since both Nazism and Marxism-Leninism were not mere political ideologies but proselytising creeds, in other words a propaganda ethos was integral to the dogma: ideology and propagation were confused. Their success lay in the fact that they were both systems of political theory and also plans of action, and Lenin himself, like Hitler, had witnessed the propaganda battles of World War I and become a believer (Taylor 1990).

At one time a formal association, the Institute for Propaganda Analysis, existed to fulfil the function of critiquing propaganda. Its publications and speakers examined the methods not only of home-grown American propagandists like Charles Coughlin, and the methods of totalitarian dictatorships, but even the propaganda put out by US corporations under such disguises as educational toolkits. It was founded in response to a strong popular belief that the United States had been propagandised into joining the First World War, in particular by the activities of the Creel committee, with its 'Minutemen'. Ironically, its demise happened because the kind of analysis it offered became too politically incorrect. A nation at war does not want to be reminded that it, also, is in the propaganda business, and, moreover, the professional critics of propaganda could thereby be released and co-opted into the propaganda industry, which is exactly what happened.

Yet to visit the United States today is to witness a propaganda war without parallel since the Second World War itself. The iconography of patriotism is everywhere to behold, posters of weeping Statues of Liberty, eagles holding the stars and stripes. Right-wing commentators compose polemical books excoriating liberals, and liberals reply, while seldom also has the nation been so divided in ferocious debate between the sacred and the secular realms. Republicans are accused by Democrats of exploiting Nine-eleven (as with the controversy over Bush campaign advertising showing 'footage of the charred hulk of the World Trade Center and flag-draped remains' (Guardian 5 March 2004)); Republicans blame the previous Democrat regime for letting it happen. The propagandising of the media is embodied in the 'Fox effect', the halving of foreign coverage on mainstream news and media from 1989: as Rampton and Stauber (2003) comment, 'the more TV people watched, the less they knew'. And propaganda is now official policy since the passing by Congress of House Resolution 3969 (Lantos and Hyde), which instructs the Secretary of State to 'make public diplomacy an integral component in the planning and execution of United States foreign policy' (Rampton and Stauber 2003). To live in the United States today is to receive the perfect tutelage in propaganda. Maybe it should be a formal education.

Propagandists are in the business of normalising the abnormal, of naturalising the perverse. Their agency can transform the deeply destructive into the contextual given, the uninterrogated social parameter within which we are expected to operate. The depravities of power and ideology transmute into the latest, newest, current agenda whose despotism we are not expected to question, or even notice. It is all part of the modern propaganda phenomenon. Propaganda addresses directly the problem of cognitive clutter today, the perceptual fog we inhabit: it casts this aside and beckons us through the retreating mist. It paints luminous tableaux, at once disgusting and alluring, that we cannot ignore. It alternately assaults and seduces our consciousness.

But to dismiss the power of propaganda is perverse, for that would be to deprecate a prime agency of change over the past 200 years. Business itself is both a target and a prime mover. Wal Mart, for example, accused of paying low wages, fights back not with new policies but with public relations advertising. Since the 1930s there does not appear to have been a visible attempt to educate students about manipulation techniques, and the Institute's ten points of propaganda analysis have been long forgotten. Yet a strong case could be made for saying that such an education could be essential to the evolution of citizens and a civic culture that are truly mature and independent. People spend much of their lives 'reading' media, and the aspiration therefore to create media literacy through the teaching of propaganda-critical techniques is not a trivial one. When we speak of the engineering of consent (perhaps 'acquiescence' would be a more accurate word) we hear claims that public opinion in the United States is a commodity to be purchased. Such a sentiment exaggerates, but like many caricatures it contains at its core an important truth.

Propaganda is ubiquitous. While such saturation is an obvious and definitive characteristic of totalitarian regimes, in democracies it is more concealed, because it is more sophisticated and naturalised as part of supposedly objective mass media communication. If we do not have labels for phenomena we tend not to recognise them, and thus the underlying unities of the myriad forms of modern propaganda will be neglected: they will simply be defined by their objective characteristics, for example 'public relations'. The breadth of propaganda media must be fully recognised, for instance, bureaucratic propaganda, and even aspects of military strategy, or that new forms of propaganda have emerged, such as certain research institutes with their pastiche academic titles like 'Research Fellow', to which the media referred during the Iraq crisis, forgetting 1,400 full-time US college faculty specialists in Middle Eastern Studies (Rampton and Stauber 2003). Even propaganda scholars treat the term conservatively. The perception that new forms of propaganda have arrived and old ones continue means that the work of propaganda analysis is never complete.

Bibliography

Aaker, David, and Myers, John G. (1989), *Advertising Management*, Prentice Hall, Englewood Cliffs NJ.

Adams, J.A.D. (1993), '1948 or 1984', *Times Literary Supplement*, 12 March.

Adams, William C., *et al.* (1986), 'Before and after the day after: the unexpected results of a televised drama', *Political Communication and Persuasion*, 3:3, pp. 191–213.

Albritton, James E. (1978), *Advertising as a Subsystem of Propaganda*, conference proceedings of the Southern Sociological Society.

Aldgate, Anthony, and Richards, Jeffrey (1994), *Britain Can Take It*, Edinburgh University Press, Edinburgh.

Allen, Robert C., ed. (1995), *To be Continued . . . : Soap Operas Around the World*, Routledge, London.

Altheide, D., and Johnson, J. (1980), *Bureaucratic Propaganda*, Allyn & Bacon, Boston MA.

Alubo, S. Ogoh (1991), 'Mass mobilization and legitimation crisis in Nigeria', *Political Communication and Persuasion*, 8, pp. 43–62.

Anderson, Jack (1996), *Inside the NRA*, Dove Books, Beverley Hills CA.

Ang, Ian, and Stattan, John (1995), 'The end of civilization as we knew it: chances and the postrealist soap opera', in Robert C. Allen (ed.), *To be Continued . . . : Soap Operas Around the World*, Routledge, London.

Ansolabehere, S., and Iyengar, S. (1995), *Going Negative*, Free Press, New York.

Austin, J.L. (1962), *How to do Things with Words*, Oxford University Press, London.

Banker, S (1992), 'The ethics of political marketing practices: the rhetorical perspective', *Journal of Business Ethics*, 11, pp. 843–848.

Bateman, Thomas S., Tomoaki, Sakono, and Makoto, Fujita Roger (1992), 'Me and my attitude: film propaganda and cynicism towards corporate leadership', *Journal of Applied Psychology*, 77:5, pp. 768–771.

Baudrillard, J. (1988), 'Simulacra and simulation', in M. Poster (ed.), *Selected Writings*, Stanford University Press, Stanford CA.

Bennett, Richard (1995), *The Black and Tans*, Barnes & Noble, New York.

Bennett, W. Lance (1996), *The Politics of Illusion*, third edition, Longman, London.

Bennett, W. Lance, and Manheim, Jarol B. (1993), 'Taking the public by storm: information, cuing and the democratic process in the Gulf conflict', *Political Communication*, 10, pp. 331–351.

Binyon, Michael (1986), 'Reagan faces cool welcome on prairies', *Times*, 29 September.

Bird, Elizabeth S., and Dardenne, Robert W. (1988), 'Myth, chronicle and story: exploring the narrative qualities of news', *Sage Annual Reviews of Communication Research*, Sage, London.

Blain, Michael (1988), 'Fighting words: what we can learn from Hitler's hyperbole', *Symbolic Interaction*, 11:2, pp. 257–276.

Blau, Peter M. (1964), *Exchange and Power in Social Life*, Wiley, New York.

Block, Robert (1994), 'The tragedy of Ruanda', *New York Review*, 20 October.

Blumenthal, Sidney (1984), *The Permanent Campaign*, Simon & Schuster, New York.

Boardman, Philip C. (1978), 'Beware the semantic trap: language and propaganda', *Etcetera*, 35:1, pp. 78–85.

Bown, Matthew Cullerne, and Taylor, Brandon, eds (1993), *Art of the Soviets*, Manchester University Press, Manchester.

Branham, Robert James (1991), 'The role of the convert in eclipse of reason and "The Silent Scream"', *Quarterly Journal of Speech*, 77:99, pp. 407–426.

Bryant, Sir Arthur (1942), *The Years of Endurance*, Collins, London.

Burke, Kenneth (1970), *A Grammar of Motives*, University of California Press, Berkeley CA.

Butler, David, and Kavanagh, Dennis (1995), *The British General Election of 1992*, Macmillan, Basingstoke.

Calder, Angus (1991), *The Myth of The Blitz*, Jonathan Cape, London.

Cantril, Hadley (1963), *The Psychology of Social Movements*, Wiley, New York.

Carnes, Mark C. (1996), *Past Imperfect; History according to the Movies*, Cassell, London.

Chagal, David (1981), *The New Kingmakers*, Harcourt Brace, New York.

Chakotin, S. (1971), *The Rape of the Masses: The Psychology of Totalitarian Political Propaganda*, Haskell House, New York.

Chang, Jung (1991), *Wild Swans*, Flamingo, London.

Cohen, Stephen P. (1990), *The Indian Army*, Oxford University Press, Bombay.

Cook, Guy (1992), *The Discourse of Advertising*, Routledge, London.

Craig, Patricia (1994), 'The clash of symbols', *Times Literary Supplement*, 16 December.

Crelinston, Ronald D. (1989), 'Terrorism and the media: problems, solutions and counter-problems', *Political Communication and Persuasion*, 6, pp. 311–339.

Crofts, Stephen (1995), 'Global neighbours?', in Robert C. Allen (ed.), *To be Continued . . . : Soap Operas Around the World*, Routledge, London.

Crofts, William (1989), *Coercion or Persuasion: Propaganda in Britain after 1945*, Routledge, London.

Dallek, Robert (1984), *Ronald Reagan: The Politics of Symbolism*, Harvard University Press, Cambridge MA.

De Sousa, Ronald (1990), *Rationality of Emotion*, MIT Press, Cambridge MA.

Demick, D.H., Carson, D., and Wilson, J. (1996), 'A Chronology of Public Service Advertising: a Northern Ireland Example', working paper, School of Management, University of Ulster at Jordanstown; 'Proceedings of the thirtieth Marketing Education Group Conference', Strathclyde, July.

Derrida, Jacques (1981), *Dissemination*, University of Chicago Press, Chicago.

Detweiler, John S. (1992), 'The religious right's battle plan in the civil war of values', *Public Relations Review*, 18:3, pp. 247–255.

Diamond, E., and Bates, S. (1988a), *Hot Spots*, New York, 15 February.

Diamond, E., and Bates, S. (1988b), *Hot Spots*, New York, 1 October.

Didion, Joan (1994), '"Something horrible" in El Salvador', *New York Review*, 14 July.

Dobkin, Bethami A. (1992) 'The rhetorical dimensions of narrative form in ABC News coverage of terrorism', *Western Journal of Communication*, 56, pp. 143–160.

Douglas, Mary (1982), *Natural Symbols*, Pantheon Books, New York.

Douglas, Mary (1996), *Thought Styles: Critical Essays in Good Taste*, Sage, New York.

Douglas, Mary, and Isherwood, Baron (1979), *The World of Goods*, Basic Books, New York.

Dowling, Ralph (1989), 'Print journalism as political communication', *Political Communication and Persuasion*, 6, pp. 289–309.

Draper, Derek (1997), *Blair's One Hundred Days*, Faber, London.

Drescher, David (1987), 'A typology of international political communication: factual statements, propaganda and noise', *Political Communication and Persuasion*, 4, pp. 83–91.

Edsall, T.B. (1994), 'America's sweetheart', *New York Review*, 6 October.

Education, Department for (1994), 'Our Children's Education: The Updated Parents' Charter, 1994' (Citizens' Charter), Stationery Office, London.

Eliade, Mircea (1991), *Images and Symbols*, Princeton University Press, Princeton NJ.

Ellul, Jacques (1973), *Propaganda; The Formation of Men's Attitudes*, Vintage Books, New York.

Emlyn-Jones, Chris (1987), 'Speech, the mighty ruler: persuasion and power in democratic Athens', in Jeremy Hawthorn (ed.), *Propaganda, Polemic and Persuasion*, Stratford-upon-Avon Studies, second series, Edward Arnold, London.

Ewen, Stuart (1988), *All-consuming Images*, Basic Books, New York.

Festinger, L. (1957), *A Theory of Cognitive Dissonance*, Stanford University Press, Stanford CA.

Figes, Orlando (1997), *A People's Tragedy*, Pimlico Books, London.

Fiske, John (1984), 'Popularity and ideology: a structuralist reality of *Dr Who*', *Sage Annual Reviews of Communication Research*, 12:7.

Foege, Alec (1990), *The Empire God Built: Inside Pat Robertson's Media Machine*, Wiley, New York.

Foucault, M. (1975), *Discipline and Punish: The Birth of the Prison*, trans. A. Sheridan, Penguin Books, Harmondsworth.

Foulkes, A.P. (1983), *Literature and Propaganda*, Methuen, London.

Frankl, Victor (1963), *Man's Search for Meaning*, Simon & Schuster, New York.

Franklin, Bob (1998), 'Civic free newspapers: "propaganda on the rates"', *Local Government Studies*, 14:3, pp. 35–56.

Galanter, Marc (1989), *Cults*, Oxford University Press, New York.

Gardiner, Juliet, and Wenborn, Neil (1995), *The* History Today *Companion to British History*, Collins & Brown, London.

Geertz, Clifford (1984), *Local Knowledge: Further Essays in Interpretative Anthropology*, Basic Books, New York

Geraghty, Christine (1995), 'Social issues and realist soaps: a study of British soaps in the 1980s/1990s', in Robert C. Allen (ed.), *To be Continued . . . : Soap Operas Around the World*, Routledge, London.

Gibbs, R.W. (1994), *The Poetics of the Mind: Figurative Thought, Language, and Understanding*, Cambridge University Press, Cambridge.

Gold, Greg J., and Raven, Bertram H. (1992), 'Interpersonal influence strategies in the Churchill–Roosevelt bases-for-destroyers exchange', *Journal of Social Behaviour And Personality* 7:2, pp. 245–272.

Goldberg, Vicki (1991), *The Power of Photography*, Abbeville Press, New York.

Goodrich, Chauncey A. (1884), *Select British Eloquence*, Harper, New York.

Griffin, Alison (1995), 'National and cultural identity in a Welsh-language soap opera', in Robert C. Allen (ed.), *To be Continued . . . : Soap Operas Around the World*, Routledge, London.

Griffiths, Richard (1983), *Fellow Travellers of the Right*, Oxford University Press, Oxford.

Gronow, Jukka (1997), *The Sociology of Taste*, Routledge, London.

Grunberger, Richard (1991), *A Social History of the Third Reich*, Penguin Books, London.

Guillermoprieto, Alan (1995), 'The shadow war', *New York Review*, 2 March.

Gustainis, J. Justin (1988), "Waist-deep in the Big Muddy': rhetorical dimensions of the Tet offensive', *Political Communication and Persuasion*, 5:2, pp. 81–82.

Harris, P., and O'Shaughnessy, N.J. (1997), 'BSE and marketing communication myopia: daisy and the death of the sacred cow', *Risk Decision and Policy*, 2:1, pp. 29–39.

Harrison, M. (1995), 'Politics on air', in D. Butler and D. Kavanagh (eds), *The British General Election of 1992*, Macmillan, Basingstoke.

Harrop, M., and Scammell, M. (1993), 'A tabloid war', in D. Butler and D. Kavanagh (eds), *The British General Election of 1992*, Macmillan, Basingstoke.

Hawthorne, Jeremy, ed. (1987), *Propaganda, Persuasion and Polemic*, Edward Arnold, London.

Herzstein, Robert Edwin (1978), *The War that Hitler Won: The most Infamous Propaganda Campaign in History*, Hamish Hamilton, London.

Hiebert, Ray E. (1993), 'Public relations, propaganda and war: a book review and essay on the literature', *Public Relations Review*, 19:3, pp. 293–302.

Himmelfarb, Gertrude (1994), 'A sentimental priesthood', *Times Literary Supplement*, 11 November.

Hirschman, Albert O. (1991), *The Rhetoric of Reaction*, Belknap Press of Harvard University, Cambridge MA.

Hodge, Robert, and Kress, Gunthar (1988), *Social Semiotics*, Cornell University Press, Ithaca NY.

Holbrook, Morris B. (1987), 'The study of signs in consumer aesthetics: an ego-centric review', in Jean Umiker-Sebeok (ed.), *Marketing and Semiotics*, Mouton de Gruyter, New York.

Hovland, C.I., and Janis, I.L., eds (1959), *Personality and Persuadability*, Yale University Press, New Haven CT.

Hudson, Liam (1994), 'The wretched connection', *Times Literary Supplement*, 2 December.

Huff, Darrell (1981), *How to Lie with Statistics*, Pelican Books, London.

Huntington, Samuel P. (1996), *The Clash of Civilisations and the Remaking of the World Order*, Simon & Schuster, New York.

Jamieson, Kathleen Hall (1988), *Eloquence in an Electronic Age*, Oxford University Press, Oxford.

Jenkins, Lord (2001), *Gladstone*, Pan Books, London.

Johnson, Dennis W. (1997), 'Political Communication in the Information Age', seminar on 'Political Communication in the Information Age', Wissenschaftszentrum Berlin/Bertelsmann Stiftung, February.

Johnson, Dennis W. (2001), *No Place for Amateurs: How Political Consultants are Reshaping American Democracy*, Routledge, New York.

Jones, Nick (1997), *Campaign 1997*, Indigo Books, London.

Jones, Nick (1999), *Sultans of Spin*, Orion Books, London.

Jowett, Garth S. (1987), 'Propaganda and communication: the re-emergence of a research tradition', *Journal of Communication* 37:1, pp. 97–114.

Jowett, Garth S. (1993), 'Propaganda and the Gulf War', *Critical Studies in Mass Communication*, 10, pp. 286–300.

Jowett, Garth S., and O'Donnell, Victoria (1992), *Propaganda and Persuasion*, second edition, Sage, London.

Kammen, Michael (1978), *A Season of Youth: The American Revolution and the Historical Imagination*, Knopf, New York.

Karganovic, S. (1974), 'Consumer socialism or the socialist way of life?' *Literaturnaya Gazeta* (Moscow), 13 March.

Kazin, Michael (1995), *The Populist Persuasion: An American History*, Basic Books, New York.

Keen, Sam (1986), *Faces of the Enemy*, Harper & Row, New York.

Kellner, Douglas (1995), *Media Culture*, Routledge, London.

Kevles, Daniel J. (1994), 'Greens in America', *New York Review*, 6 October.

Keynes, John Maynard (1985), *Essays in Biography*, Macmillan, Basingstoke.

Kim, Jin K., Shoor-Ghaffari, Pirouz, and Gustainis, J. Justin (1990), 'Agenda-setting functions of a media event: the case of *Amerika*', *Political Communication and Persuasion*, 7, pp. 1–11.

Klein, Gary (1998), *Sources of Power: How People make Decisions*, MIT Press, Cambridge MA.

Klein, Naomi (2001), *No Logo*, Flamingo, London.

Klemperer, Victor (1998), *I Shall Bear Witness: Diaries, 1933–1941*, Weidenfeld & Nicolson, London.

Knightley, Philip (1995), *The First Casualty*, Harcourt Brace, New York and London.

Kraus, S., and Davis, D. (1976), *The Effects of Mass Communication on Political Behavior*, Pennyslvania State University Press, University Park PA.

Kuhn, Deanna (1991), *The Skills of Argument*, Cambridge University Press, Cambridge.

Kulik, Karol (1975), *Alexander Korda*, W.H. Allen, London.

Kurz, Howard (1998), *Spin Cycle*, Touchstone Books, New York.

Larson, C.U. (1995), *Persuasion: Reception and Responsibility*, Wadsworth, New York.

Lashmar, Paul, and Oliver, James (1998), *Britain's Secret Propaganda War, 1948–1977*, Sutton, London.

Lasswell, Harold D. (1971), *Propaganda Techniques in World War I*, MIT Press, Cambridge MA.

Leathers, D. (1986), *Successful Nonverbal Communication: Principles and Applications*, Macmillan, New York.

Le Carré, John (2002), 'The making of a master criminal', *Daily Telegraph*, 14 October.

Lee, Alfred McClung, and Lee, Elizabeth Briant (1979), *The Fine Art of Propaganda*, International Society for General Semantics, San Francisco.

Lee, Alfred McClung, and Lee, Elizabeth Briant (1986), 'Whatever happened to "propaganda analysis"?', *Humanity and Society*, 10:1, pp. 11–24.

Lee, Elizabeth Briant, and Lee, Alfred McClung (1986), 'Coughlin and propaganda analysis', *Humanity and Society*, 10:1, pp. 25–35.

Levitin, Teresa E., and Miller, Warren E. (1979), 'Ideological interpretations of presidential elections', *American Political Science Review*, 73, pp. 751–71

Lewin, K. (1947), 'Group decision and social change', in T.M. Newcomb and E.L. Hartley (eds), *Readings in Social Psychology*, Holt, New York.

Leymore, V.L. (1975), *The Hidden Myth*, Basic Books, New York.

Lidz, Victor (1984), 'Television and moral order in a secular age', *Sage Annual Review of Communication Research*, 12:11.

Lieber, Tamar, and Bar-Nachum, Yossi (1994), '"What a relief": when the press prefers celebration to scandal', *Political Communication*, 11:1, pp. 35–48.

Loewen, James W. (1995), *Lies my Teacher told Me*, Touchstone Books, New York.

Lule, Jack (1990), 'The political use of victims: the shaping of the *Challenger* disaster', *Political Communication and Persuasion*, 7, pp. 115–128.

Lupia, Arthur (1994), 'Short cuts versus encyclopedias: information and voting behavior in California insurance reform elections', *American Political Science Review*, 88, pp. 63–76.

Lyne, John, and Howe, Henry F. (1990), 'The rhetoric of expertise: E.O. Wilson and sociobiology', *Quarterly Journal of Speech*, 76, pp. 134–151.

MacIntyre, Alasdair (1981), *After Virtue: A Study in Moral Theory*, Duckworth, London.

Magnet, Julia (2001), 'His grasp of spin is chilling', *Daily Telegraph*, 16 November.

Marreco, Anne (1967), *The Rebel Countess*, Weidenfeld & Nicolson, London.

Mason, Geoff (1989), *Philosophical Rhetoric*, Routledge, London.

May, Jacob (1982), 'My Gain–Zero Profit in Language Use', International Sociological Association Conference, Odense University, DK-5230.

Mayhew, Leon H. (1997), *The New Public*, Cambridge University Press, Cambridge.

Mayrowitz, J. (1986), *No Sense of Place*, Oxford University Press, Oxford.

Mazrui, Ali A. (1976), 'The political sociology of oratory: power and persuasion in black Africa', *Revista mexicana de sociologia* 38:3, pp. 669–683.

McCloskey, Donald N. (1990), *If You're So Smart: The Narrative of Economic Expertise*, University of Chicago Press, Chicago.

Mckie, D. (1995), '"Fact is free but comment is sacred", or, Was it the *Sun* wot won it?', in I. Crewe and B. Gosschalk (eds), *Political Communication: The General Election Campaign of 1992*, Cambridge University Press, Cambridge,

Melder, Keith (1992), *Hail to the Candidate: Presidential Campaigns from Banners to Broadcasts*, Smithsonian Institute, Washington DC.

Meyer, Michael (1994), *Rhetoric, Language and Reason*, Pennsylvania State University Press, University Park PA.

Mitchell, Greg (1993), *Campaign of the Century*, Random House, New York.

Moloney, Kevin (2001), 'The rise and fall of spin: changes of fashion in the presentation of UK politics', *Journal of Public Affairs*, 1:2, pp. 124–135.

Moore, R. Laurence (1994), *Selling God: American Religion in the Marketplace of Culture*, Oxford University Press, New York.

Mussolf, Lloyd (1991), 'Congress, policy proposals and the articulation of values', *Political Communication and Persuasion*, 8, pp. 93–108.

Nichols, John Wasting (1984), 'The propaganda dollar', *Foreign Policy*, 56, pp. 124–140.

Nimmo, Dan (1970), *The Political Persuaders*, Prentice Hall, Englewood Cliffs NJ.

O'Shaughnessy, Andrew Jackson (2000), *An Empire Divided*, University of Pennsylvania Press, Philadelphia PA.

O'Shaughnessy, John (1995), *Competitive Marketing: A Strategic Approach*, Routledge, London.

O'Shaughnessy, John (1992), *Explaining Buyer Behaviour*, Oxford University Press, New York.

O'Shaughnessy, John, and O'Shaughnessy, Nicholas (2003), *The Marketing Power of Emotion*, Oxford University Press, New York.

O'Shaughnessy, John, and O'Shaughnessy, Nicholas (2004), *Persuasion in Advertising*, Routledge, London.

O'Shaughnessy, Nicholas J. (1990), *The Phenomenon of Political Marketing*, Macmillan, Basingstoke.

Oliver, Nick (1995), 'Dedicated Followers of Fashion? Management Fads and the Case of Just-in-time', working paper, Judge Institute of Management Studies, Cambridge.

Orren, Gerry (1985), 'What's new about the Media', in Project on New Communications Technologies, Public Policy and Democratic Values, Harvard University, Cambridge MA, December

Orwell, George (1969), *Nineteen eighty-four*, Penguin Books, London.

'Our Children's Education: The Updated Parents' Charter, 1994', Department for Education, London.

Overing, Joanna (1997), 'The role of myth: an anthropological perspective', in G. Hosking and G. Schöpflin (eds), *Myths and Nationhood*, Routledge, London.

Papademus, Diana (1989), 'Nuclear propaganda: a review essay', *Humanity and Society*, 8.

Patterson, Gordon (1990), 'Freud's Rhetoric: Persuasion and History', the 1909 Clark Lectures, *Metaphor and Symbolic Activity*, 5:4, pp. 215–233.

Pennington, N., and Hastie, R. (1993), 'A theory of explanation-based decision making', in C. Klein, J. Orasanu, R. Calderwood and C.E. Zsambok (eds), *Decision Making in Action: Models and Methods*, Ablex, Norwood NJ.

Perelman, Chaim (1982), *The Realm of Rhetoric*, University of Notre Dame Press, Notre Dame IN.

Perris, Arnold (1985), *Music as Propaganda: Art to Persuade, Art to Control*, Greenwood Press, Westport CT.

Perry, James M. (1968), *The New Politics*, Weidenfeld & Nicolson, London.

Petty, R.E., and Cacioppo, J.T. (1979), 'Issue involvement can increase or decrease persuasion by enhancing message-relevant cognitive responses', *Journal of Personality and Social Psychology*, 37.

Petty, Richard, and Cacioppo, John (1986), *Communication and Persuasion: Central and Peripheral Routes to Attitude Change*, Springer, New York.

Petty, R.E., Cacioppo, J.T., and Goldman, R. (1981), 'Personal involvement as a determinant of argument-based persuasion', *Journal of Personality and Social Psychology*, 41.

Plimmer, Charlotte, and Plimmer, Denis (1981), 'Black ivory', in *The British Empire*, Ferndale Editions, London.

Political Communication and Persuasion (1988), 5, pp. 81–82.

Pollay, R.B. (1986), 'The distorted mirror: reflections on the unintended consequences of advertising', *Journal of Marketing*, 50, pp. 18–36.

Pollock, John (1998), *Kitchener*, Constable, London.

Pratkanis, Anthony R., and Aronson, Elliot (1991), *The Age of Propaganda: The Everyday Use and Abuse of Persuasion*, Freeman, New York.

Prelli, Lawrence J. (1989), *A Rhetoric of Science*, University of South Carolina Press, Columbia SC.

Preston, Paul (1995), *Franco*, Fontana Press, London.

Preston, Paul (2000), *Comrades! Portraits from the Spanish Civil War*, Fontana Press, London.

Rakow, L.F. (1989), *Information and Power: Toward a Critical Theory of Information Campaigns*, Sage Annual Review of Communication Research 18, Sage, London.

Rampton, Sheldon, and Stauber, John (2003), *Weapons of Mass Deception: The Uses of Propaganda in Bush's War on Iraq*, Tarcher/Penguin, New York.

Reich, Robert (1987), *Tales of New America*, Times Books, New York.

Rentschler, E. (1996), *The Ministry of Illusion: Nazi Cinema and its Afterlife*, Harvard University Press, Boston MA.

Rhodes, Anthony (1993), *Propaganda, the Art of Persuasion: World War II*, Mayor Books, Wigston, Leicester.

Richardson, Jeremy (1995), 'The market for political activism: interest groups as a challenge to political parties', *Western European Politics*, 18:1, pp. 116–139.

Ridley, Jasper (2001), *Bloody Mary's Martyrs*, Constable, London.

Roberts, Andrew (1004), *Eminent Churchillians*, Weidenfeld & Nicolson, London.

Robins, K., Webster, F., and Pickering, M. (1987), 'Propaganda, information and social control', in Jeremy Hawthorn (ed.), *Propaganda, Polemic and Persuasion*, Edward Arnold, London.

Rohatyn, Dennis (1990), 'The (mis)information society', *Bulletin of Science, Technology and Society*, 10:2, pp. 77–85.

Rokeach, Milton (1971), 'The measurement of values and value systems', in Gilbert Abcarian and John W. Soule (eds), *Social Psychology and Political Behaviour*, Merrill, Columbus OH.

Rothschild, Michael (1978), 'Political advertising: a neglected policy issue in marketing', *Journal of Marketing Research*, 15, pp. 58–71.

Rozin, Paul, Millman, L., and Nemeroff, C. (1986), 'Operation of the laws of sympathetic magic in disgust and their domains', *Journal of Personality and Social Psychology*, 50, pp. 703–712.

Rutherford, Ward (1978), *Hitler's Propaganda Machine*, Bison Books, London.

Sabato, Larry (1983), *The Rise of Political Consultants: New Ways of Winning Elections*, Basic Books, New York.

Salmon, Charles T. (1989–1990), 'Campaigns for social "improvement": an overview of values, rationales and impacts', *Sage Annual Reviews of Communication Research* 18, Sage, London.

Schick, Suzanne (1985), 'Propaganda analysis: the search for an appropriate model', *Etcetera*, spring, pp. 63–71.

Schlesinger, P., and Tumber, H. (1994), *Reporting Crime: The Media Politics of Criminal Justice*, Clarendon Press, Oxford.

Schöpflin, George (1997), 'The function of myths and a taxonomy of myths', in G. Hosking and G. Schöpflin (eds), *Myths and Nationhood*, Routledge, London.

Schudson, Michael (1982), *Advertising: The Uneasy Persuasion*, Basic Books, New York.

Schumpeter, J.A. (1996), *Capitalism, Socialism and Democracy*, Allan & Unwin, London.

Schwartz, Tony (1973), *The Responsive Chord*, Basic Books, New York.

Searle, John R. (1995), *The Construction of Social Reality*, Alan Lane The Penguin Press, London.

Segev, Tom (2000), *One Palestine, Complete: Jews and Arabs under the British Mandate*, Metropolitan Books, New York.

Seymour-Ure, C., and Scott, S. (1995), 'Characters and assassinations: portrayals of John Major and Neil Kinnock in the *Daily Mirror* and the *Sun*', in I. Crewe and B. Gosschalk (eds), *Political Communication: The General Election Campaign of 1992*, Cambridge University Press, Cambridge.

Simmons, Annette (2000), *The Story Factor: Secrets of Influence from the Art of Storytelling*, Perseus Publishing, New York.

Simpson, John (1994), 'Not just a tribal war', *Spectator*, 23 July, pp. 8–9.

Singh, Amardeep (1989), 'Social marketing and the AIDS crisis', *Sage Annual Review of Communication Research* 18, Sage, London.

Smith, B.L, Lasswell, H.D, and Casey, R.D (1946), *Propaganda, Communication and Public Opinion*, Princeton University Press, Princeton NJ.

Sniderman, Paul M., Brody, Richard A., and Tetlock, Philip E. (1991), *Reasoning and Choice: Explorations in Political Psychology*, Cambridge University, Cambridge.

Snyder, Louis (1976), *Encyclopedia of the Third Reich*, McGraw-Hill, New York.

Soley, L.S., and Reid, Michael (1978), cited in Michael Rothschild, 'Political advertising: a neglected policy issue in marketing' *Journal of Marketing Research*, 15:1, pp. 58–71.

Sproule, J. Michael (1987), 'Propaganda studies in American social science: the rise and fall of the critical paradigm', *Quarterly Journal of Speech*, 73:1, pp. 60–78.

Stark, Frank M. (1980), 'Persuasion and power in Cameroon', *Canadian Journal of African Studies*, 14:2, pp. 273–293.

Stern, Barbara B. (1988), 'How does an ad mean? Language in service advertising', *Journal of Advertising*, 17:2, pp. 3–14.

Steuter, Erin (1990), 'Understanding the media/terrorism relationship: an analysis of ideology and the news in *Time* magazine', *Political Communication and Persuasion*, 7, pp. 257–271.

Stevens, Robert (2001), 'Eviscerating Oxford', *Spectator*, 14 July.

Tasker, Yvonne (1993), *Spectacular Bodies: Gender, Genre and the Action Cinema*, Routledge, London.

Taylor, Philip M. (1990), *Munitions of the Mind: War Propaganda from the Ancient World to the Nuclear Age*, Collins, London.

Thomas, Hugh (1986), *The Spanish Civil War*, Penguin Books, London.

Thomas, Keith (1994), 'As you like it', *New York Review*, 22 September.

Thompson, Michael (1979), *Rubbish Theory*, Oxford University Press, Oxford.

Thorburn, David (1988), *Sage Annual Reviews of Communication Research*, chapter two, Sage, London.

Tomaselli, Keyan (1987), *The Cinema of Apartheid*, Routledge, London.

Tyrrell, Wm Blake, and Brown, Frieda S., eds (1991), *Athenian Myths and Institutions*, Oxford University Press, Oxford.

Uklanski, Piotr (1999), *The Nazis*, Patrick Frey, Zurich.

Umberson, Debra, and Henderson, Kristin (1992), 'The social construction of death in the Gulf War', *Omega: Journal of Death and Dying*, 25:1, pp. 1–5.

Vanderwicken, Robert (1995), 'Why the news is not the truth', *Harvard Business Review*, May–June, pp. 144–150.

Vansittart, Sir Robert (1941), *Black Record*, Hamish Hamilton, London.

Velleman, J. David (2000), *The Possibility of Practical Reason*, Clarendon Press, Oxford.

Vickers, Brian (1988), *In Defence of Rhetoric*, Clarendon Press, Oxford.

Warren, Donald (1996), *Radio Priest: Charles Coughlin, the Father of Hate Radio*, Free Press, New York.

Webber, Anne (1992), *Social Psychology*, Harper Collins, New York.

Webster, Duncan (1988), *Look Yonder! The Imaginary America of Populist Culture*, Routledge, London.

Whyte, Kenneth (1994), 'The face that sank a thousand Tories', *Saturday Night*, February.

Wiener, Martin J. (1981), *English Culture and the Decline of the Industrial Spirit, 1850–1950*, Penguin Books, London.

Williams, Gordon (1987), 'Remember the *Llandovery Castle*: cases of atrocity propaganda in the First World War', in Jeremy Hawthorn (ed.), *Propaganda, Persuasion and Polemic*, Edward Arnold, London.

Zajonc, R.B., and Markus, H. (1991), 'Affective and cognitive factors in preferences', in H.M. Kassarjian and T.S. Robertson (eds), *Perspectives in Consumer Behavior*, Prentice Hall, Englewood Cliffs NJ.

Zimmerman, Warren (1995), 'The captive mind', *New York Review*, 1 February.

Index